We Preach Not Ourselves

Paul *on* Proclamation

Michael P. Knowles

Brazos Press

a division of Baker Publishing Group
Grand Rapids, Michigan

Published by Brazos Press
a division of Baker Publishing Group
P.O. Box 6287, Grand Rapids, MI 49516-6287
www.brazospress.com

Printed in the United States of America

Library of Congress Cataloging-in-Publication Data
Knowles, Michael (Michael P.)
   We preach not ourselves : Paul on proclamation / Michael P. Knowles.
      p. cm.
   Includes bibliographical references and indexes.
   ISBN 978-1-58743-211-8 (pbk.)
   1. Paul, the Apostle, Saint. 2. Preaching—Biblical teaching. 3. Bible. N.T. Corinthians, 2nd, I-VI—Criticism, interpretation, etc., I. Title.
BS2655.P8K56 2007
251.0092—dc22   2007042595

An earlier version of some of the material in chapter one appeared as "Paul's 'Affliction' in Second Corinthians: Reflection, Integration, and a Pastoral Theology of the Cross" in the *Journal of Pastoral Theology* 15.1 (Spring, 2005): 64–77.

For we do not proclaim ourselves; we proclaim Jesus Christ as Lord and ourselves as your slaves for Jesus' sake.

2 Corinthians 4:5

Contents

Texts and Translations

Unless otherwise indicated, biblical texts in English are cited from the New Revised Standard Version. Greek texts are cited from Eberhard and Erwin Nestle, *Novum Testamentum Graece*, ed. Kurt Aland et al., 27th edition (Stuttgart: Deutsche Bibelgesellschaft, 1993), accessed via Gramcord for Windows 2.3 (Vancouver, WA: Gramcord Institute, 1998) and its various program components. The Louw and Nida *Greek-English Lexicon of the New Testament* has also been accessed via Gramcord, although references have been checked against the printed text. In addition to those listed below, abbreviations for the names of biblical books, translations, standard reference works, and journals follow the protocols set out in Patrick H. Alexander et al., *The SBL Handbook of Style for Ancient Near Eastern, Biblical, and Early Christian Studies* (Peabody, MA: Hendrickson, 1999). Several studies that have proven especially helpful (and thus are frequently cited) are referred to by the names of their respective authors: full bibliographic information appears below.

Abbreviations

ABD   *Anchor Bible Dictionary*, ed. D. N. Freedman et al. 6 vols. New York: Doubleday, 1992.

Barrett   C. K. Barrett. *The Second Epistle to the Corinthians*. 2nd ed. BNTC. London: Adam and Charles Black, 1973.

Furnish   Victor Paul Furnish. *II Corinthians: A New Translation with Introduction and Commentary*. AB 32A. Garden City, NY: Doubleday, 1986.

L&N   Johannes P. Louw, Eugene A. Nida, et al., eds. *Greek-English Lexicon of the New Testament: Based on Semantic Domains*. 2nd ed. 2 vols. New York: United Bible Societies, 1989.

Matera   Frank J. Matera. *II Corinthians: A Commentary*. NTL. Louisville: Westminster John Knox, 2003.

NEB   The New English Bible

NIV   The Holy Bible: New International Version

NRSV   New Revised Standard Version Bible

RSV   Revised Standard Version Bible, 2nd ed.

TCGNT   Bruce M. Metzger. *A Textual Commentary on the Greek New Testament*. London: United Bible Societies, 1975.

TDNT   *Theological Dictionary of the New Testament*, ed. Gerhard Kittel and Gerhard Friedrich. Tr. Geoffrey W. Bromiley. 10 vols. Grand Rapids: Eerdmans, 1964-1976.

Thrall   Margaret E. Thrall. *A Critical and Exegetical Commentary on the Second Epistle to the Corinthians*. 2 vols. ICC. Edinburgh: T. & T. Clark, 1994, 2000.

TNIV   The Holy Bible, Today's New International Version

Preface

The bulk of this study was completed in the course of a yearlong research leave generously granted by McMaster Divinity College, McMaster University, in Hamilton, Ontario. Being granted freedom from academic and administrative responsibilities for an extended period of time created a precious opportunity for drawing together and refining ideas developed over the course of several years of teaching and reflection. Numerous colleagues have listened patiently, offering wise counsel and gracious encouragement in response to various aspects of this work, at various stages of its development. Prominent among them were Lee Beach, Deborah Bowen, Janet Clark, and Kurt Richardson. Paul Miller brought the wisdom of pastoral experience as well as keen intellectual acumen to this project, taking time from his congregational responsibilities to read each draft chapter. My student research assistants were consistently helpful: Michael Ford tracked down bibliographic material, while Luz Iglesias carefully proofread the entire text and gently pointed out the parts that didn't make sense. Matt Lowe helped to compile the indexes. To these and other students (all of whom have demonstrated admirable patience), I owe a commensurate debt of gratitude. I also wish to thank Stan Porter for having generously lent several difficult-to-obtain titles from his extensive personal library. Above all, I am indebted to Sylvia Keesmaat and Rodney Clapp of Brazos Press for carefully reading what I imagined would be the "final version," and then another "final version," and for providing an extensive series of critiques that were at once generous, wide-ranging, and detailed, rendering the study as a whole considerably clearer, more readable, and (I hope) more relevant to the ministry of preaching in our day.

Introduction

Paul and Preaching

This book seeks to discover what Paul's second letter to the Corinthians (less known but no less powerful than 1 Corinthians) has to say about preaching, in particular the spirituality of preaching. But before we can explore Paul's theology of Christian proclamation, we need to answer a few basic questions. What *is* preaching, exactly, and what does it mean to preach from Paul in particular? Is it enough to proclaim his theology, or can his method instruct us as well? What models does Paul himself follow? With respect to the context of his ministry, what was the situation in Corinth—socially, politically, and in terms of popular piety or religion? How did Paul arrive in Corinth, and what was his relationship with the congregation? In particular, why does he feel the need to defend himself, and what are we likely to learn from him for our own ministries of proclamation?

This study is intended for the benefit of pastors and preachers, many if not most of whom labor throughout their careers in relative obscurity, their successes and failures known at most to members of their own families and congregations. Although few would dare compare themselves directly to so important a figure in Christian tradition as Paul, the apostle's experience has much to say to those who are, far more than Paul himself, truly "unknown" (2 Cor. 6:9). Indeed, the acceptance of Paul's letters into the Christian canon constitutes permission for readers to apply the content of these letters as widely as possible to their own circumstances. This is especially true for those who exercise ministries of preaching and teaching. Paul is, after all, the preacher par excellence of Christian tradition, single-handedly responsible for formulating the basic theological categories of subsequent Christian thought. In 2 Corinthians, however, Paul feels obliged to account for his ministry in the face of vociferous and stinging critique. In the course of defending himself (while claiming to be doing nothing of the sort), he succeeds in articulating a coherent theological and practical justification for the preaching of the Christian gospel: not just his own, but preaching in general.

This study does not expound the entire text of 2 Corinthians, but concentrates on 2 Corinthians 1:1–6:13, the section in which Paul's apostolic self-defense is most clearly focused. Nor does it explore every issue in this section of text that has aroused scholarly interest and debate—for these are truly legion. While such debates are important, it must be kept in mind that Paul's writing both proceeds from and is directed toward real-life situations involving the concrete experiences of Christian leaders and congregations. For that reason alone, it is worth comparing those experiences (however distant in terms of time and culture) with our own, and seeking to read each in light of the other. But once again, because 2 Corinthians has long since been incorporated into the church's canon, such comparisons are meant to flow in a particular direction. Accepting this text as canonical and authoritative obliges us to read our contemporary experience in light of the text before we may read the text in light of our experience.[1] That is, the text itself indicates the meaning of the context in which it is later preached, not the other way around. That the opposite is frequently attempted (both consciously and unconsciously) does not obviate the basic theological claim that the Christian canon speaks and demands that we listen—indeed, provides us voice and

1. As theologian John Webster astutely observes, "Interpretation of the clear word of God is not . . . first of all an act of clarification but the event of being clarified" ("Biblical Theology and the Clarity of Scripture," in Craig Bartholomew et al., ed. *Out of Egypt: Biblical Theology and Biblical Interpretation* [Grand Rapids: Zondervan, 2004], 379).

words with which to speak—rather than giving us license to listen selectively to whatever parts of its message we happen to find agreeable, or, worse yet, limiting the gospel itself to what little we are already prepared to hear.

In order for our comparison to be as accurate as possible, it will first be necessary to set out something of Paul's situation, socially and historically as well as theologically. With regard to the letter's general setting, the Western church of the twenty-first century has little in common with that of Corinth in the post-Augustan Roman Empire. If nothing else, the social and cultural settings are significantly different, and we must carefully explore such differences if we are to avoid unconsciously reading the biblical text as a distant mirror of our own expectations and cultural assumptions. Historically, early Christians were vastly outnumbered by a plethora of well-established religious alternatives: followers of "the Way" would have been barely noticeable in terms of social influence or significance, as Paul points out (1 Cor. 1:26–29). Their numbers were painfully few, and the only traditions and history to which they might appeal were those of Judaism, with which only some in the congregation would have been familiar. Because many would have lacked any background in Israel's monotheistic heritage, and because distinctively Christian traditions of belief and conduct were equally novel and unfamiliar, Paul's apologia appeals to and expounds the basic outlines of a Christian worldview. The fact that, at least in Corinth, Christianity is both a new and a foreign religion means that its adherents need to be reminded of the basis for their recent shift in religious allegiance.[2] This gives great value to his correspondence for later generations, although for very different reasons than it served in the first century. We live in a culture that has been "Christianized" for so long that we have all but forgotten what is distinctive about this faith. Indeed, Christianity in the nominally Christian West has over the years been so successfully domesticated, abbreviated, and relegated to the sphere of harmless private devotion that we find ourselves shocked by the unfamiliar contours of Pauline spirituality. As much for us, then, as for the believers of ancient Corinth, Paul offers a much-needed refresher on the content, meaning, and cost of Christian proclamation.

2. Novelty was likely an asset rather than a liability: "Everywhere a process was afoot of syncretizing the old religions with new ones streaming in especially from the east, and the odder and vaguer these were, the greater their attraction" (Guenther Bornkamm, *Paul*, tr. D. M. G. Stalker [New York: Harper and Row, 1971], 7).

Spirituality and Worship

A key feature of the background of this letter is its context in worship. In the early church (though not reflected in Acts because of Luke's tendency there to highlight public venues), most preaching would have taken place in synagogues or private homes,[3] with the latter setting particularly relevant in the case of meetings for worship. The rigid distinction between "preaching" (i.e., to non-adherents) and "teaching" (to the church alone) once proposed by C. H. Dodd[4] has been abandoned, and there is widespread acknowledgment that teaching and preaching alike (to the extent that these can be distinguished) would have taken place in gatherings of the Christian community. Similarly, Paul's correspondence would have been read aloud to the congregants in the course of their worship gatherings (as 1 Thess. 5:27 and Col. 4:16 indicate).[5] So whereas later Christian communities may appreciate Paul's exposition of a christocentric worldview, and congregational leaders will want to see how Paul dealt with the pastoral crises of his day, preachers in particular have much to learn from his explanation of how preaching relates to both theological and pastoral concerns as these come together in the setting of corporate worship. As worship is the proper human response to divine self-revelation, so preaching itself is an act of praise. It is doxological in the sense that it arises from and responds to God's saving action, and insofar as it contributes to doxology by recalling for its hearers their true identity as those who are being transformed by God. Since this doxological characteristic of Paul's letters transcends social and historical particularities, subsequent preachers are able to learn from and to some extent model their own practice on that of one of the early church's first, most effective, and most influential preachers.

In keeping with this emphasis on worship, a key proposal of this study is that preaching is a function not primarily of form, of communicative

3. Stanley Kent Stowers, "Social Status, Public Speaking and Private Teaching: The Circumstances of Paul's Preaching Activity," *NovT* 26 (1984): 59–82.

4. C. H. Dodd, *The Apostolic Preaching and Its Development* (London: Hodder and Stoughton, 1936).

5. Recitation of Paul's letters would have been necessary given literacy rates in the first-century Mediterranean world of 10–15% for adult males, and less than 5% for women (see William V. Harris, *Ancient Literacy* [Cambridge: Harvard University Press, 1989], 248–84, 328–30).

medium (whether verbal or visual, electronic or in person), or of any particular concept or theory (important as these may be), but of spirituality. "Spirituality," although not a term the apostle would have used,[6] bespeaks a general disposition and outlook oriented to the spiritual realm. In theistic religions, it implies (over and above an interest in the inner self for its own sake) an engagement of the human "spirit" with God or the gods. As used here in an explicitly Christian context, the term "spirituality" refers to the direction of mind and will toward the transcendent God of Israel and of Jesus, above all as enabled *by* Jesus.[7] The term "worship" denotes various concrete physical behaviors (whether individual or corporate, liturgical or political) that express this broader orientation. As one aspect of this subset, preaching is informed by, articulates, and intends to sustain spirituality. It alerts listeners to various dimensions and implications of the divine-human relationship, and encourages particular kinds of responses. In particular, properly "Christian" preaching focuses on the person of Christ as instrumental to the relationship between God's creation, God's creatures, and their Creator.

6. All the more so for Paul's Hellenistic congregants, according to D. T. Runia ("The Pre-Christian Origins of Early Christian Spirituality," in Pauline Allen, Wendy Mayer, and Lawrence Cross, eds., *Prayer and Spirituality in the Early Church*, Vol. 2 [Brisbane: Centre for Early Christian Studies, Australian Catholic University, 1999], 11–24), the nearest equivalent to "spirituality" would have been *philosophia*: "The well-known Platonist formulation of the philosophical *telos*, 'becoming like unto God to the extent possible,' may be taken as representative of the spiritual quest of Greek philosophy as a whole at the time that the early Christians first came into contact with it."

7. Among the many available definitions of Christian spirituality, see, e.g., Walter Principe, "Toward Defining Spirituality," *Studies in Religion/Sciences Religieuses* 12.2 (1983): 139: "Spirituality . . . points to those aspects of a person's living a faith or commitment that concern his or her striving to attain the highest ideal or goal. For a Christian this would mean his or her striving for an ever more intense union with the Father through Jesus Christ by living in the Spirit"; Gordon S. Wakefield, "Spirituality," in Gordon S. Wakefield, ed., *The Westminster Dictionary of Christian Spirituality* (Philadelphia: Westminster, 1983), 362: "Christian spirituality is not simply for 'the interior life' or the inward person, but as much for the body as the soul, and is directed to the implementation of both the commandments of Christ, to love God and our neighbor"; Michael Downey, *Understanding Christian Spirituality* (Mahwah, NJ: Paulist, 1997), 43: "As a lived experience, Christian spirituality is a way of living for God in Christ through the presence and power of the Holy Spirit."

These more general definitions allow us to approach Paul's preaching in the following terms. In the course of defending himself and his ministry of proclamation, Paul articulates a Jesus-centered spirituality that can best be described as "cruciform," a spiritual vision essentially shaped by Jesus's crucifixion and resurrection. This is not to say that Paul's interpretation corresponds exactly to Jesus's vision of his heavenly Father as recorded, for instance, in John or the Synoptic Gospels. The Gospels focus largely on *Jesus's* spirituality—his relationship to God and the activities that proceed from it—in the course of his earthly ministry prior to crucifixion. Paul, by contrast, concentrates on the conclusion of Jesus's life, proposing crucifixion and resurrection as categories that provide a primary template or archetype for Christian spirituality, discipleship, and ministry. This is especially true, as we will see, for the task of preaching.

According to Michael Gorman, *"Paul conceives of identification with and participation in the death of Jesus as the believer's fundamental experience of Christ."* And, he notes, "No letter stresses cruciformity as the norm of existence in Christ more than 2 Corinthians."[8] The master narrative of Jesus's crucifixion and exaltation is most succinctly narrated in Philippians 2:6–11, but four fundamental patterns of cruciformity are evident throughout the Pauline corpus:

1. cruciformity as faithful obedience, or cruciform *faith*.
2. cruciformity as voluntary self-emptying and self-giving regard for others, or cruciform *love*.
3. cruciformity as—paradoxically—life-giving suffering and transformative potency in weakness, or cruciform *power*.
4. cruciformity as requisite prelude to resurrection and exaltation, or cruciform *hope*.[9]

8. Michael J. Gorman, *Cruciformity: Paul's Narrative Spirituality of the Cross* (Grand Rapids: Eerdmans, 2001), 35, 32 (emphasis original); cf. 44: *"the narrative of the crucified and exalted Christ is the normative life-narrative within which the community's own life-narrative takes place and by which it is shaped"* (emphasis original). Gorman's argument is also briefly summarized in the chapter titled "Paul's Spirituality" from his *Apostle of the Crucified Lord: A Theological Introduction to Paul and His Letters* (Grand Rapids: Eerdmans, 2004), 115–29.

9. Gorman, *Cruciformity*, 93.

Although "faith" is to be understood in the first instance as Jesus's faithful, trusting obedience in submitting to crucifixion, it also refers to the manner in which those who place their own trust in Jesus participate in his death, share the benefits of his obedience, and pattern their lives accordingly. In practical terms, Paul explains that a cruciform pattern of Christian discipleship entails suffering and persecution, even "suggesting that the suffering associated with faith is to be expected."[10] "Love" is Paul's shorthand term for a cruciform ethical orientation that consists of seeking the advantage of others rather than one's own, based on the example of Jesus's self-offering for the sake of humanity (e.g., 1 Cor. 10:23–24, 33; 13:5; 2 Cor. 5:14–15, etc.).[11] Submitting to "Christ's law" (1 Cor. 9:21) and being impelled by "the love of Christ" (2 Cor. 5:14) means for Paul the renunciation of social status and apostolic rights (especially the right to financial support), self-enslavement to congregants through preaching and pastoral care, and submission to continued personal suffering despite the temptation to evade it. Gorman traces Paul's application of this ethic in 1 Corinthians to lawsuits, marital and social relations, and the exercise of spiritual gifts. In 2 Corinthians, cruciform love takes the form of reconciliation, forgiveness, and generosity in the collection for the Jerusalem church.[12]

Likewise, Gorman's discussion of cruciform "power" draws in large measure on evidence from the Corinthian correspondence. According to Paul, "the word of the cross . . . is the power of God" (1 Cor. 1:18 RSV). Not only is the cross itself the paradoxical manifestation of God's "power-in-weakness," but "the message about the cross"—that is, the proclamation of a crucified Messiah—announces the cruciform nature of divine power.[13] Paul's own ministry is characterized by weakness: lack of oratorical prowess, public disgrace and physical suffering, the dishonor of manual labor, and a general attitude of humility and meekness. Yet, Paul insists, "whenever I am weak, *then* I am strong" (2 Cor. 12:10), for only through such human weakness is God's power manifest, both in Paul's life and in the lives of his congregants.[14]

10. Ibid., 149.
11. Ibid., 158–62.
12. Ibid., 214–67, esp. 238–44.
13. Ibid., 277–78.
14. Ibid., 281–93.

Finally, the prospect of believers sharing the pattern of Jesus's death and resurrection, or of humiliation followed by exaltation, constitutes the essence—and eschatological focus—of cruciform "hope." According to Gorman, this is a two-stage process, whereby (ethically) believers now "die to" and are forgiven their sins and (devotionally) are made "more than conquerors" amid physical tribulation (Rom. 8:37), while awaiting future resurrection (see 2 Cor. 4:1–18). Specifically, *"The power of the resurrection operates in the present as the power of conformity to the death of Christ, which in turn guarantees a place in the future resurrection."*[15] Even so, passages such as 2 Corinthians 3:18 ("all of us . . . *are being transformed*") require an acknowledgment that "this process of transformation begins in the present."[16]

Particularly as he articulates it in the Corinthian correspondence, cruciform spirituality emerges as a definitive feature of Paul's theology, lifestyle, and apostolic proclamation. Paul's assertion is that God acts in the lives of Jesus's followers as God acted in the life of Jesus, by allowing humiliation and death to provide the occasion for a uniquely divine gift of new life. Although the experiential dimensions of this approach emerge in 2 Corinthians 1:8–10 (describing Paul's affliction suffered "in Asia"), 2 Corinthians 4:5 offers a convenient summary of its theological content—and of the role of the preacher in communicating it: "For we do not proclaim ourselves; we proclaim Jesus Christ as Lord and ourselves as your slaves for Jesus' sake." Both of these passages will be examined more fully in subsequent chapters. But, for the moment, it is enough to point out that for Paul the cruel death and unexpected resurrection of Jesus provide not only the *content* of his preaching, nor merely the *means* by which preaching is made possible; they determine also the *manner* and the *method* by which he preaches.

How Does Paul "Preach"?

Admittedly, to approach homiletics from the perspective of Pauline spirituality is to break ranks with the predominant emphases of current scholarship in at least two regards. Recent homiletical discussion has

15. Ibid., 332 (emphasis original).
16. Ibid., 337.

17

concentrated more on questions of sermonic form than of content, and thereby appears to take the issue of spirituality more or less for granted. Conversely, studies of Paul's letters by New Testament scholars have concentrated traditionally more on the content of his proclamation than on its method (although recent publications have begun to reverse this trend). The approach taken here is to understand preaching as something more than a convenient vehicle for the promulgation of Pauline theology, and to investigate ways in which the content of that theology entails both a spiritual disposition (an orientation to the reality and activity of God) and a specific homiletical method.

Along the same lines, Daniel Patte argues that faithful presentation of Paul's theology—as, indeed, of Christian faith as a whole—amounts to more than simply repeating or "translating" a series of propositional truths. Rather, it requires a conscious "imitation" of Paul's faith experience (as Paul seems to imply in 1 Cor. 11:1). Preaching, says Patte, announces "the power of God for salvation" (Rom. 1:16) that is manifest not only in the death and resurrection of Jesus, but also "in the process of preaching the message" and "in the experience of the hearers."[17] Specifically, since "Paul sees God at work in situations which are Christ-like, that is, in situations which include both a cross-like experience and a resurrection-like experience," so preachers are called to recognize the same pattern in the lives of those whom they encounter:

> Paraphrasing 1 Corinthians 2:2–5 and 1 Thessalonians 1:5, we can say that our sermons will be the demonstration of our powerlessness and our lack of knowledge; that they will simultaneously demonstrate our faith—how could we perceive these revelations and manifestations of God in our fellow church members without faith?—with "full conviction" about the promise of the gospel, and that they will also be a "demonstration of power" since they will show that the power of God is at work in the church.[18]

Nancy Lammers Gross similarly invites preachers to imitate Paul's theological method:

17. Daniel Patte, *Preaching Paul* (Philadelphia: Fortress, 1984), 25. This study summarizes the more complex analysis Patte offers in *Paul's Faith and the Power of the Gospel: A Structural Introduction to the Pauline Letters* (Philadelphia: Fortress, 1983), which seeks to uncover the structure, significance, and "operating principles" of Christian faith by which Paul interprets his experience.

18. Patte, *Preaching Paul*, 33, 61, 69.

When we ask the question, "What was it Paul did?" we *do not* find it to be the case that Paul took timeless truths and *applied* them to the current situation. Rather, Paul was a moderator in the conversation between the Christ event as pointed to in the Hebrew Scriptures and testified to by apostolic witnesses, and the situations in which the hearers of his letters found themselves.[19]

To preach on such a model requires one not to "engage" the Pauline text so much as to be engaged by the reality of Christ to which the text bears witness, in the confidence that "the text has the potential and power to disclose to the interpreter a world of its own"—the "world" of God's saving action with Christ as its center.[20]

Although one way of construing the post-Pauline sermon envisages its preacher as responding solely to Paul, and only through Paul to the revelatory tradition that he transmits, it is also possible to envisage the preacher as responding to the source of revelation itself (that is, to the saving action of God expressed in Christ and reflected throughout the history of his followers), to which the preacher has been alerted *by* Paul. The testimony of church history is that Paul mediates the "Word of God" to later preachers, even as later preachers to some extent mediate God's Word to their own hearers, but neither the apostle nor his interlocutors thereby replace God. God may well be savingly active through Paul and other preachers, but the initiative always remains God's own. While it may prompt others to respond to the "voice" of God, preaching is at best a response to that voice, not a substitute for it. This appears most clearly when preaching is located within a service of congregational worship, and is understood as an aspect of that worship. The best preaching, like true worship, directs attention away from itself and toward God's self-revelation in human form.

But just as neither Paul nor the preacher of Paul can replace God, neither can the preacher replace Paul. Perhaps we may say that in proclaiming the apostolic message, the voice of the preacher both echoes and answers that of Paul: it is simultaneously dependent on Paul and separate from

19. Nancy Lammers Gross, *If You Cannot Preach Like Paul . . .* (Grand Rapids: Eerdmans, 2002), 61. The corollary implied by the title is announced in an epigraph to the volume: "If you cannot preach like Paul then do what Paul did; don't just say what Paul said."
20. Ibid., 101–2.

him.[21] Acknowledging canonical authority, and borrowing an analogy from musical theory, we may say that the voice of Paul represents a recurrent—dominant—leitmotif within the compositions of subsequent preachers, or that the latter present a series of close "variations" on Pauline "themes," while remaining true to the Christological core of his teaching. Or, perhaps more accurately, we may conceive of the preacher as a voice which, while autonomous, seeks to be "in harmony" or "in concert" with that of the apostle, who sets the original pitch, tone, or rhythm of the dialogue, even as Paul seeks to remain true to the tradition he has received.[22]

Indeed, the form in which Paul's preaching has come down to us implies an invitation to respond. According to Heikki Koskenniemi, the main function of a Hellenistic letter—such as those Paul wrote to fledgling

21. Although the question cannot be fully explored here, the ensuing discussion of the dialogical nature of preaching is indebted to the diverse and complex oeuvre of Russian philosopher and literary theorist Mikhail Mikhailovich Bakhtin (1895–1975). Bakhtin held that communication is predominantly a social operation, so that meaning is essentially fluid, not fixed. For Bakhtin, each word or "utterance" is part of an ongoing continuum of re-definition, deriving its semantic content from previous communicative acts and contributing meaning to future such acts that echo it in turn. Communication consists of voices in dialogue, constantly shaping the meaning of words and ideas partly by concurring with what has gone before and partly, through re-use, by proposing more contextually adequate definitions and applications. His term for this process is "dialogism." For Bakhtin as for the contemporary preacher, the ultimate dialogical referent of human communication is God. For an introduction to Bakhtin (and, in particular, the religious dimensions of his thought), see, e.g., Katerina Clark and Michael Holquist, *Mikhail Bakhtin* (Cambridge: Harvard University Press, 1984); Ruth Coates, *Christianity in Bakhtin: God and the Exiled Author* (Cambridge: Cambridge University Press, 1998); Barbara Green, *Mikhail Bakhtin and Biblical Scholarship* (SBLSS 38; Atlanta: SBL, 2000); Susan M. Felch and Paul J. Contino, *Bakhtin and Religion: A Feeling for Faith* (Evanston: Northwestern University Press, 2001).

22. In this sense, the preacher's use of Paul is analogous to Paul's own use of Hebrew scripture in relation to the church of his day: "The text was written by some human author long ago, written to and for an ancient community of people in Israel, but original writer and readers have become types whose meaning emerges with full clarity only in the church—that is, only in the empirical eschatological community that Paul is engaged in building. Even utterances that appear to be spoken to others in another time find their true addressees in *us*" (Richard B. Hays, *Echoes of Scripture in the Letters of Paul* [New Haven: Yale University Press, 1989], 167; emphasis original). Indeed, Hays boldly proposes (178–92) that Paul's interpretative methods should serve as a direct model for our own.

congregations in places including Corinth, Thessalonica, and Philippi—was "the continuance of a dialogic conversation in writing."[23] Literary theorists of Paul's day note that letters do not set forth a one-sided oration: they represent only half of an ongoing, multi-voiced dialogue (*dialogos*) that imitates as closely as possible the tone and manner of the writer's own discourse. Within a few centuries, theorists will adopt the broader term *homilia* (social intercourse) to express the intentionally relational function of written correspondence.[24] Already in this earlier period the dialogic nature of the letter appears closely tied to two other rhetorical functions that Koskenniemi identifies, namely *philophronēsis*, the expression and maintenance of a friendly relationship between sender and recipient(s), and *parousia*, whereby the letter serves as a substitute form of authorial presence.[25] So pervasive are these features that they can equally be illustrated from the Roman world: the Roman Stoic and moralist Lucius Annaeus Seneca (also known as "Seneca the Younger," ca. 4 BC–AD 65) writes to his friend Lucilius, "Whenever your letters arrive, I imagine that I am with you, and I have the feeling that I am about to speak my answer, instead of writing it" (*Moral Epistles* 67.2 [Gummere, LCL]).

Because the writer is unable (or, in Paul's case, temporarily unwilling) to be present, a Hellenistic letter conveys the voice and concerns of the writer, inviting the recipient to respond and thereby further extend the give-and-take that is constitutive of their larger relationship. This dialogical tone, appealing directly to the interests and sympathies of the recipients, is frequently evident in 2 Corinthians:

> We do not want you to be unaware, brothers and sisters, of the affliction we experienced in Asia.
>
> 2 Corinthians 1:8

> For if I cause you pain, who is there to make me glad but the one whom I have pained?
>
> 2 Corinthians 2:2

23. Heikki Koskenniemi, *Studien zur Idee und Phraseologie des griechischen Briefes bis 400 n. Chr.* (AASF B 102.2; Helsinki: Suomalainen Tiedeakatemia, 1956), 42–47; cf. the summary in William G. Doty, *Letters in Primitive Christianity* (GBS; Philadelphia: Fortress, 1973), 12, also quoted by Thomas G. Long, *Preaching and the Literary Forms of the Bible* (Philadelphia: Fortress, 1985), 112, 115–16.

24. Koskenniemi, *Studien*, 43–44; cf. Doty, *Letters*, 8.

25. Koskenniemi, *Studien*, 35–42.

Are we beginning to commend ourselves again? Surely we do not need, as some do, letters of recommendation to you or from you, do we?

2 Corinthians 3:1

We entreat you on behalf of Christ, be reconciled to God.

2 Corinthians 5:20

We have spoken frankly to you Corinthians; our heart is wide open to you.

2 Corinthians 6:11

This is, in part, what makes Paul's correspondence seem so accessible to later audiences, who hear themselves addressed by such words. This phenomenon is not limited to instances of exhortation or ethical instruction: because Paul directs his words to a specific audience, subsequent readers and hearers find themselves engaged by and invited to answer the apostle's epistolary rhetoric. There is a distinct sense, therefore, in which the preacher of Paul's message furthers in oral form something very similar to what Paul himself was attempting by means of his letters. That is, preachers simultaneously "answer" the apostle and articulate new configurations of his voice to which their own hearers may respond in turn, further extending a theological and spiritual dialogue begun by the "word of the cross" itself (1 Cor. 1:18).

An emphasis on spirituality suggests that Christian preaching of every age may learn from and legitimately model itself after Paul's example on the following grounds. By way of general principle, preaching is an activity directed to the glory of the same God whom Paul worshiped and served. More specifically, as Paul responded to the activity of God in his own circumstances according to the paradigm of Jesus's cross and resurrection, so preachers and congregants may do likewise. What Paul did, therefore, other preachers may seek to do, even while knowing that their own preaching will not be as powerful, permanent, or paradigmatic as that of the one they imitate.

Notwithstanding its translation into the many languages of the modern world, Paul's voice is always that of the "other"; it is "foreign" in every sense.[26] Not only is it in Koine Greek, a form of language no longer spoken

26. The quality of "otherness" (alternatively, "outsidedness" or "exotopy") is for Bakhtin an essential feature of the dialogical dynamic. By this he means that each

22

anywhere in the world, it also speaks out of a distant, foreign culture, one that we can recover only in part. We must work hard to recognize and appreciate the cultural contexts and norms that Paul would have taken for granted. In addition to knowing the semantic range of words that he uses, we must inquire, for example, into the political implications of the title *Kyrios* ("Lord"), or the social significance of crucifixion. We will want to ask what role slaves played in the ancient city of Corinth; how patronage and social distinctions likely functioned in a small, voluntary association such as that of the Corinthian church; and what influence the presence of the mighty Roman army would have had on its view of the world. Not least is the matter of Paul's own apostolic commissioning, whereby the voice of none other than the risen Christ has called him to proclaim the Lord's death and resurrection. These and a host of other questions will help us to identify the "voices" and meanings that Paul's audience would have understood, and to which the apostle either appealed or responded in shaping his message. Only once we have done that will we be able to attempt a further "translation" of sorts so as to hear and communicate the voice of Paul to the hearers of our day.

But two qualifications are in order. First, the "otherness" and "foreignness" of the text and its world are assets rather than obstacles to preaching, for they remind preachers and hearers alike that the message in question has a life outside the pulpit, one that cannot be disarmed, domesticated, or consumed by modern renderings. As Fred Craddock aptly observes,

> To say the distance of the text is welcomed is to say that the preacher, sometimes weary of his or her own voice, is glad to hear another voice, the voice of the text, speak to the congregation. The text provides the occasion for the preacher, who is always speaking, to be spoken to. . . . Also welcomed is the opportunity to move inside the strange world of the text, getting away for awhile from the pulpit and pews, to discern afresh whether preacher and congregation are truly being addressed by another Word or only hearing echoes of their own voices.[27]

---

voice neither subsumes nor is subsumed by the others with which it is in dialogue, but always remains external to them, and they to it. See further Michael Holquist, "Existence as Dialogue," in *Dialogism: Bakhtin and His World* (London: Routledge, 1990), 27–39; Green, *Bakhtin and Biblical Scholarship*, 33–35.

27. Fred Craddock, "Preaching to the Corinthians," *Int* 44 (1990): 158–59.

Second, we do well to recall that Paul's message appears as strange and as counterintuitive within his own social and historical setting as it does in ours. For Paul, the message of the cross, and the cruciform spirituality that it conveys, constantly contradict the expectations of his hearers. Likewise the Corinthians are perplexed and frequently in conflict with him because he conducts himself in a manner contrary to the cultural norms of their day. The more we come to understand the causes and dimensions of this conflict, the more accurately we will be able to distinguish between cultural dissonance, on the one hand, and underlying theological principles, on the other.

Paul would claim that although articulated in human language, the counterintuitive quality of the Christian message derives from its ultimately non-human origin, and its function as divine revelation. To the extent that it echoes or represents the "voice" of God, its meaning is not solely or wholly reliant on semantic antecedents or social contexts. Paul's preaching of the cross, then, presents to the Corinthians a distinctively divine word in human language, a word of the ultimate Other. Perhaps an initial clue to this distinctiveness appears precisely in its perplexing denial of cultural norms and expectations. Particularly in the construct of crucifixion, as we shall see, Paul claims that this divine voice countermands and silences *all* merely human voices in order to make its own heard. On the one hand, revelation does not call human voices into a partnership of dialogical equals, but insists that its own voice prevail. Yet it does so in the most paradoxical manner possible, by initially allowing even its own voice—that of Jesus of Nazareth—to fall silent at the cross in order to be heard anew under terms and conditions determined by God alone.

As we seek to articulate the gospel by entering into dialogue with voices from the past, Paul's foremost among them, we are confronted by the necessity of silence. We are challenged by the voicelessness of the crucified Jesus and the fact that no human voice (not even Paul's) can fully express the "unsearchable" judgments and "inscrutable" ways of God (Rom. 11:33). We arrive at this conclusion not on the philosophical grounds that God is "beyond" human language (a premise denied by the Incarnation), but by the fact that if the voice of Jesus fails, then so too must all human voices. Even so—and as a further reversal of expectation—it turns out that our voicelessness and silence need be no more final than Jesus's own. On the contrary, preachers are bidden to enter into the conditions of his silence so that we may become subject to the necessity of God's self-articulation, and so that our preaching may subsequently depend not merely on our own voices, but also on the voice of God.

For this is Paul's own task, which preachers and congregants alike may properly imitate. Both in person and by letter, by word and example, Paul proclaims Christ's death and resurrection: he embodies and articulates a spirituality of the cross. Because the Messiah is no longer physically present to the church, Paul proposes his own preaching and cruciform lifestyle in Christ's stead; because he cannot be present in Corinth, Paul sends letters instead; because Jesus is no longer on earth, Paul contends that the life of the congregation presents Christ to the world, insofar as congregants too live out the pattern of their Lord's death and resurrection. Likewise preachers present Christ to all who see and hear them, as they are seized, shaped, and inspired to speak by the lethal, life-giving dynamic of Jesus's cross.

For the most part, the chapters that follow are addressed to practitioners—active or soon-to-be-active preachers of the Christian message. Notwithstanding the many footnotes and references to scholarly discussion, they are intended primarily as a guide to the practical implications of Paul's preaching. Readers who wish to explore the social and historical background of 2 Corinthians will find such matters discussed in the next two sections, titled "The Setting of the Letter: Corinth and its First Christian Congregation" and "Conflict in Corinth." Others who are more immediately interested in engaging Paul's text may turn to one of the subsequent chapters, each of which examines a section of his letter:

- Chapter One: "Affliction and Consolation" (2 Cor. 1:1–2:13)
- Chapter Two: "Triumph and Captivity, Sacrifice and Sufficiency" (2 Cor. 2:14–17)
- Chapter Three: "Confidence and Conviction" (2 Cor. 3:1–18)
- Chapter Four: "Not Ourselves" (2 Cor. 4:1–15)
- Chapter Five: "Glory and Hope" (2 Cor. 4:16–5:15)
- Chapter Six: "Ambassadors for Christ" (2 Cor. 5:16–6:13).

Each of these can be read as a more-or-less self-contained discussion of the passage and its implications for preaching, while the seventh and final chapter draws together a brief series of observations and conclusions from the study as a whole.

The Setting of the Letter: Corinth and Its First Christian Congregation

Following Luke's account in Acts 18, it would appear that Paul arrived in Corinth about AD 50 and remained there for "a year and six months" (Acts 18:11) in order to preach and establish a congregation. Paul's description of this initiative indicates that he began ministry in Corinth "in weakness and in fear and in much trembling" (1 Cor. 2:3), an estimation confirmed by Luke's report that Paul needed the encouragement of a direct word from the Lord: "Do not be afraid, but speak and do not be silent; for I am with you, and no one will lay a hand on you to harm you" (Acts 18:9–10). The Greek-speaking orator and historian and a near-contemporary of Paul, Dio Chrysostom (ca. AD 40–120) notes the fickle and dangerous nature of Hellenistic audiences:

> the audience might cheer and applaud with enthusiasm, or raise an uproar, shouting the speaker down; they might sit, silent and indulgent, or pelt the speaker with stones out of rage; they might listen raptly in awe, or respond with jeering, hissing, derisive laughter, or crude jokes. In short, the audience had it in its power to terrify and dominate the speaker if it cared to.[28]

Paul's various detractors and opponents later concur that "his bodily presence is weak, and his speech contemptible" (2 Cor. 10:10). No wonder, then, that he is unsure of himself.

First and Second Corinthians (as well Paul's letter to the Romans, written from Corinth) offer vital clues to the nature of the congregation, which includes both Jews and Gentiles (1 Cor. 7:18–20), slaves and freeborn or freed (1 Cor. 7:21–24), those of Roman and of Greek extraction.[29] In general, Paul finds the congregation to be spiritually immature (1 Cor. 3:1–4) and unreflective (1 Cor. 14:20); they are badly divided (1 Cor. 1:10–13), likely along the lines of social stratification, for such divisions manifest themselves particularly in the context of community gatherings (1 Cor. 11:18–19). By

28. This summary of material from Dio Chrysostom's *Discourses* is provided by Duane Litfin, *St. Paul's Theology of Proclamation: 1 Corinthians 1–4 and Greco-Roman Rhetoric* (SNTSMS 79; Cambridge: Cambridge University Press, 1994), 126–27.

29. For a full treatment of the social environment of ancient Corinth and its Christian community in particular, see Wayne A. Meeks, *The First Urban Christians: The Social World of the Apostle Paul* (New Haven: Yale University Press, 1983), esp. 47–72.

modern standards the congregation is probably small.[30] Even though it incorporates still smaller groups from several households, Paul can speak of the "whole church" gathering in one place (1 Cor. 14:23).[31] By the time Paul writes to Rome, the "whole church" gathers in the house of Gaius (Rom. 16:23; cf. 1 Cor. 11:18, 20). How many souls might fit under the roof of a Roman-style house? Perhaps thirty or forty is a reasonable guess. Paul mentions, at most, sixteen members of the congregation by name, two of these (Stephanas and Chloe) in connection with other believing members of their respective households who likely joined them in worship.[32] Most clubs or voluntary associations in the Greco-Roman world (of which there were many) were equally modest, typically incorporating "from a dozen to thirty or forty, rarely more than a hundred members."[33] At least in this respect, the Corinthian congregation is thus quite similar to many of our own churches today: small, struggling, and of limited social significance.

One of the more entertaining—and intractable—difficulties in Pauline scholarship is that of reconstructing the chronology of Paul's letters and previous visits to Corinth. The letter we know as Second Corinthians is probably his fourth to the congregation (cf. 1 Cor. 4:17; 5:9; 2 Cor. 2:3–4; 7:8), and they have written at least one reply (1 Cor. 7:1). First Corinthians is likely sent from Ephesus where, Paul says, he has encountered both opportunity and adversity (1 Cor. 16:5–9). In the same passage, he announces a forthcoming visit to Corinth, the details of which bring much complaint from church members, not least because he appears to change his plans and arrives unexpectedly (2 Cor. 1:23, 2:1). Indeed, this "painful visit" seems to have been occasioned by some personal hurt or betrayal directed at Paul, causing even more strife within the congregation (2 Cor. 2:5–8). Even so, Paul wants to fulfill his original plan, but does not wish to arrive in Corinth without first gaining some sense of

30. Pace Gerd Theissen, who concludes on the basis of Acts 18:10, in which the Lord tells Paul that "many people [*polus . . . laos*]" in Corinth are his followers, that "the congregation at Corinth was large" (*The Social Setting of Pauline Christianity: Essays on Corinth*, tr. John H. Schütz [Philadelphia: Fortress, 1982], 89).

31. Cf. Meeks, *First Urban Christians*, 75–76, and, further, L. Michael White, "House Churches," in Eric M. Meyers, ed., *The Oxford Encyclopedia of Archaeology in the Near East* (New York: Oxford University Press, 1997), 3:118–21.

32. Cf. Theissen, *Social Setting*, 94–95; also Furnish, 24–26 (with an introduction to the social, religious, and historical background of Roman Corinth, pp. 4–26).

33. Meeks, *First Urban Christians*, 31.

27

what reception might await him. So he sends Titus to evaluate the situation. Apparently the Corinthian Christians are as anxious as Paul is, for they are said to have welcomed Titus "with fear and trembling" (2 Cor. 7:15). Hoping to meet Titus on his way back, Paul continues the journey overland, reporting that he is "afflicted in every way [by] disputes without and fears within" (2 Cor. 7:5). Much to Paul's relief, however, Titus brings a favorable report (2 Cor. 7:6–7, 13–15).

This, then, is the setting in which much of 2 Corinthians seems to have been composed (cf. 2 Cor. 9:2, 4). Now that Titus has allayed some of his fears, Paul writes another letter to the congregation (some or all of what we know as Second Corinthians), this time to explain his delay in arriving. Indeed, he hopes to justify not only his recent actions but also his ministry as a whole, which detractors have evidently called into question. Building on the success of his recent visit, Titus returns to Corinth with this letter in hand (2 Cor. 8:6), accompanied by "another brother" whom Paul declines to name (2 Cor. 12:18).

Even if some of the details are uncertain, this reconstruction of the Corinthian situation indicates the pastoral realities of Paul's ministry. Not unlike the way in which Jesus's profoundly flawed and ordinary disciples have been polished and sanctified beyond recognition by the piety of succeeding generations, preachers in particular seem to accord Paul almost superhuman qualities. So penetrating and profound is his theology that he appears, at least in the minds of some, virtually detached from the messiness of everyday life. But nothing could be further from the truth. We see in this exchange of letters and visits a pastor/theologian wrestling for the allegiance of his congregation, beset by personal doubts, on the one hand, and public opposition, on the other. Paul is at times far from certain that he is even welcome in the congregation he once founded. Like Jacob preparing to encounter Esau, he dares not visit without preparing the way by means of letters and personal emissaries. Although Paul had entrusted the congregation to the care of others, new leaders have arrived or arisen who oppose and denigrate him. He calls such individuals "super-apostles," an ironic admission of how much superior to him they consider themselves to be (2 Cor. 11:5, 12:11). On more than one occasion, Paul is reduced to pleading with his former congregation to believe that everything he has done has been solely out of sincerity, love, and pastoral concern (2 Cor. 1:12, 23; 2:4, etc.). Yet he is painfully aware that the more he does so, the more they will accuse him of self-justification (2 Cor. 3:1).

In this light, the apostle takes on startlingly human dimensions, and there is much here that contemporary pastors and preachers will find painfully familiar. Criticism, conflict, and opposition even to endeavors initiated with the best intentions are part and parcel of every pastor's experience. Conflict and congregational ministry seem to go hand in hand, and far from being above this sort of turmoil, Paul writes in the thick of it. The explanation that he provides of ministry in general and preaching in particular applies well beyond his own situation, giving new meaning to words of encouragement that Paul had originally directed only to a select few: "Yes, everything is for your sake, so that grace, as it extends to more and more people, may increase thanksgiving, to the glory of God" (2 Cor. 4:15). Of course, the fact that one faces conflict provides no justification for the course of action that has given rise to it, and such opposition may be amply justified! Nor can we claim for ourselves the foundational status or full apostolic authority once bestowed on Paul. So before we rush to adduce parallels between the radically different social and historical situations of the apostle's world and our own, we need to be clearer about the kind of opposition he faced.

Conflict in Corinth

Much critical ink has been spilled over the identity of Paul's opponents in Corinth. But before we categorize his opponents as (for example) Judaizers, Gnostics, or Hellenistic Jewish missionaries, the difficulties Paul encounters can more easily be explained in light of contemporary social and historical circumstances, to the extent that these can be reconstructed. Largely because of its strategic location, Corinth is a wealthy boomtown at the time of Paul's ministry there. Destroyed in 146 BC, Corinth had been rebuilt in magnificent splendor as a Roman colony. Its population is dominated by the upwardly mobile and *nouveaux riche*, who amply illustrate the social opportunism characteristic of the age:

> Late Hellenism stressed an individual's ability to determine his own worth. When the Roman emphasis on social stratification penetrated Greek society, people gained both a framework for measuring worth and an incentive to reach higher. In theory, higher status was attained through wealth and/or

some other social advantage. But this was meaningless unless acknowledged by others. Consequently, people competed for attention. They paraded their lives before their contemporaries in an attempt to earn applause and esteem. Assertiveness and pride characterized their efforts and boasting was *de rigueur*. When people turned to appraise their counterparts they looked for the same indications of worth and status which they valued for themselves: namely, impressive displays meriting public applause and esteem.[34]

Particularly is this so of the citizens to whom Paul writes: "In Corinth, perhaps more than anywhere else, social ascent was the goal, boasting and self-display the means, personal power and glory the reward."[35] Popular religion fits perfectly into this more general pattern:

> The great allure of the cults may be summed up in a few words: "the visible show of the divinity at work." People yearned to see divine power. They wanted to be thrilled by it and even terrified by it. Accordingly, the cults publicized the feats of the gods. . . . Converts did not regard the god's power passively, but wanted to experience that power for themselves. The more powerful one's god the more strength one expected to receive and manifest.[36]

The Corinthians and their contemporaries thus understand "salvation" not as present moral transformation or even as safe passage to the afterlife, but rather in terms of "health, wealth, protection, and sustenance." As Savage explains, far from challenging the devotee ethically or existentially, popular religion largely "confirmed an individual in the pursuit of happiness and satisfaction."[37] Accordingly, much of what Paul has to say (particularly on the subject of crucifixion) and the

34. Timothy B. Savage, *Power Through Weakness: Paul's Understanding of the Christian Ministry in 2 Corinthians* (SNTSMS 86; Cambridge: Cambridge University Press, 1996), 25. This dynamic is helpfully set out by Peter Garnsey and Richard Saller, "Patronal Power Relations," with multiple examples from Corinth and elsewhere in the empire in John K. Chow, "Patronage in Roman Corinth," and Richard Gordon, "The Veil of Power," all in Richard A. Horsley, ed., *Paul and Empire: Religion and Power in Roman Imperial Society* (Harrisburg: Trinity, 1997), 96–137.

35. Savage, *Power Through Weakness*, 41.

36. Ibid., 29, citing R. MacMullen, *Paganism in the Roman Empire* (New Haven: Yale University Press, 1981), 126.

37. Savage, *Power Through Weakness*, 28, 34, 159.

manner in which he conducts his ministry run directly counter to the Corinthians' expectations of how religion should function. Whereas they place a premium on self-aggrandizement and personal advantage, Paul exemplifies self-abasement; where they look for boasting and eloquence as indicative of spiritual authority, Paul is contemptibly plainspoken, boasting only when forced to; against their expectation of present affirmation and reward, Paul replies, "If for this life only we have hoped in Christ, we are of all people most to be pitied" (1 Cor. 15:19). Even in the matter of financial support, Paul chooses to work for a living rather than allowing them to boast of prospering him (1 Cor. 4:12; 2 Cor. 11:8–9). Even Paul's habit of teaching in synagogues and private homes designates him as being of low social standing, further contradicting the congregants' aspirations to social advancement.[38] Savage summarizes the situation as follows:

> In each of the areas in which the Corinthians find fault with Paul—his boasting, his physical presence, his speech and his support—we have discovered not only that his converts are drawing inspiration from the social outlook of the day but also that Paul responds by adopting a position which represents the exact antithesis of what they would have desired in a religious leader. While the Corinthians will find his position offensive, Paul insists that it actually works for their good. The reason for this fundamental disagreement between Paul and his converts would seem to boil down to a conflict between two opposing perspectives: the worldly outlook of the Corinthians and Paul's own Christ-centered viewpoint.[39]

Savage's ultimate purpose is to elucidate the way in which, throughout 2 Corinthians, Paul defends himself and his congregational ministry by demonstrating that the very features his audience despises are those most consonant with the gospel of Jesus's cross and resurrection that he proclaims. Although he acknowledges apostolic proclamation to be an important aspect of Paul's ministry, Savage does not single it out for special attention, or suggest ways in which the rich results of his study

38. Stowers, "Circumstances of Paul's Preaching Activity," 81: "Public speaking and often the use of public buildings required status, reputation, and recognized roles which Paul did not have. Public speaking, on the one hand, often necessitated some type of legitimation or invitation or, on the other hand, demanded that the speaker somehow force himself on his audience."
39. Savage, *Power Through Weakness*, 99.

might be relevant for preachers of a later day. To this question we now turn, following Paul in 2 Corinthians as he continues to defend himself and his ministry of proclamation in particular against the opposition and outright misunderstanding that have arisen. In doing so, we bear in mind a series of key issues and principles that help bridge the gap between the church of Corinth and the church of today. Paul is, in the first instance, a pastor, calling his congregation to faithfulness in Christ. Since his own life and preaching are fundamentally shaped by the cross and resurrection of Jesus, to preach from Paul draws us into the darkness of Christ's death and the light of resurrection. Doing this brings us also, like Paul and the early apostles, into direct conflict with many values and social standards of our day—even values and standards that prevail in the contemporary church.

1

Affliction and Consolation
(1:1–2:13)

The basic task of every preacher, according to Paul, is to interpret the
lives of their congregants—and all human experience—in light of Jesus's
cross and resurrection, and to find there the foundational pattern of God's
saving intervention in response to ongoing human need. He comes to
this pastoral and theological insight in the course of personal trials that
severely test, yet ultimately affirm his faith. The unexpected conclusion
to which this leads him is that it is not personal strength, gifts, or ability,
but ongoing weakness and insufficiency that draw even preachers near
to Christ—not only at the outset, but throughout the course of their
discipleship and ministry. In fact, Jesus's crucifixion and resurrection
determine not only the preacher's message, not only the shape of Christian experience in general, but the act of preaching in particular, because
preaching is an act of utter dependence on the grace and generosity of a
life-giving God. Implying that Christian confession calls into question all
other claims of personal, social, and political allegiance, Paul explores the
practical dimensions of proclaiming Christ crucified and risen against the
competing standards of popular culture and the religious expectations of
his young converts in Corinth.

The Letter Opening: Establishing the Theological Context for Proclamation (1:1–2)

> Paul, an apostle of Christ Jesus by the will of God, and Timothy our brother, to the church of God that is in Corinth, including all the saints throughout Achaia: Grace to you and peace from God our Father and the Lord Jesus Christ.
>
> 2 Corinthians 1:1–2

The opening of what we know as Paul's second letter to this fledgling congregation establishes the basic theological parameters of Christian proclamation, whether offered in person or by letter, by voice or written text. Paul begins by announcing that he is "an apostle of Christ Jesus by the will of God," a statement that expresses three key features of his ministerial identity. Ancient Hellenistic letters were "signed" at the outset rather than at the end, and this one is no exception. Although to some degree unrepeatable by virtue both of the format and of the letter's canonical status, Paul's self-description is nonetheless instructive. First, he is an "apostle," by which he means that he has been specially commissioned for the task of preaching the gospel by an encounter with the risen Christ (1 Cor. 9:1, 17; 15:8–9). Later preachers are not wise to make the same claim; they can, however, legitimately point to Christ's resurrection as the ultimate warrant for their own message (a premise we will later explore in greater detail). Second, Paul makes it clear that he has not taken on this title or task by his own volition: rather, he is an apostle "by the will of God," constrained by a purpose that outweighs his own (cf. 1 Cor. 9:17). Third, he is an apostle "of Christ Jesus." Certainly Paul belongs to Christ, having been made a "slave of Christ" (so 1 Cor. 7:22), but this phrase reiterates in addition the source and origin of Paul's apostolic calling.[1] And it is this sense of being owned and commissioned by Christ that explains (both for Paul and for preachers in the Christian tradition) the christocentric content of his apostolic proclamation.

But one further theological claim lies implicit within this seemingly conventional and familiar use of titles. Paul's declaration that he is "an apostle of *Christ Jesus*" identifies the Jewish Messiah with a precise

---

1. Gordon D. Fee, *The First Epistle to the Corinthians* (NICNT; Grand Rapids: Eerdmans, 1987), 30 (on 1 Cor. 1:1); cf. Barrett, 53.

historical figure. Paul's sense of apostolic identity, and therefore also his preaching, are rooted in an appreciation of Jesus that combines a concrete historical reference with a tradition of theological interpretation. The one whom Paul proclaims is both the man from Nazareth and the Messiah of Jewish expectation: in the combined formulation "Christ Jesus" the mundane and the metaphysical are inseparable. This seems particularly relevant to our recurrent tendency to focus on one at the expense of the other. Too many preachers affirm Jesus's humanity but confess embarrassment at claims of divinity, or vice versa.

But Paul is not alone here. Timothy may not share the title of "apostle," but he is nonetheless Paul's coauthor and "brother." Just as Paul, Timothy, and Silvanus together first preached the gospel in Corinth (2 Cor. 1:19), so this letter represents a shared ministry, as Paul and Timothy jointly greet those who have been transformed by Christ.[2] Whether in person, then, or by letter, even apostolic preaching is multi-vocal, a work carried out in partnership and community. Appropriately, then, the first note of this joint endeavor is to remind the recipients of their *theological* identity: they are "the church of God that is in Corinth," those who have together been made "saints" by God's saving purpose. Whatever other social distinctives they may or may not enjoy, their single, most determinative characteristic is a product neither of culture nor of society (much less of their own making), but a gift of God. The same, surely, applies to all preachers and their congregations, who share a common theological identity in Christ. Likewise all preaching—whether acknowledged as such or not—is necessarily an expression of community and (at best) has in view the formation of Christian community on the basis of a new identity bestowed by Christ alone.

The theologically definitive character of these opening phrases is even clearer in the greeting itself: "Grace to you and peace from God our Father and the Lord Jesus Christ." Much has been written about the distinctive nature of this characteristic Pauline salutation. In place of the verb *chairein* (more or less the equivalent of "greetings, welcome") with which Hellenistic letters tended to open (Acts 15:23; 23:26; James 1:1), Paul shrewdly selects its more theologically explicit cognate, *charis*, "grace." This he combines with the Greek equivalent of the typical Hebrew greeting, *shalom*, "peace." The

2. Additionally intriguing is the virtual certainty that Paul has made use of an amanuensis (2 Thess. 3:17; cf. 1 Cor. 16:21), an anonymous scribe whose task is essential to the transmission of Paul's message.

salutation "grace and peace" thus implicitly acknowledges the mixed religious ancestry of his audience. The word order communicates to Gentiles first, but also to Jews (reversing the order in Rom. 1:16; 2:9–10, but perhaps reflecting the priorities of Paul's own ministry: Rom. 15:16, 18). To the Jews Paul announces that God has effected reconciliation and established harmony, "peace," in the person of Jesus (cf. Rom. 5:1; Eph. 2:14–17, etc.). Insofar as *shalom* is a theological concept with concrete social and political ramifications, Paul thus declares Jesus to be the ultimate manifestation of God's gracious reign, anticipated by the entire course of Israelite history.

Of course, Paul—together with the "Lord" and "Father" on whose behalf he speaks—is not the only one who promises "peace" to the people of Corinth. This was also the claim of Rome and its vast empire: *Pax Romana*, obtained by military conquest, maintained by crippling taxation, and ordered in a strict social hierarchy with the founding city and its citizens at the top.[3] With regard to Corinth in particular, Julius Caesar's re-establishment of the city as a Roman colony in 46 BC had conferred Roman citizenship on the settlers (mostly freed slaves) and their descendants.[4] For Paul to insist that true "peace" originated instead with an obscure victim of Roman power—the crucified Jesus—might be seen as inviting dangerous political ingratitude on the part of the Corinthian believers.

No less potentially treasonous are the titles Paul employs. It would hardly have escaped notice that both "Father" and "Lord" (as well as, incidentally, "Savior" and "Son of [a] god") were titles with significant political overtones, for these applied in the first instance to the Roman emperor. By the turn of the common era, Caesar Augustus had been accorded the supreme honorific, *Pater Patriae*, "Father of the Fatherland," designating him as patron and benefactor of the empire as a whole. The same title passed to his sons and successors, as did the semi-divine designation *Kyrios*, "Lord."[5] Thus to refer to Jesus as *Kyrios*, or to the God

---

3. See further Klaus Wengst, *Pax Romana and the Peace of Jesus Christ*, tr. John Bowden (Philadelphia: Fortress, 1987), 7–54.

4. Pace Gerd Theissen, *The Social Setting of Pauline Christianity: Essays on Corinth*, tr. John H. Schütz (Philadelphia: Fortress, 1982), 99.

5. See the titles and inscriptions cited by T. H. Kim, "The Anarthrous *huios theou* in Mark 15, 39 and the Roman Imperial Cult," *Bib* 79 (1998): 234–36n34, n36, esp. the examples referring to Claudius and Nero. The title *Pater Patriae* was not automatically accorded to emperors, but only to those deemed to have made a significant contribution to the welfare of the empire.

of Israel as "Father," was to fly in the face of Roman political domination and, worse yet, to deny allegiance (that is, gratitude and obligation) to the true patron and "Lord" of every Roman subject.[6] For the Corinthians at the time of Paul's writing, this might have been Claudius (in office AD 41–54), or, more likely, his adopted son, the ruinously dissolute Nero (AD 54–68). But the personal virtue of a particular emperor was of secondary concern. What mattered most was publicly ascribing "honor to whom honor is due," as Paul acknowledges (Rom. 13:7). As Seneca, Paul's near contemporary, pointedly observes, "Homicides, tyrants, traitors there will always be: but worse than all these is the crime of ingratitude" (*On Benefits* 1.10.4).[7] On the other hand, perhaps it is too much to imagine that—at least initially—many outside the small circle of Christian believers would have taken such claims seriously, much less be offended by them. More likely these would have seemed sufficiently ridiculous as to occasion little more than a snicker of derision or a snort of disbelief.

The implications of *charis*, "grace," are equally profound and far-reaching for those of Greco-Roman religious background, for whom this term describes a key feature of the divine-human relationship:

> [*Charis*] is often translated "grace" or "favor." In fact, it refers to a whole nexus of related ideas that we would call reciprocity. When one gives something to a god, one is giving *charis* in the sense that the offering is pleasing; but equally one is storing up for oneself a feeling of gratitude on the part of the god, which is also *charis*. The whole two-way relationship can be called one of *charis*. . . . The worshipper establishes with the god a relationship not of strict indebtedness but rather one where the god remembers the gift and feels well disposed in future.[8]

---

6. As Chow ("Patronage in Roman Corinth," in Richard A. Horsley, ed., *Paul and Empire: Religion and Power in Roman Imperial Society* [Harrisburg: Trinity, 1997], passim) observes, the dynamic of patron-client relations, extending hierarchically from the Emperor down to the common slave, applied to every aspect of Corinthian social organization: even "the name of the colony, *Colonia Laus Julia Corinthiensis*, stood as a constant reminder of the grace of Julius Caesar who helped to refound the colony" (106).

7. Cited by Garnsey and Saller, "Patronal Power Relations" in Richard A. Horsley, ed., *Paul and Empire: Religion and Power in Roman Imperial Society* (Harrisburg: Trinity, 1997), 96.

8. Simon Pulleyn, *Prayer in Greek Religion* (Oxford: Clarendon, 1997), 4, 13; see, more comprehensively, David A. deSilva, "Patronage and Reciprocity: The Context of Grace in the New Testament," *Ashland Theological Journal* 31 (1999): 32–84.

The usual translation, "favor," has a similar range of meaning. By doing the gods a "favor," one hopes to receive "favor" or to be viewed "favorably" by them in turn. Or having received divine favor, the worshiper gives an offering or sacrifice of "thanks" (which *charis* can also mean) in return. The exchange is neither mechanical nor automatic, but describes a way of relating to the gods that mirrors the way social obligations work in human society. Thus both the noun, *charis*, and the related verb, *chairein* (which means "to please or favor" here), express the essential notion of reciprocal obligation that undergirds prayer in particular within Hellenistic religion.[9]

According to Lochman, "most people in the Hellenistic age lived under the shadow of fatalistic constraints, surrendered to the superior might of ominous 'principalities and powers.'"[10] In other words, divine "favor" was not easy to come by, and the firm grip of the gods neither gentle nor kind. The fate of King Oedipus, who must fulfill a cruel destiny of patricide and incest, provides a case in point—all the more so for our purposes as his terrifying and tragic story unfolds in Corinth.[11] Although Christians of a later age seem no longer astonished by the concept of *charis*, Paul's audience would surely have been stunned to learn of the God who not only set their lives free from bondage to implacable fate, but by virtue of Jesus's self-offering had poured out on them a rich abundance of unearned and un-repayable "favor." The NRSV neatly captures this sense in its translation of 2 Corinthians 8:9: "For you know the generous act [*charis*] of our Lord Jesus Christ, that though he was rich, yet for your sakes he became poor, so that by his poverty *you might become rich*." Likewise the parallelism of Romans 5:15 underscores the gratuity of "grace":

> For if the many died through the one man's trespass,
>   much more surely have the *grace* of God

9. So David E. Aune, "Prayer in the Greco-Roman World," in Richard N. Longenecker, ed., *Into God's Presence: Prayer in the New Testament* (Grand Rapids: Eerdmans, 2001), 26–27. See further M. P. Knowles, "Reciprocity and 'Favour' in the Parable of the Undeserving Servant (Luke 17.7–10)," *NTS* 49 (2003): 256–60.

10. Jan Milič Lochman, *The Theology of Praise* (Atlanta: John Knox, 1982), 7–8.

11. *Oedipus the King*, by the Greek tragedian Sophocles (ca. 496–406 BC), relates how Oedipus's desperate attempts to avoid a prophecy that he will murder his father and marry his mother invariably serve to fulfill it.

and the *free gift* [*dorea*] in the *grace* of the one man, Jesus
Christ,
abounded for the many.[12]

Thus with a single phrase, *charis hymin* ("grace to you"), Paul rebuts an
entire worldview, on the grounds that the sense of human obligation that
it expressed has been overturned by Christ.[13] The generosity of Israel's
God has trumped any obligation to the gods of Rome.

To this may be compared, in a much earlier context, the equally
radical implications of Israelite theology in light of Babylonian cultic
ideology. Defeated militarily and exiled in Babylon, the Israelites were
subject not only to physical oppression but also to a theology that declared them to be "slaves or indentured servants of the gods, created
for the express purpose of ministering to their needs."[14] According to
Babylonian mythology, human beings were created from the blood of
a defeated and slain god, Kingu (an enemy of Marduk, patron god of
Babylon). If, then, ordinary Babylonians understood their lot to be one
of perpetual servitude, with Babylonian society as a whole structured
around the tending of temples and shrines, how much more so did
this apply to slaves of the state, over whom the servants of Marduk
had themselves proven victorious. Scholars concur that the Israelite
account of creation was written in just such a setting for the express
purpose of rebutting a Babylonian worldview. The alternative? That
Israel's God had created humanity not as debased slaves, but as trusted
stewards "in his image," with the responsibility of tending and caring
for the whole of creation (Gen. 1:27–28).[15]

12. Indeed, Rom. 5:15–17 employs a range of parallel terms to express the same
idea: *charisma* ("gift as an expression of *charis*," 5:15a, 16b), *dorea* ("gift," 5:15b, 17),
dorema ("gift," 5:16a), and three occurrences of *charis* itself. Cf. Rom. 3:24.

13. Gorman (*Cruciformity: Paul's Narrative Spirituality of the Cross* [Grand Rapids:
Eerdmans, 2001], 26) points out that Paul's emphasis on the magnitude and magna-
nimity of divine grace likely reflects the circumstances of his own conversion.

14. J. Richard Middleton and Brian J. Walsh, *Truth Is Stranger Than it Used to
Be: Biblical Faith in a Postmodern Age* (Downers Grove, IL: InterVarsity, 1995), 115;
cf. the more extensive treatment in J. Richard Middleton, *The Liberating Image: The
Imago Dei in Genesis 1* (Grand Rapids: Brazos, 2005), 149–67.

15. For comprehensive expositions of this theme, see Middleton and Walsh,
Truth Is Stranger, 115–25, and, more fully, Middleton, *Liberating Image*, passim
(esp. 185–231).

Such examples suggest the vast scope and radical agenda of Christian (and Jewish) preaching. Far from limiting itself to the concerns of personal devotion, the proclamation of salvation as practiced by Paul (like the compilers of Hebrew scripture) goes beyond even social and political concerns to confront the reigning "myths" of contemporary culture. In our day and age, these myths are less obviously theological, except to the extent that avowedly secular governments employ such slogans as "In God we trust," "God save the Queen," or "God keep our land glorious and free." Our own ideologies tend to be material and economic, defining human value in terms of sexual identity, social influence, or the production and consumption of material goods. Notwithstanding the fact that he counsels submission to the state, apparently for the sake of avoiding offense (Rom. 13:1–7; cf. 1 Cor. 10:32), Paul is unequivocal in his confrontation of contemporary social and political ideologies (as we will see in later chapters).[16] By declaring "grace to you and peace," he asserts a carefully delineated divine purpose for humanity against whatever definitions of personal or national identity are established by prevailing cultures and political entities for the benefit of their citizens.

The implications for contemporary Christian preaching of the simple phrase, "Grace to you and peace from God our Father and the Lord Jesus Christ," are so extensive as to require volumes of exposition in their own right. We will have occasion later in this study to examine in greater detail some consequences for our present day of God's decisive reformulation of human identity. But for the moment, we must be content with observing in more general terms that if preachers are to follow Paul, it will mean not only confronting, but also offering alternatives to the peace that "the world gives" (John 14:27), which is a peace based on material acquisition and military supremacy. It will oblige us to question the religious (and not infrequently blasphemous) claims of kings and presidents.[17] And it will pose the challenge of preaching real grace in a "pay-as-you-go"

16. According to Neil Elliott ("Romans 13:1–7 in the Context of Imperial Propaganda," in Horsley, ed., *Paul and Empire*, 184–204), Paul counsels (temporary) submission only because the power of the state is repressively absolute, and open revolt would invite destruction.

17. For recent examples from the American context, see Stephen B. Chapman, "Imperial Exegesis: When Caesar Interprets Scripture," in Wes Avram, ed., *Anxious about Empire: Theological Essays on the New Global Realities* (Grand Rapids: Brazos, 2004), 91–102, and, more broadly, Michael Northcott, *An Angel Directs the Storm: Apocalyptic Religion and American Empire* (London: Tauris, 2004), 1–13 and passim.

world. We are not, according to the gospel Paul proclaims, self-made, self-authenticating, or self-fulfilled. We are a "new creation," living by forgiveness, joyfully dependent on the generosity of God. The preacher's task is nothing less than to declare the full scope of this "indescribable gift" (2 Cor. 9:15) in the face of innumerable counterclaims and the less-than-God-given alternatives they propose.

That "grace and peace" are gifts "from God *our Father* and the *Lord* Jesus *Christ*" again notes the incarnate and transcendent identity of the human Jesus who is equally "Lord" and "Christ," and declares the consequences of his saving work. Paul's phrase reminds the believers that, by virtue of having been reconciled to God, they are able—like Jesus—to call on God as "Father." The same premise is spelled out more fully by the free quotation of 2 Samuel 7:14 in 2 Corinthians 6:18: "I will be your father, and you shall be my sons and daughters, says the Lord Almighty."[18] Yet here it is not God but Paul who (after the manner of all preachers) makes this declaration. The apostle's opening statement thus models an astonishing economy of theological expression. In a single phrase he not only sums up the essential content of Christian proclamation, but also implicitly models the task of the preacher as one who declares on God's behalf the unique saving accomplishment of Christ, in pointed contradistinction to all other such offers: "Grace to you and peace from God our Father and the Lord Jesus Christ."

Little distinguishes this salutation theologically from that, say, of Paul's letters to the Thessalonians or Philippians, whom the apostle also addresses as the beneficiaries of the salvation offered by Jesus as Lord and Christ. Once past the salutation, however, Paul begins immediately to address the specific situation in Corinth.

Human Affliction and Divine Deliverance

At least in popular Christian imagination, Paul's dramatic conversion on the road to Damascus represents the single defining moment of his religious biography, an account sufficiently important as to be recorded

---

18. Cf. Rom. 8:15, Gal. 4:6, and, for the formula as a whole, see esp. 1 Cor. 8:6 (TNIV): "for us there is but one God, the *Father*, from whom all things came and for whom we live; and there is but one *Lord*, Jesus *Christ*, through whom all things came and through whom we live."

not once but three times in the Acts of the Apostles (Acts 9:3–9; 22:6–11; 26:12–18).[19] It seems curious, therefore, that Paul's own writings, which incorporate any number of other biographical details, contain what is at best only a single, oblique reference to this event (Gal. 1:15–17). Considerably clearer and more prominent, by contrast, are the multiple accounts of his personal suffering and affliction (1 Cor. 4:11–13; 2 Cor. 4:8–10; 6:4–10; 11:23–28; 12:7–10). Taken together, these passages present a list of reversals, afflictions, and difficulties that is nothing short of astonishing. They offer a comprehensive Greek vocabulary of suffering: hunger and thirst; lack of clothing, deprivation, poverty, homelessness, and obscurity; overwork, fatigue, and sleeplessness; reviling, humiliation, insult, slander, and the specific accusation of being an imposter; punishment, physical beatings, floggings, and being "knocked down"; affliction, persecution, distress, hardship, weakness, multiple imprisonments, even mob violence, with the result that Paul describes himself as not only beset by perplexity and sorrow, but "often near death" (2 Cor. 11:23). In addition to such general categories, he has kept tally of particular events:

> Five times I have received from the Jews the forty lashes minus one. Three times I was beaten with rods. Once I received a stoning. Three times I was shipwrecked; for a night and a day I was adrift at sea; on frequent journeys, in danger from rivers, danger from bandits, danger from my own people, danger from Gentiles, danger in the city, danger in the wilderness, danger at sea, danger from false brothers and sisters; in toil and hardship, through many a sleepless night, hungry and thirsty, often without food, cold and naked.
>
> 2 Corinthians 11:24–27

Were all this not enough, there is also his constant "anxiety" for his congregations and a persistent (albeit unidentified) physical affliction for which not even repeated prayer avails (2 Cor. 12:7–9).

The rhetorical intensity of these passages, as well as the frequency and variety of troubles to which they attest, provide some indication of their importance for Paul, all the more so for our purposes as the great majority

---

19. Recent discussion of Paul's conversion from a variety of perspectives, including a history of its interpretation, is offered in Richard N. Longenecker, ed., *The Road From Damascus: The Impact of Paul's Conversion on His Life, Thought, and Ministry* (Grand Rapids: Eerdmans, 1997).

of them occur in the Corinthian correspondence.[20] Indeed, 2 Corinthians 1:3–11 in particular suggests that Paul's post-conversion experience of trial and suffering is determinative for him both experientially and conceptually. This passage records a moment of profound integration in which Paul is able to interpret his experience in light of foundational theological categories, and his theological paradigms in light of personal experience. For the sake of greater clarity, we will approach these issues in an order opposite to that in which Paul himself relates them, dealing first with his reasons for writing (1:12–2:13), then with his reported moment of insight (1:8–11), and finally with the approach that he takes as he begins his letter (1:3–7). Our interest in these passages is not merely historical, or generally theological; rather, what emerges is the extent to which Paul's ministry, and his ministry of apostolic proclamation in particular, is a direct expression of his continuous participation in and imitation of the life of Jesus of Nazareth.

Reasons for Writing (1:12–2:13)

Indeed, this is our boast, the testimony of our conscience: we have behaved in the world with frankness and godly sincerity, not by earthly wisdom but by the grace of God—and all the more toward you. For we write you nothing other than what you can read and also understand; I hope you will understand until the end—as you have already understood us in part—that on the day of the Lord Jesus we are your boast even as you are our boast. Since I was sure of this, I wanted to come to you first, so that you might have a double favor; I wanted to visit you on my way to Macedonia, and to come back to you from Macedonia and have you send me on to Judea. Was I vacillating when I wanted to do this? Do I make my plans according to ordinary human standards, ready to say "Yes, yes" and "No, no" at the same time? As surely as God is faithful, our word to you has not been "Yes and No." For the Son of God, Jesus Christ, whom we proclaimed among you, Silvanus and Timothy and I, was not "Yes and No"; but in him it is always "Yes." For in him every one of God's promises is a "Yes." For this reason it is through him that we say the "Amen," to the glory of God. But it is God who establishes us with you in Christ and has anointed us, by putting his seal on us and giving us his Spirit in our hearts as a first installment. But I call on God as witness

20. Among the exceptions are Rom. 8:35–39, Phil. 1:17, and 1 Thess. 2:1–2.

against me: it was to spare you that I did not come again to Corinth. I do not mean to imply that we lord it over your faith; rather, we are workers with you for your joy, because you stand firm in the faith. So I made up my mind not to make you another painful visit. For if I cause you pain, who is there to make me glad but the one whom I have pained? And I wrote as I did, so that when I came, I might not suffer pain from those who should have made me rejoice; for I am confident about all of you, that my joy would be the joy of all of you. For I wrote you out of much distress and anguish of heart and with many tears, not to cause you pain, but to let you know the abundant love that I have for you. But if anyone has caused pain, he has caused it not to me, but to some extent—not to exaggerate it—to all of you.

2 Corinthians 1:12–2:5

Although the letter opens on a note of consolation, Paul expends considerably more effort, some verses further on, in his attempt to explain his recent change of travel plans. This, commentators propose, is Paul's more immediate reason for writing. However we reconstruct the chronology of events leading up to this letter, it is clear that Paul has failed to show up in Corinth when he had promised. From the intensity (as well as the details) of Paul's reply, we may infer that this unexpected change of schedule has led some in the congregation to question his honesty, his motives, the genuineness of his concern for the church, even the authenticity of his ministry in general. The first of these charges is implied by Paul's insistence that he has conducted himself "with frankness and godly sincerity" (1:12), his assurance that he is not trying to deceive or confuse his audience (1:13), and his protest that a change of mind on this occasion should not be taken as proof of indecision or duplicity in general (1:17–18). While he concedes that he wants to avoid more conflict for his own sake also (2:3, 5), he strongly contends that both his change of travel plans (2:1–2) and his painful pastoral directives have been motivated entirely by loving concern: "For I wrote you out of much distress and anguish of heart and with many tears, not to cause you pain, but to let you know the abundant love that I have for you" (2 Cor. 2:4). It is not as if Paul has been blessed by a supportive or appreciative congregation: his ministry (like those of more than a few pastors) operates largely on the defensive, a fact that causes Paul to fall back on the theological foundations of his apostolic calling.

Thus, a recurrent motif in this section of the letter is the explicit contrast between human and divine origins for Christian ministry. Paul claims to have conducted himself "not by earthly [*sarkikē*, literally, 'fleshly'] wisdom but by the grace of God" (1:12; cf. 10:4). Similarly, he protests that he does not make his travel plans *kata sarka*, "according to the flesh" (1:17; NRSV: "according to ordinary human standards"; NIV: "in a worldly manner"). On the contrary, his ministry and conduct are of God: "it is *God* who has established us with you in Christ and has anointed us" (1:21). That is, even as Jesus is the "anointed" one of God, the *Christos*, so, he insists, God has "anointed [*chrisas*]" apostles and preachers of the gospel. If his detractors believe themselves to be of God, filled with the Spirit of God, no less so is Paul (1:22; cf. 1 Cor. 14:37; 2 Cor. 10:7). His defense, in other words, is the claim that he and his congregation share the same grace, and not that he has been granted special favor over them. As much as they are "in Christ," so too is he, and on that basis alone they should acknowledge the legitimacy of his ministry among them.

Even more striking are the two oaths (somewhat obscured in translation) by which Paul appeals to God for vindication. Verse 18 reads literally, "But 'God is faithful' that our word to you is not yes and no." Paul swears by the fidelity of God that his own "word" is likewise faithful, referring not only to his travel plans but (by implication) to his disposition toward the congregation in general, including his preaching (1:19). In much the same manner, 1:23 employs the strongest possible language of adjuration: "I call on God as witness against me: it was to spare you that I did not come again to Corinth."

Paul's audacity—even theological arrogance—is breathtaking. The most limited sense of self-awareness would keep most preachers from professing anything like this degree of charity or sincerity. Although many would claim to have sensed (at some point) a divine call to ministry, few of us are free from self-doubt, whether to a healthy or an unhealthy degree. And it is hard to imagine most congregations perceiving such apparent assurance as anything more than self-serving rhetoric. Yet what would it take for us to be granted the legitimate right to claim God's Word and witness in support of our own ministry? Paul's boldness and confidence emerge from a painful yet powerful confluence of theological vision with personal experience.

45

Insight and Integration (1:8–11)

> We do not want you to be unaware, brothers and sisters, of the affliction we experienced in Asia; for we were so utterly, unbearably crushed that we despaired of life itself. Indeed, we felt that we had received the sentence of death so that we would rely not on ourselves but on God who raises the dead. He who rescued us from so deadly a peril will continue to rescue us; on him we have set our hope that he will rescue us again, as you also join in helping us by your prayers, so that many will give thanks on our behalf for the blessing granted us through the prayers of many.
>
> 2 Corinthians 1:8–11

Paul reports that while in Asia Minor he and his companions—the "we" is significant—were confronted by a severe, life-threatening affliction (*thlipsis*). While he does not pause here to identify the experience, the fact that catalogues of tribulation occur only in the Corinthian correspondence (with four of the five in Second Corinthians) suggests that some such occurrence is painfully fresh in his mind. It seems likely that his experience in Asia Minor is included somewhere on these lists. By comparison, Paul writes in 1 Corinthians 15:32 of having "fought with wild animals in Ephesus," where 1 Corinthians was written (1 Cor. 16:8).[21] Here, the threefold juxtaposition of "putting ourselves in danger every hour" (1 Cor. 15:30), "I die every day!" (15:31), and "I fought with wild animals" (15:32) suggests mortal peril. Yet Paul mentions this situation only in passing. It is simply an illustration, requiring no comment in its own right. By contrast, the events underlying 2 Corinthians 1:8–9 are of another order of magnitude. Paul laments: "We were so utterly, unbearably crushed that we despaired of life itself. Indeed, we felt that we had received the sentence of death." As Furnish (113) points out,

> The noun *apokrima* (*sentence*) stands nowhere else in biblical Greek, but was used by other ancient writers as a technical term for any official decree which, coming in response to a petition or inquiry, settled a case.

21. This need not be taken literally, since the verb in question (*theriomachein*) can have the figurative sense of "to encounter serious conflict." On the interpretation of this phrase, see the summary by Hans Conzelmann, *1 Corinthians: A Commentary on the First Epistle to the Corinthians*, tr. James W. Leitch (Philadelphia: Fortress, 1975), 277–78, and, more fully, R. E. Osborne, "Paul and the Wild Beasts," *JBL* 85 (1966): 225–30; and A. J. Malherbe, "The Beasts at Ephesus," *JBL* 87 (1968): 71–80.

Simply put, Paul had been convinced that he and his companions would die.

If this example is in any measure relevant for Paul's successors and imitators, preachers not least among them, then the first, most obvious lesson to be drawn is that affliction and despair are not antithetical to the life of faith. Preachers in particular feel the pressure to live "exemplary" lives before their congregations, with "exemplary" often being equated with qualities such as being "victorious," "faith-filled," "unfailingly joyful," and the like. Paul too firmly embraces such responsibility, even chiding the congregation for not emulating him more closely: "Be imitators of me," he insists, "as I am of Christ" (1 Cor. 11:1; cf. 4:16). Yet here he freely confesses what can only be described as absolute despair, and the absolute *failure* of faith. Note that this is not despair at being unable to live up to the expectations of his congregation, board of deacons, or major donors. This is the final despair of one who, while clinging stubbornly to life, feels it being wrenched from his grasp. From the perspective of greater maturity, Paul will later be able to confess, "living is Christ and dying is gain" (Phil. 1:21); he will be torn between pastoral responsibilities and his eager desire to be more fully "with Christ" (Phil. 1:23). But on this earlier occasion the certainty of faith apparently eludes him, and he is unable to meet the prospect of death with equanimity. The language with which he describes his situation is, in every sense, "hyperbolic": *kath hyperbolēn hyper dynamin ebarēthēmen* (2 Cor. 1:8) means literally, "we were overweighed to the utmost, beyond strength." This from the man who takes credit for having faithfully preached the Christian gospel and cofounded the congregation to which he now writes!

Although the image of a despairing, fearful, utterly beaten Paul is hardly a familiar one, it does offer a certain comfort. For this is an image with which—at least on occasion—more than a few pastors and preachers can identify. Even for Paul, the life of faith is hardly one of constant "victory." In regard to the most personal of trials he will later testify, "Three times I appealed to the Lord about this . . . but he said to me, 'My grace is sufficient for you'" (2 Cor. 12:8–9). Here and throughout his ministry, the message he preaches is neither triumphalist nor exclusive of suffering, but testifies rather to the sufficiency of grace. Such grace, it turns out, emerges out of weakness, emptiness, and the prospect of death. As we will see, imitating Paul as Paul imitates Christ entails participation in, rather than escape from, the suffering that is so characteristic of the human condition.

The fact that he and his companions have—against all expectation—survived their ordeal causes Paul to reflect anew on the nature of Christian experience. The experience leads to (or reinforces) what may be the most important insight of Paul's entire ministry. He concludes that they have been allowed to suffer this affliction in order, he says, that "we would rely not on ourselves but on God *who raises the dead*" (2 Cor. 1:9). The latter formula is a conventional Jewish expression of piety (so Barrett, 65), but here it takes on new meaning in light of Jesus's paradigmatic death and resurrection.[22] Paul realizes that his own experience is essentially similar to that of Jesus on the cross and thereafter.

In one sense, this should not seem remarkable. Identification with Christ's crucifixion in anticipation of sharing his new life is an essential feature of the gospel Paul preaches (Rom. 6:6–8), and there is no question that the crucifixion is central to the message he has already proclaimed in Corinth (so 1 Cor. 1:23; 2:2, etc.). He explains to the Thessalonian believers that their experience of suffering and persecution effectively imitates Jesus's crucifixion (1 Thess. 1:6; 2:13–15), and his statement that "in spite of persecution [they] received the word with joy inspired by the Holy Spirit" likewise reflects the power of the resurrection.[23] Even so, he says, their definitive imitation of Christ awaits the moment of his glorious return (1 Thess. 4:14–17). Along the same lines, Paul's previous letter to Corinth interpreted resurrection as applying to those who have died, and therefore as taking place at the moment of Christ's return (1 Cor. 15:18–23). In Asia Minor, however, Paul realizes that the paradigm of death and resurrection applies fully to Christian discipleship *prior* to the parousia. For, he says, the outcome (if not the implicit divine purpose) of that experience "was to make us rely not on ourselves but on God who *raises the dead*; he delivered us from so deadly a peril, and he will deliver us; on him we have set our hope that he will deliver us again" (2 Cor. 1:10, RSV).

22. Gorman (*Cruciformity*, 343) initially overlooks the paradigmatic and cruciform nature of this experience, referring to it in pedagogical terms: "believers . . . learn not to depend on themselves but on God . . . Paul espouses suffering as both tutor and guarantor of hope." In his subsequent study, however, he notes that whatever Paul's affliction may have been, "God comforted as only God can do, by bringing life out of death" (*Apostle of the Crucified Lord: A Theological Introduction to Paul and His Letters* [Grand Rapids: Eerdmans, 2004], 294).

23. So Patte, *Preaching Paul*, 34.

In other Pauline correspondence the pattern of crucifixion and resurrection applies primarily to forensic justification before God (so Rom. 5:6–10; 1 Cor. 15:3, 17; Gal. 2:19–20; 3:1–2; 6:14) or as a metaphor for spiritual renewal and moral transformation (Rom. 6:3–11; 8:9–11). Nor does Paul abandon these interpretative categories in light of his recent experience: in 2 Corinthians, Christ's resurrection still applies both forensically (2 Cor. 5:17–18) and ethically (5:15). But in Asia Minor, the prospect of literal physical death is so immediate that it brings to the fore the need for physical resurrection, or something very nearly like it. In this moment of extreme peril, imitation of Jesus's death and resurrection extends beyond forgiveness and moral conduct to imply the divine gift of life itself in the face of deadly persecution and suffering. Only God could have rescued him, and God alone, Paul is certain, will rescue him in the future.

This is not the first time that the apostle has changed his mind in response to a direct encounter with the risen Lord, for Luke records his conversion in just such terms (Acts 9:1–9; 22:6–11; 26:12–20). In 2 Corinthians 1:8–10, Paul reports a moment of theological insight and integration that is hardly less profound. He had arrived in Asia Minor with a strong theological grid: "We proclaim Christ crucified" (1 Cor. 1:23). Paul reveals an equally strong sense of God's sovereignty and saving initiative by using the historical accomplishment of God's Messiah as the theological lens through which he now interprets his own and all of human experience. While holding this view—indeed as a direct result of embracing it—Paul comes close to death (2 Cor. 11:23). This experience is so powerful that it demands to be interpreted in light of his no-less-powerful theological convictions. Yet conviction and experience, concept and praxis, prove equally and mutually determinative. Insight and integration come for Paul at the moment of recognizing the same truth in both: that Jesus's experience of death and resurrection has been repeated in the apostle's own life as nearly as is possible prior to the final and irreversible encounter with physical death. Paul is overwhelmed to the point of being crushed; he despairs of life, yet finds himself alive. It is not only a "near-death" experience but a "near-resurrection" experience as well.

Particularly significant is the fact that Paul is not alone in this. His narrative is consistently cast in the first person plural, so that it was, he says, "we" who were crushed, "we" who despaired, and "we" who could rely only on God; God rescued "us" and will do so again. At the very least, he shares this experience with Timothy, his "son" in the faith and cowriter of the epistle. This alone is sufficient to indicate the legitimacy of generalizing his experience as paradigmatic (at least) for those of us who, like Paul and Timothy, lead, preach, proclaim the Christian gospel, and suffer as a result. We will return later to Paul's application of this principle in his own experience, and to the situation of his Corinthian converts.

In the meantime, other instances of Israel's God sustaining his servants in circumstances of profound weakness and failure come immediately to mind. Joseph, the young brother sold into slavery, then imprisoned on false charges, only to rise to a position nearly equal that of pharaoh, is one example. Moses is another. Having fled from Egypt to escape prosecution for the murder of an Egyptian official, Moses is plainly unwilling to return, even when compelled by vivid theophany. Far from acquiescing to the call for him to lead God's people, Moses equivocates at length, finally appealing to his limitations as a public speaker (Exod. 4:10–12). When not even that succeeds, Moses simply concludes, "O my Lord, please send someone else," thereby eliciting God's wrath (Exod. 4:13–14). But when such protests fail, he finds himself as spokesman and leader of his nation. A similar principle obtains in the selection of David, considered too small and insignificant by his own family, as king over Israel (1 Sam. 16:6–13). Indeed, according to Deuteronomy this is what explains the choice of Israel as a whole to be God's people:

> It was not because you were more numerous than any other people that the LORD set his heart on you and chose you—for you were the fewest of all peoples. It was because the LORD loved you and kept the oath that he swore to your ancestors, that the LORD has brought you out with a mighty hand, and redeemed you from the house of slavery, from the hand of Pharaoh king of Egypt.
>
> Deuteronomy 7:7–8

According to the psalms that bear his name, the legacy of divine protection and sustenance is characteristic of David's reign. Psalm 23:4, for example, can be translated, "Even though I walk through *the darkest valley*," or in the more familiar phrasing of the King James Bible, "though I walk through *the valley of the shadow of death*."[24] The key term, *tzalmaveth*,

---

24. Compare also, among modern translations, Segond, "la vallée de l'ombre de la mort," or, as an ancient example, the Septuagint (LXX) rendering, "for even should I

means something along the lines of "profound darkness" (as in the familiar words of Isaiah 9:2, "those who lived in a land of *deep darkness*—on them light has shined"). But translations that include mention of "death" convey something more of the word's etymology and poetic intent, implying mortal danger and darkness akin to that which covers the dead (e.g., Job 38:17). All the more so because it implies the closeness of death, Psalm 23:4 speaks of an experience very much like that of Paul in Asia Minor:

> Even were I to walk in a ravine as dark as death
> I should fear no danger, for you are at my side.[25]

That is, only by actually experiencing the "valley"—a metaphor no less current today than in ancient times—does the psalmist find deliverance and consolation. This, too, is a lived theology of deliverance in the face of adversity and enemies.[26]

Such examples are not, ultimately, anachronistic, for they show that the principle of divine redemption intervening at the point of weakness, inability, or apparent failure is not unique either to Jesus or to Paul. Rather, this is a consistent pattern or principle of divine-human interaction that finds its fullest expression in the death and restoration of the Messiah. In the case of Jesus's disciples, such a pattern is all the more compelling because it contradicts historical tradition. In all four gospels, Peter insists that he will follow Jesus regardless of the cost, if necessary even to the point of death (Matt. 26:33, 35; Mark 14:29, 31; Luke 22:33; John 13:37–38). But Peter ultimately abandons him like everyone else; Matthew and Mark explicitly state that "*all* the disciples deserted him and fled" (Matt. 26:56; cf. Mark 14:50). Only the women have the courage—and probably also a sense of their own powerlessness—to wait at the foot of the cross (Mark 15:40–41 and parallels). According to Luke, the first counter-example among the male disciples is Stephen, whose death directly imitates that

---

go amidst the shadow of death." The Jewish Publication Society edition (*Tanakh: The Holy Scriptures. The New JPS Translation According to the Traditional Hebrew Text* [Philadelphia: Jewish Publication Society, 1985]) acknowledges both alternatives.

25. *The New Jerusalem Bible* (Garden City, NY: Doubleday, 1985).

26. Notwithstanding the extensive biblical and rabbinic evidence that Savage (*Power Through Weakness: Paul's Understanding of the Christian Ministry on 2 Corinthians* [Cambridge: Cambridge University Press, 1996], 167–68) adduces (referring in particular to Abraham, Joseph, and Moses), the point of such examples is not humility *per se*, but powerlessness before—and need of assistance from—God.

of Jesus (Acts 7:54–60). Perhaps influenced by his own involvement in Stephen's martyrdom, Paul somewhat belatedly proposes that joining Jesus at the cross is, after all, the essence of discipleship.

To digress briefly from the biblical text, subsequent illustrations of this principle emerge from many different contexts and eras of church history. Perhaps best known is the *theologia crucis* ("theology of the cross") articulated by Martin Luther (1483–1546). Although this phrase covers several related features of his theology—including the hiddenness of God, the paradoxical or counterintuitive nature of revelation, and justification by faith—what concerns us here is Luther's understanding of how God is manifest in human experience. Luther's theology of the cross was likely based at least in part on the teaching of the fourteenth-century German mystic Johannes Tauler (ca. 1300–1361), who declared, "There are many who find the Cross by means of much suffering and numerous trials, and this is the way God draws them to Himself."[27] "God," Luther similarly insisted, "can be found only in suffering and the cross."[28] For Luther, God is not only revealed in the torment and negation represented by Jesus's crucifixion, but also uses suffering and despair to bring humanity to salvation through the cross. The same principle remains axiomatic for the life of discipleship as a whole:

> [God] permits the godly to become powerless and to be brought low, until everyone supposes their end is near, whereas in these very things he is present to them in all his power, yet so hidden and in secret that even those who suffer the oppression do not feel it but only believe. . . . For where man's strength ends, God's strength begins, provided faith is present and waits on him. . . . Even so, Christ was powerless on the cross; and yet there he performed his mightiest work and conquered sin, death, world, hell, devil, and all evil. Thus all the martyrs were strong and overcame. Thus, too, all who suffer and are oppressed overcome.[29]

27. "Sermon 59 (Exaltation of the Cross II)," in *Johannes Tauler, Sermons*, tr. Maria Shrady (Classics of Western Spirituality; New York: Paulist, 1985), 164; cf. 97.

28. Jaroslav Pelikan and Helmut T. Lehmann, ed., *Luther's Works*, 55 vols. (St. Louis: Concordia, 1955–1986), 31:53. For a brief summary of Luther's *theologia crucis*, see Alister E. McGrath, *Luther's Theology of the Cross: Martin Luther's Theological Breakthrough* (Oxford: Blackwell, 1985), 148–52 ("It is through undergoing the torment of the cross, death and hell that true theology and the knowledge of God come about" [152]).

29. *Luther's Works* 21:340, cited in Regin Prenter, *Luther's Theology of the Cross* (Philadelphia: Fortress, 1971), 16.

The life of the Christian is thus for Luther a life of participation in Christ's suffering, of sharing Christ's cross and being crucified with him through the trials and opposition that the life of faith invariably occasions.[30]

"Through the mercy of our dear God, I do not want to experience anything . . . or enjoy any consolation except that of being crucified with Jesus"; "The Passion contains everything. That is where the science of the saints is learned."[31] Remarkably, these statements come not from Luther but from Paulo Franceso Danei (1694–1775), the Italian mystic and founder of the Passionist order more popularly known as "St. Paul of the Cross." His conviction that imitation of Jesus's suffering was the supreme mark of submission to God's will led him to embrace fearsome deprivations and mortification:

> Just as the most beloved Jesus willed that His most holy life here on earth . . . should be spent amid . . . continual sorrows, trials, exhausting labors, hardships, anguish, scorn, calumny, pain, whips, nails, thorns, and the most bitter death of the Cross, so He made me understand that in dedicating myself to Him, I was to lead the same life, amid every suffering. With what jubilation my soul embraced all kinds of sufferings.[32]

Turning to more contemporary examples, the following excerpts are taken from the diary of Lilias Trotter, a missionary to Algeria in the late nineteenth and early twentieth centuries. The first is dated October 26, 1894, reflecting back on three months spent in England to recuperate from exhaustion:

> Oh, God has been good to us throughout these months! On July 12th he gave me this promise, "He shall come down like rain upon the mown grass" [Ps. 72:6]. And he has made it true, hallelujah! For I was feeling mown in body and spirit. Now he has begun to show me how all must be brought down into the dust of death before living out the life of Jesus can be more than an intermittent thing.[33]

---

30. So Walther von Loewenich, *Luther's Theology of the Cross*, tr. Herbert J. A. Bouman (Belfast: Christian Journals, 1976), esp. 117–23.

31. Charles Alméras, *St. Paul of the Cross, Founder of the Passionists*, tr. M. Angeline Bouchard (Garden City, NY: Hanover House, 1960), 211–12; the first quotation is from the *Retreat Journal* of 1720, the second from a letter of Sept. 23, 1747.

32. Alméras, *St. Paul of the Cross*, 211–12; from a letter of Aug. 29, 1737.

33. Patricia St. John, *Until the Day Breaks: The Life and Work of Lilias Trotter, Pioneer Missionary to Muslim North Africa* (Bromley, Kent: OM Publishing, 1990), 25.

In May of 1901, with the life of a dear friend hanging in the balance due to smallpox, she writes:

> It has come to me freshly how every bit of weakness, ignorance and insufficiency can come full of blessedness if we unite it with the death of Christ. Each bit of it, as it sinks down into his grave, touches the spring of resurrection, like the man who was let down into Elisha's grave of old. We just need the faith to let it go down and down until it finds Christ.[34]

To rely utterly on God amid weakness is, for Trotter, to imitate Christ in crucifixion. In a diary entry dated October 27, 1924, she meditates on what she terms "the wonderful words 'weak with him.'" For, she writes,

> the world's salvation was not wrought out by the three years in which He went about doing good, but in the three hours of darkness in which He hung, stripped and nailed, in uttermost exhaustion of spirit–soul and body, till His heart broke. So little wonder for us, if the price of power is weakness.[35]

Similarly, Hudson Taylor (1832–1905), the pioneer English missionary to nineteenth-century China, wrote in 1894, at age 62: "God chose me because I was weak enough. God does not do his great works by large committees. He trains somebody to be quiet enough, and little enough,

---

The date (along with a fuller account of Trotter's life) is provided by Miriam Huffman Rockness, *A Passion for the Impossible: The Life of Lilias Trotter* (Grand Rapids: Discovery House, 2003), 134n2.

34. St. John, *Until the Day Breaks*, 84. Trotter sees this principle at work in Jesus's response to Jairus's daughter and Lazarus: "He deliberately delayed until the child was dead, for the faith of Jairus must know him as the God who quickeneth the death, and with Lazarus he deliberately stayed away until death had established its reign, so that Martha and Mary might know him as resurrection life. So the first answer to many prayers may, therefore, be the reign of death. The last spark of life may be quenched and faith and hope left alone with the dead—and with the God who raises the dead. Do not be dismayed if the first answer to some of your prayers is a revelation, not of the power of God to make alive, but of his might to slay every hope outside himself" (71–72).

35. Rockness, *Passion for the Impossible*, 297 (with corrections to date and content provided in personal correspondence from Miriam Rockness, June 12 and 28, 2004). St. John (*Until the Day Breaks*, 196) offers a paraphrase dated "September, 1924" (but without specifying the source).

and then he uses *him*."[36] In 1995, Dinis Sengulane, Anglican bishop of Lebombo, Mozambique, described how congregations under his care had undertaken to pray through the stations of the cross as a means of coming to terms with the profound suffering they had experienced in their country's lengthy civil war.[37] Mona Khauli, a Lebanese Baptist, commented in a 1998 address on "The Importance of Worship to Suffering People": "If you want to grow, come and suffer. . . . You are at your weakest, but then you are united with Christ in His suffering."[38]

Missiologist Lesslie Newbigin contends that the principle of redemptive debility lies at the core of the church's life and witness in every age. Drawing precisely on Paul's second letter to Corinth, he argues that the spiritual vitality and effectiveness of the Christian community depends on the power of God that is revealed above all in human weakness. The church, he says,

> continues to bear witness to the real meaning and goal of history by a life which—in Paul's words—by always bearing about in the body the dying of Jesus becomes the place where the risen life of Jesus is made available for others (2 Cor. 4:10).[39]

This paradox, says Newbigin, accounts both for the irrelevance and social invisibility of the Christian communities of the first century, and for their unexpected and entirely disproportionate influence:

> These communities are, as [Paul] says to the Corinthians, composed mostly of people whom the world despises. They do not look like the wave of the

36. J. C. Pollock, *Hudson Taylor and Maria: Pioneers in China* (Grand Rapids: Zondervan, 1967), 125 (emphasis original).

37. Address to "G-CODE 2000: International Anglican Conference on the Decade of Evangelism," Hendersonville, NC, Sept. 4–9, 1995. A partial report of the address appears as "Evangelism in a Context of War, Marginalization, and Poverty: A Personal Testimony," in Cyril C. Okorocha, ed., *The Cutting Edge of Mission: The Report of G-Code 2000 Global Conference on Dynamic Evangelism beyond 2000. Mid-Point Review of the Decade of Evangelism* (London: Anglican Communion Publications, 1996), 40–45.

38. Mona Khauli, "The Importance of Worship to Suffering People" (address to the Baptist World Alliance "Baptists in Worship" Conference, Berlin, Germany, Oct. 16, 1998).

39. Lesslie Newbigin, *The Gospel in a Pluralist Society* (Grand Rapids: Eerdmans, 1989), 119.

future. They are ignored by contemporary historians. They do not pretend to take control of the destiny of the Roman Empire, let alone of the whole world. What, then, is their significance?

One could answer most simply by saying that their significance is that they continue the mission of Jesus in accordance with his words: "As the Father sent me, so I send you." They share his weakness, and as they do so, they share in the powers of the new age which he brings. . . . They . . . share, in their measure, his passion.[40]

At least in the nominally Christian West, preachers are unlikely to encounter the kind of life-threatening persecution faced by Paul and his contemporaries, or even that of Christians in Mozambique and Lebanon. Our sermons are more likely to meet with public indifference than outright opposition. Correspondingly, our own suffering is more often interior than external; typically emotional, spiritual, and psychological rather than directly physical. Were we to rewrite Paul's list of afflictions from contemporary experience, we might refer to material poverty, loneliness, social dislocation, damaged or broken relationships, unfulfilled (but nonetheless godly) aspirations, physical afflictions, emotional turmoil, confusion, and frequent failure of spiritual vision and understanding. In addition, Christian leaders typically face the pressure of aging facilities (and congregations), dwindling resources, fractious parishioners, and the limitless demands involved in caring for the legitimate needs of their respective communities. Most pastors labor in relative obscurity and anonymity; their experience, not that of the megachurch or media-visible pastorate, is the norm. They not infrequently feel themselves at an end of their own resources, with nowhere else to turn.

Their situation is rendered more difficult by the social context of contemporary ministry. According to George Hunsberger, our society believes that "Personal happiness, good health, and complete freedom from pain are reasonable expectations."[41] Science and technology, medicine and pharmacology, economic security and relative affluence compared with the rest of the world have all led us to expect that suffering is abnormal,

40. Ibid, 122.

41. Quoted in William Willimon, *Shaped by the Bible* (Nashville: Abingdon, 1990), 58. Although Hunsberger cites this outlook among the "attributes of modernity," it remains current in a postmodern setting.

whether that suffering is physical or psychological, concerning bodily health, self-esteem, social standing, or financial security. Any adversity, however slight or temporary, comes as a shock. Were this not enough, our social context frequently favors a success-oriented model of ministry, both in terms of a professional career track and in terms of the message that we preach. Resner's summary is in equal measures painful and incisive:

> With "Jesus C.E.O." as a dominant christological orientation for our time, what is to prevent the capitalistic, consumer-driven, felt-needs-driven church from desiring and selecting a minister to function partly as buoyant master of ceremonies and entertainer . . . and partly as a Wal-Mart-style manager and motivator, with the goal of happier, greater, bigger, and more?[42]

As preachers, we are likely to aspire to ever-increasing personal and professional accomplishments, whether measured by the numerical size and significance of our congregations, the influence of our ministries, or (for academics!) the number of books and articles we have published. Newly ordained clergy expect that although they may begin ministry in a rural pastorate, they will quickly move toward ever-larger centers of population.[43] For many pastors, languishing in rural ministry seems an unmistakable sign of professional failure.

While lack of career advancement, failure to achieve personal goals, rejection by one's congregation, financial hardship, marriage breakdown, or having to cope with depression or other illness are not the same as the persecution and physical threats that Paul faced, the spiritual dynamic is identical. Being pushed beyond one's limits and human resources—in whatever manner is appropriate to personal circumstances—is normative for the life of Christian discipleship. As Teresa of Ávila (1515–1582) told her nuns, "It is clear that, since God leads those whom He most loves by the way of trials, the more He loves them, the greater will be their trials." Nor did she imagine that the life of the cloister would shield them from

---

42. André Resner, Jr., *Preacher and Cross: Person and Meaning in Theology and Rhetoric* (Grand Rapids: Eerdmans, 1999), 6.

43. For example, Richard Lischer offers a compelling account (*Open Secrets: A Memoir of Faith and Discovery* [New York: Broadway, 2001]) of his own dismay at being sent to an "insignificant" rural charge, and of the process of discovery and spiritual awakening to which it eventually gave rise.

difficulty: "And do you not know, sisters," she observed, "that the life of a good religious, who wishes to be among the closest friends of God, is one long martyrdom?"[44] Paul—and all those whom we have cited—repeatedly find themselves in circumstances that require utter dependence on God.

On reflection, we recognize that particular instances of dependence are simply illustrations of a larger orientation, namely that of the created being acknowledging its reliance (both original and ongoing) on the Creator. In addition to this general orientation, however, preachers and pastors in particular are faced with the humanly impossible task of commenting on God. The presumption (in one sense) of this unavoidable professional responsibility can be remedied only by the counter-presumption of faith, which is that God is indeed at work within the ministry of proclamation (cf. Phil. 2:13). Yet human pride and presumption being what they are, specific limitations and inadequacies serve as personal reminders of the larger principle: that one's ministry depends for its effectiveness and impact on more than human effort alone, and that without divine intervention it is simply incapable of bearing spiritual fruit.

Perhaps not surprisingly, the principle of death and resurrection as a paradigm for Christian spirituality is already anticipated in the teaching of Jesus, as for example in the Beatitudes (quoted here from *The Message*, Eugene Peterson's paraphrasing dramatization of scripture):

> Arriving at a quiet place, Jesus sat down and taught his climbing companions. This is what he said:
> You're blessed when you're at the end of your rope. With less of you there is more of God and his rule.
> You're blessed when you feel you've lost what is most dear to you. Only then can you be embraced by the One most dear to you.
> You're blessed when you're content with just who you are–no more, no less. That's the moment you find yourselves proud owners of everything that can't be bought.
> You're blessed when you've worked up a good appetite for God. He's food and drink in the best meal you'll ever eat . . .
> You're blessed when your commitment to God provokes persecution. The persecution drives you deeper into God's kingdom.[45]

44. Teresa of Ávila, *The Way of Perfection*, tr. and ed. E. Allison Peers (New York: Doubleday Image, 1991), 98, 128.

45. Matt. 5:1–6, 10; from Eugene H. Peterson, *The Message: The New Testament in Contemporary English* (Colorado Springs: NavPress, 1993).

Conversely, the prospect of success elicits Jesus's lamentation, even condemnation:

> But woe to you who are rich, for you have received your consolation.
> Woe to you who are full now, for you will be hungry.
> Woe to you who are laughing now, for you will mourn and weep.
> Woe to you when all speak well of you, for that is what their ancestors did to the false prophets."
>
> Luke 6:24–26

Or, to quote the Song of Mary,

> He has scattered the proud in the imagination of their hearts;
> He has brought down the mighty from their thrones, and exalted the lowly and meek;
> He has filled the hungry with good things, and the rich He has sent empty away.
>
> Luke 1:51b–53, author's translation

It seems striking, to say the least, that Jesus effectively condemns virtually everything to which we preachers normally aspire, whether in terms of ministry specifically or our goals for life in general. The reason for this is the paradoxical truth that Paul has so vividly encountered: the fullness of God's saving power emerges only on behalf of those who know themselves to be truly in need of it. This leads Paul to an otherwise inexplicable conclusion, based in his case on nothing less than a personal revelation of the crucified and risen Christ:

> He said to me, "My grace is sufficient for you, for my power is made perfect in weakness." I will all the more gladly boast of my weaknesses, that the power of Christ may rest upon me. For the sake of Christ, then, I am content with weaknesses, insults, hardships, persecutions, and calamities; for when I am weak, then I am strong.
>
> 2 Corinthians 12:9–10 RSV

But Paul (in contrast with Luther) is careful not to attribute suffering and affliction directly to divine design. Rather, he simply affirms that God's will expressed in Christ is to offer consolation for those who do suffer. Only to the extent that tribulation and suffering provide an occasion for consolation do they serve God's ultimate purposes. It is on these grounds that Paul can come to terms with his own weakness, frustration, and physical affliction, all of which serve to highlight the significance of the resurrection—that is, life-giving divine intervention—as a practical principle for the life of faith. If anything, he is therefore determined to emphasize his lack of ability and qualifications as an apostle, in regard both to the circumstances of his call ("For I am the least of the apostles, unfit to be called an apostle, because I persecuted the church of God"; 1 Cor. 15:9) and to the conditions of his ongoing ministry ("For the sake of Christ, then, I am content with weaknesses, insults, hardships, persecutions, and calamities; for when I am weak, then I am strong"; 2 Cor. 12:10 RSV).

If, as both Jesus and Paul indicate, this pattern of weakness and rescue, failure and redemption, death and resurrection is indeed normative for the life of faith, Paul's own example proves highly suggestive for those entrusted with a ministry like his. To begin with, we must keep in mind that his report in 2 Corinthians 1:8–9 of suffering in Asia is itself an instance of proclamation, implying both a specific methodology and a specific conceptual content. His approach is not categorical, in the sense of making theological categories determinative of experience, regardless of the fit. But neither does it amount to an absolutizing of experience, constructing theology on the basis of self-description. Rather, as previously noted, the model that his example suggests is one of "lived theology," involving the integration of equally powerful categories of principle and praxis. Because God raised Jesus from the dead, Paul himself did not die; conversely, because Paul did not die, his trust in a God who raises the "dead" has been validated.

This, surely, is how preachers function for their congregations. They are not the only theologians within the community, perhaps not even the best theologians. But that is not the point. For their appointed task—if only by virtue of presuming to preach—is to reflect aloud on the nature of their own and all human experience in light of Jesus's experience, above all his experience of death and resurrection. In this sense, to accept the role of preacher is to agree to be a sort of "test case" for the Christian life, with all its vicissitudes. It is to "listen out loud," as it were, to the voice of Christ in scripture, and to add one's own voice by way of commentary. By no means is the preacher the only one to have experienced Christ; the experience of at least some to whom preachers speak may well be different, deeper, and especially more mature. Nonetheless, those who presume to preach must have at least *some* experience of Christ, on which basis they wish their own voices to be heard. Simply put, the task of the preacher is to exemplify the process by which followers of Jesus make coherent sense of experience in light of Christian faith, and make sense of Christian faith in light of experience. The only way for this to take place is for preachers to be engaged in that process themselves.

Of course, preachers and theologians are at various times called on to answer any number of vexing theological questions, and to address a wide range of social and pastoral concerns. But rather than addressing particular issues in their own right (in his case, "Why does God allow suffering?" or "How long must tribulation last?"), Paul here accounts for all such essential yet ultimately secondary concerns within a single, foundational theological category: death and resurrection. The dynamic transformation between Good Friday and Easter Sunday becomes an all-encompassing heuristic for Christian ministry as a whole, and his in particular:

> We are treated as impostors, and yet are true; as unknown, and yet are well known; as dying, and see—we are alive; as punished, and yet not killed; as sorrowful, yet always rejoicing; as poor, yet making many rich; as having nothing, and yet possessing everything.
>
> 2 Corinthians 6:8–10

It may be a matter of historical accident that in this instance Paul does not identify the precise occasion or nature of his own suffering. But his reticence, whether accidental or not, contains an important lesson. While, on the one hand, the preacher seeks to articulate a lived theology, the focus of that articulation is not the experience itself. For that—as the unfortunate experience of many congregations will attest—too easily devolves into an implicit solicitation of sympathy and, ultimately, pastoral codependency. By remaining somewhat discreet about the nature of his suffering, Paul's proclamation remains focused on theological interpretation. The experience is real, but his emphasis is on the shape that a theology of the cross gives to Christian pilgrimage and ministry. Stated differently, this is the difference between a theology that is experienced and a theology that is merely an expression of the preacher's experience.[46] If anything,

---

46. I am grateful to Dr. Paul Miller for framing the distinction in these terms.

Paul emphasizes the experience of his listeners over his own, as we will see shortly from 2 Corinthians 1:3–11 (which, not accidentally, occurs *prior* to his references to personal experience). In this way the task of preaching is for Paul simultaneously pastoral and theological, aimed at affirming both a theological worldview centered on the person of Jesus of Nazareth and the concrete experience of the hearers, with the preacher's own faith experience providing the immediate grounds for speaking out of the former into the latter.

How might this work in practice? One contemporary example is philosopher Nicholas Wolterstorff's *Lament for a Son*. This is the diary of a broken heart, offering Wolterstorff's intensely personal meditations on the death of his 25-year-old son in a mountain-climbing accident. As Wolterstorff grieves his loss, he too ponders the meaning of the Beatitudes:

> Blessings to those who mourn, cheers to those who weep, hail to those whose eyes are filled with tears, hats off to those who suffer, bottoms up to the grieving. How strange, how incredibly strange.[47]

But in the process of reflecting on his own pain, his theological premises and personal experience each illuminate, validate, and enrich the other. This leads Wolterstorff to a profound insight:

> God is not only the God of the sufferers but the God who suffers. The pain and fallenness of humanity have entered into his heart. Through the prism of my tears I have seen a suffering God . . .
>
> God is love. That is why he suffers. To love our suffering sinful world is to suffer. God so suffered for the world that he gave up his only Son to suffering. The one who does not see God's suffering does not see his love. God is suffering love . . .
>
> To believe in Christ's rising from the grave is to accept it as a sign of our own rising from our graves. . . . So I shall struggle to live the reality of Christ's rising and death's dying. In my living, my son's dying will not be the last word.[48]

47. Nicholas Wolterstorff, *Lament for a Son* (Grand Rapids: Eerdmans, 1987), 84.
48. Ibid., 81, 90, 92–93.

The prime example for Wolterstorff of divine suffering is, of course, the crucifixion, and the essential meaning of the crucifixion is divine love. Yet God's "last word," he says, despite the great suffering of Jesus and humanity alike, is resurrection. Both crucifixion and resurrection assume new significance in light of his personal tragedy, just as his tragedy takes on new meaning in light of both.

Equally personal and compelling is James Van Tholen's sermon, "Surprised by Death." Returning to the pulpit after a seven-month absence for cancer surgery and chemotherapy, Van Tholen, a Christian Reformed pastor in Rochester, New York, chooses to preach on Romans 5:6, "For while we were *still* weak, at the right time Christ died for the ungodly."[49] Having preached so often on the subject of grace, he says, he has now come to understand it better, because he will soon meet his God. He confesses his own weakness, fear, and failure, in consequence of which all he has left on which to rely is grace. Still, his ultimate focus is not on his own experience, but on the shape it is given by Jesus. "I cannot be [the] focus," he insists,

> because the center of my story—*our* story—is that the grace of Jesus Christ carries us beyond every cancer, every divorce, every sin, every trouble that comes to us. The Christian gospel is the story of Jesus, and that's the story I'm called to tell.[50]

Van Tholen offers himself as an example of the life of faith, not as an instance of spiritual excellence or success, but as an illustration of the sufficiency of grace.

Yet even when issues of literal life and death are not at stake, preaching itself is inherently cruciform, for it is by definition an act of human weakness that depends for validation on nothing less than the direct intervention of God. According to Charles Campbell, preaching that is specifically Christian intentionally imitates Jesus's own powerlessness and renunciation of violence by refusing to use coercion or manipulation. Just as Jesus moved "from ministry to crucifixion, from authoritative power to helplessness," so preachers submit to similar limitations:

49. "Surprised by Death: A young pastor discovers what grace looks like while battling cancer," *Christianity Today* 43.6 (May 24, 1999), 57–59.

50. Ibid., 59. Van Tholen died in January of 2001.

Not only is the preacher's *message* shaped by the story of Jesus . . . but the very *act* of preaching itself is a performance of Scripture, an embodiment of God's reign after the pattern of Jesus. . . . Preachers accept a strange kind of powerlessness, which finally relies on God to make effective not only individual sermons, but the very practice of preaching itself; like the Word made flesh, the preacher's words must be "redeemed by God" to be effective. . . . Faithful preaching thus enacts on behalf of the entire church an interpretive performance of the story of Jesus.[51]

Thus, preaching is an exercise in theological testimony. In the words of William Willimon,

Whatever we say, it must take the form of witness, of proclamation. We can only testify to what we have seen and heard. We can, in our congregational life together, witness that God really has formed a new people. We cannot coerce the hearer with arguments.[52]

For preachers to engage such a methodology entails enormous risk. That is because, as the foregoing examples indicate, preaching is an exercise in more than biblical exegesis, cultural analysis, or effective communication skills. At its core, as we have argued from the outset, preaching is an exercise in spirituality. For this reason, preaching necessarily entails the risk of self-disclosure (whether partial or complete, and whether the details appear positive or negative). In particular instances either preacher or congregation, or both, may be unable to offer or accept the level of trust that such engagement requires. But beyond this largely social and psychological concern is a much deeper risk, and that is the risk that neither "resurrection" nor anything resembling it will in fact take place, either for the preacher or for the hearers. There is always the risk that suffering will not be redeemed, and that faith is void. This is, after all, the inescapable nature of faith. There is no guarantee as to its outcome, other than the assurance, experienced and attested so vividly by Paul,

51. Charles L. Campbell, *Preaching Jesus: New Directions for Homiletics in Hans Frei's Postliberal Hermeneutic* (Grand Rapids: Eerdmans, 1997), 214, 216 (emphasis original). Campbell adds the important qualification that non-coercive preaching is not to be confused with passivity or reluctance to assert strong moral and theological claims.

52. William Willimon, *Peculiar Speech: Preaching to the Baptized* (Grand Rapids: Eerdmans, 1992), 91.

that what God did for Jesus God will also do for Jesus's followers. But that outcome is not up to us. Preachers can only acknowledge that they find themselves in the way that leads to death, in trust that life will ensue. To the extent that they too find themselves "rescued," and to the extent that they too are lifted from theological helplessness (or even despair!) by a "near-resurrection" experience, they will be able to bear witness to their hearers regarding such redemption. To that extent they will serve as examples and illustrations of "lived theology" in much the same way that Paul did for the Corinthian congregation.

Nor can preachers do more than identify the ways of suffering and death in which their congregants find themselves, and testify to the promise that God, in Christ, raises the dead. Preachers cannot, of their own accord, either insist on such "resurrection" or enable it themselves, for that is something beyond human ability which—by definition—only God can accomplish. Despite—or because of—its frequent misuse along these lines, the cross of Jesus cannot become a means of justifying injustice.[53] Because resurrection is the sole prerogative of God, no preacher can pronounce a "final word" on the meaning of suffering for particular individuals and situations. As partners in and witnesses to a larger theological dialogue, preachers urge their hearers to engage *God* in conversation, even (or especially) if that conversation is likely to be angry, outraged, or uncomprehending—if, in short, that conversation is likely to take the thoroughly biblical form of a lament.

Incidentally, if "life" and "rescue" do *not* ensue for them as for Paul, preachers have a responsibility to declare as much. To that extent also they must testify not simply to their theological expectations of experience (which is not quite the same thing as faith), but to a genuinely "lived" theology. Here too they may find a warrant in the example of Paul for speaking honestly, not pretending that matters are other than they themselves have actually experienced them. Paul testifies explicitly to intense personal affliction, and to the frustration of having his petitions for deliverance go unanswered (2 Cor. 12:8–9). In this situation, however, two observations may prove helpful. First, preaching may at this point

53. As rightly pointed out by James F. Kay, "The Word of the Cross at the Turn of the Ages," *Int* 53 (1999): 44–45. The problematic nature of the cross in light of institutional injustice is sensitively explored by Resner, *Preacher and Cross: Person and Meaning in Theology and Rhetoric*, 143–47; and by Gorman, *Cruciformity*, 368–81.

become more explicitly dialogical, with the preacher attending to the testimony of others that, for them, "life" has indeed ensued. The voice of the preacher is always an echo of prior voices, evoking further echoes and responses that may or may not affirm what he or she has to say. By acknowledging that they represent only one voice in a larger conversation, preachers may become open to hearing other, more hopeful voices, among them Paul's own.

Second, we need to attend carefully to the perspective that Paul himself offers. We noted earlier the precise wording of 2 Corinthians 1:8: *kath hyperbolēn hyper dynamin ebarēthēmen*, literally, "we were overweighed to the utmost, beyond strength." As he later reflects on the ultimate, eschatological outcome of faith, Paul explicitly recalls the wording of the previous passage: "For this slight momentary affliction is preparing us," he says, "for *an eternal weight of glory beyond all measure* [*kath hyperbolēn eis hyperbolēn aiōnion baros doxēs*]" (2 Cor. 4:17). The echo is intentional: however overwhelming his affliction in Asia may have seemed at the time, the "weight" of future glory ultimately appears even greater.[54] Even as the suffering was itself "to the extreme" or "beyond measure" (*kath hyperbolēn*), that which awaits believers is (although the wordplay fails in translation) still greater, to an "extreme of extremes" (*kath hyperbolēn eis hyperbolēn*). There is no question that Paul has testified to a "near resurrection" of sorts in Asia Minor, a rescue from grave peril that seemed at least "resurrection-like." Yet the implication of his wordplay is that the full redemption of the repeated "near-death" experiences of Christian pilgrimage will take place only beyond the present life. At that moment, whereas suffering itself had once seemed "beyond measure," the all-the-more-immeasurable glory of divine reversal will so outweigh it as to make it seem a "slight momentary affliction." As Paul indicates in various ways throughout this letter, complete identification with the resurrection of Jesus will not take place until then. Suffering and affliction will continue, and for the present will be reversed only in part.

Indeed, in his letter to the Romans, Paul insists that participation in suffering is not only unavoidable, but in fact essential to the Christian life. God's gift of the Spirit, says Paul, serves as a legal token of adoption, making believers "children of God, and if children, then heirs, heirs of God

---

54. Implicit here is a wordplay on the Hebrew stem *kbd*, different forms of which can denote either "weight" or "glory."

and joint heirs with Christ." But then he adds a crucial qualification: "*if*, in fact, we suffer with him *so that* we may also be glorified with him" (Rom. 8:16–17). As his own experience indicates, identification with Christ's suffering is an indispensable precursor to identification with Christ's glorification: participation in "death"—in all its various manifestations—must precede participation in resurrection. And this hints at the ultimate (if humanly uncomforting) response to the unredeemed aspects of Christian suffering: full resurrection awaits physical death.

Although the point should be obvious, Paul's method implies that Christian theology is articulated in the process, as he notes, of working out one's salvation, even "with fear and trembling" (Phil. 2:12). Theology is never merely abstract: it is always inescapably rooted in personal experience of the presence and/or apparent absence of God. Conversely, Christian experience, to the extent that it is influenced or directed by God, reveals inherently "theological" contours. In Asia, Paul encounters the resurrection as a lived reality, rediscovering it experientially after having preached it for a considerable length of time. It is not that the resurrection was less "true" previously, as if Paul did not previously believe the resurrection, or his grasp of it had hitherto been shallow or merely theoretical. Rather, the theological reality of the resurrection has gained a personally experiential and more holistic dimension, however much he might have preferred to avoid the process that has led to this new understanding. The same is probably true of much theological insight, which often emerges out of tribulation (pietistic denials notwithstanding). In even broader terms, Paul acknowledges that he always carries around his own biography ("unfit to be called an apostle, because I persecuted the church of God," 1 Cor. 15:9), which may account for his theological method: "What you have learned and received and heard and seen in me, do" (Phil. 4:9 RSV). That is, Paul can proclaim himself as an example of grace and transformation in the person of an unworthy as well as suffering recipient.

Although the respective experiences of Jesus and Paul prove mutually illuminating, it is the former rather than the latter that ultimately takes priority. Lest the point be lost, it is essential to observe once more that Paul does not absolutize his own experience. On the contrary, his brush with death implies the irrelevance of experience in its own right. That is, personal experience represents less a source of meaning in its own right than a proving ground according to which the interpretative value of Jesus's death and resurrection is either confirmed or not. Personal experience enables a hearer such as Paul to choose between alternative, even conflicting voices that each call for affirmation: either that of a prosperity-oriented culture (whether Hellenistic or North American) for which suffering is anathema, or that of Christian tradition according to which suffering and consolation are inextricably bound together. Fortunately for the future of the church, the apostle is able to discern the same pattern of divine action in Christian tradition and personal experience alike. Therefore, just as Paul serves as an imperfect yet living example of Christian faith for his congregation, so (guided by Paul's experience) may preachers and pastors serve as examples of lived theology for their own congregants.

Paul's immediate purpose in this section of the letter is to defend himself against accusations of ministerial failure, although his response is both novel and unexpected. Called to account by the congregation for perceived inadequacies, Paul defends himself by drawing attention to the extent of his suffering on behalf of the gospel and, indirectly, for the sake of believers such as those who are at this moment questioning both his credentials and his pastoral commitment. By recounting his trials in Asia Minor, Paul models the basic orientation of the Christian preacher as one who reflects on his or her experience in the brutal light of the cross, and frequently must confess abasement and failure (albeit discreetly or only in part). In that confession he finds common cause with the suffering of his congregants, and thus is able to speak for their hope and consolation.

The spiritual vision that Paul articulates may prove unpalatable to Western audiences more oriented to the language of entitlement and personal "rights." It is entirely antithetical, for instance, to the outlook and interests of the so-called "prosperity gospel." Preachers and pastors whose skills have rightly earned them more than the average amount of professional acclaim or material compensation will hardly see it as an attractive alternative. And it will almost certainly arouse consternation among advocates for the rights of victims, as they seek to reverse the sense of powerlessness that comes with victimization. But for preachers and congregants who suffer or stumble (whatever their social or cultural setting), Paul offers a compelling account of the spiritual life: reversals, humiliation, and affliction offer an opportunity for identification with Jesus. In some measure, he testifies, identification with Jesus's abasement will itself be reversed. Just as God raised Jesus from death, so his failing followers encounter God's grace as their own foretaste of resurrection. Such deliverance is only partial, however, for Paul also testifies that on this side of death and the eschaton God's grace is "sufficient" but not overwhelming. Nonetheless, preaching such a message offers profound meaning and consolation to those hearers who know that their situation exceeds the usual capabilities of human intervention, who are caught in circumstances beyond their control, or whose endeavor to follow Jesus has itself occasioned debilitating opposition and rejection.

Responding to Criticism (1:3–7)

> Blessed be the God and Father of our Lord Jesus Christ, the Father of mercies and the God of all consolation, who consoles us in all our affliction, so that we may be able to console those who are in any affliction with the consolation with which we ourselves are consoled by God. For just as the sufferings of Christ are abundant for us, so also our consolation is abundant through Christ. If we are being afflicted, it is for your consolation and salvation; if we are being consoled, it is for your consolation, which you experience when you patiently endure the same sufferings that we are also suffering. Our hope for you is unshaken; for we know that as you share in our sufferings, so also you share in our consolation.
>
> 2 Corinthians 1:3–7

Now that we have reviewed key aspects of the apostle's theological outlook, we arrive at last where Paul begins, with an opening word of comfort directed at his congregation. For Paul believes that they stand in need of the same consolation he himself has already received. Perhaps wisely, Paul seeks to minister to his detractors before offering an account of his own ministry. The letter begins by focusing on the nature and character of God: "Blessed be the God and Father of our Lord Jesus Christ, the Father of mercies and the God of all consolation" (2 Cor. 1:3).[55] Paul will, of course, have much to say about his own situation and the congregation's stormy response to him. But he feels impelled to allow theological concerns to take precedence (if only for a moment) over personal or

55. "Paul's decision to use a benediction rather than a thanksgiving is related to the personal nature of this letter . . . Whereas the letter of thanksgiving tends to offer a prayer of thanks for what God has done for the community, Paul employs a benediction to praise the God who has consoled him in his apostolic afflictions" (Matera, 40).

pastoral considerations. His apologia opens with a firm focus on God: specifically, the persistently compassionate and merciful God of Israel's covenant history. At the outset, then, he declares his intention to focus on God not as an abstract figure or series of concepts, but as one who engages humanity with concrete acts of deliverance that proceed from and demonstrate a compassionate divine character. Keeping in mind that Paul's letters represent a kind of preaching in written form, this opening models for us the starting point and true focus of all Christian proclamation, notwithstanding—or perhaps precisely because of—other pressing pastoral and relational concerns.

The gracious nature of Israel's God, Paul contends, is demonstrated historically, relationally, and experientially. Historically, Paul refers to Jesus and to Jesus's relationship with God as Father. But just as God is the "Father of our Lord Jesus Christ," so "the Father of mercies and the God of all consolation" refers to more than the historical experience of Israel, from which this language derives. For, as we have seen, standing over the whole of Paul's train of logic is the event of resurrection, the paramount instance of divine mercy and consolation demonstrated in the vindication of God's anointed Son. Only by examining the opening sections of this letter in reverse order does the logic of his reasoning become clear. Paul begins with the fact of Jesus's crucifixion, the supreme instance of unjust human suffering. Yet, he implies, God has "consoled" Christ by raising him from death. When, in turn, Jesus's followers share abundantly in "the sufferings of Christ" (1:5), they find themselves "consoled by God" (1:4). Since Jesus's death and resurrection exemplify divine consolation in the face of human suffering, Paul can rejoice that "our consolation is abundant *through* Christ" (1:5).

All of this is intensely personal for Paul, as it is for all those who preach out of a deep awareness of God's grace in their lives. Just as Christ's death and resurrection make sense of Paul's personal experience of abasement and consolation, so his experience in turn provides a model by which the believers at Corinth can make sense of their own difficult experience:

> If we are being afflicted, it is for *your* consolation and salvation; if we are being consoled, it is for *your* consolation, which you experience when you patiently endure the same sufferings that we are also suffering. Our hope for you is unshaken; for we know that as you share in our sufferings, so also you share in our consolation.
>
> 2 Corinthians 1:6–7

The consolation of which Paul speaks is historical in the sense that it emerges out of the history of Israel and, above all, the personal history of Jesus; it is relational in the sense that it proceeds from God's covenant relationship with Israel, Jesus, and all humanity; it is experiential in the sense that God's saving concern continues to be demonstrated in the personal and collective experience of Christian believers. It is not too much to suggest that all preachers, reflecting on the example of Christ, function for their own congregations as does Paul for his: however imperfectly, they in turn contemplate, model, and testify to the gracious consolation of human suffering that God has set forth preeminently in his Son.

Matera (42) rightly characterizes this passage as "a bold move" on Paul's part, for in it the apostle claims to be afflicted "for [*hyper*]" the "consolation and salvation" of others, even as he proclaims that Christ has suffered and died "for [*hyper*]" them and their sins (1 Cor. 15:3; 2 Cor. 5:14–15).[56] Even so, he does not imagine himself to be their Savior. The difference between his own exemplary role and that of Christ points to the function of proclamation as the preaching of theological premises through the filter of one's own encounter with God. The affliction and consolation encountered by Paul, and by those who share this ministry, benefit other believers only to the extent that the ministers can explain its meaning—its theologically referential character—in relation to Christ. Here preachers may run into one of several dangers. They may absolutize the pattern of their own spiritual experience (loyal followers often do this for them), or they may avoid mention of it altogether. Or, perhaps, they will either deny or fail to interpret both their own tribulations and those of their congregants in light of Christ. As we observed earlier, Paul avoids all these in order to model what might be called a "triangulated hermeneutic," drawing into conjunction God's gracious reversal of Jesus's suffering, that of the apostle himself, and that of the believers to whom he preaches. Thus his apostolic function is to point to the redemptive action of God in the midst of their affliction, and to remind them of their resemblance to Christ. Preachers in turn do not simply invite listeners to identify with their own experience of affliction and comfort, any more than they seek merely to identify with the congregation. Rather, the experiences of both are relativized, validated, and redefined in relation to

56. Further, Gorman, *Cruciformity*, 202–3.

a third, much larger reality: the Messiah's execution at the hands of men and his vindication at the hands of God.

Admittedly, there is something of a gap in this logic. At least as regards the episode from Asia Minor, Paul did not require another preacher to interpret the theological shape of his experience. By all appearances, this is an insight he has found on his own. Why, then, should other Christian sufferers need Paul or one of us to interpret their experience? If God is active at all, then surely they will find consolation in the kind of "near-resurrection" that has so comforted the apostle. Perhaps the only answer is that Paul sees himself in something of a special category by virtue of his apostolic office. Notwithstanding his assertion that his audience must "patiently endure the *same* sufferings that we are also suffering" (1:6), Paul's experience is unquestionably more intense and, it would seem, more theologically transparent. In any event, whether other believers might come to the same conclusion without benefit of Paul's explanation is now a moot point, for the explanation is there in his letter for all to read. Our congregants may well be able to interpret their experiences in light of Jesus's cross and resurrection without benefit of our preaching. But in case some do not arrive at such insight on their own, the example of Paul suggests this is the preacher's proper task, part of the responsibility of Christian proclamation.

Still, one final qualification is in order. As we have sought to emphasize throughout, the fact that God, not the preacher, is the author both of resurrection proper and of "near-resurrection" experiences means that while Christian proclamation properly bears witness to such an interpretation, it cannot impose this perspective on its audience. To the extent that Paul remains true to his own experience, the verification of the truth of his preaching must take place in the experience of each hearer. Paul suggests as much, for, he says, the Corinthian believers discover God's consolation only "when [they] patiently endure the same sufferings that we are also suffering" (2 Cor. 1:6). This implies that it is not the task of the preacher to prove the resurrection (for how would one do that?), but rather—on the basis of the preacher's own encounter with Christ—to point to the hearers' own spiritual experiences as the only "proof" they require.[57] Of course, being invited by a preacher to adopt the paradigm and perspective of the crucifixion/resurrection is itself an important aspect of any

57. So also Patte, *Preaching Paul*, 56–61.

listener's "spiritual experience." Even so, since God continues to be savingly active—consistent with Jesus's death and resurrection—in the lives of these hearers, the preacher is more like a commentator on the sidelines of congregational life, not presuming to create a particular reality in their lives, but merely observing and offering a theological interpretation of a reality that God alone is responsible for (literally) bringing to life.

The Fellowship of Consolation

Paul's appeal to the experience of the Corinthian believers bespeaks the fundamentally pastoral orientation of Christian preaching—even preaching that insists on a strong theological foundation. In his letter to the Philippians, he speaks of the "fellowship" or "community" of Christ's sufferings ([tēn] koinōnian [tōn] pathēmatōn autou, Phil. 3:10). And while in that letter Paul speaks of resurrection as something he has not yet fully attained (3:11–13a), it is nonetheless clear from 2 Corinthians that he understands there to be also a koinōnia of consolation, patterned precisely on Jesus's resurrection. The similar language of 2 Corinthians incorporates both possibilities: "as you are partners," he tells them, "participants [koinōnoi] in the sufferings, so in the consolation also" (2 Cor. 1:7).[58]

As Paul's own approach implies, for such a fellowship or partnership to emerge requires the preacher to be deeply in tune with the needs and tribulations of the congregants. Here the etymological origins of "sympathy"—that is, "suffering with"—seem altogether appropriate. Yet, once again, the koinōnia into which Paul invites his fellow believers is "communion" not primarily with himself, but with the Christ (similarly in 1 Cor. 1:9, "God is faithful; by him you were called into the *fellowship* of his Son, Jesus Christ our Lord"; cf. 1 Cor. 10:16). Accordingly, what Paul models for us in the first chapter of 2 Corinthians is neither an inherently effective rhetorical technique nor a clever or persuasive theological argument, but an all-encompassing experiential orientation. Conscious of the glaring weakness and outright folly of the Christian message (as a result of which hearers are unlikely to be convinced on the grounds of either intellectual plausibility or material benefit), Paul proposes an

---

58. Author's translation: although the NIV and NRSV both refer to "*our* sufferings" and "*our* comfort/consolation," there are no personal or possessive pronouns at this point in the original Greek.

overarching spiritual vision—a metanarrative expressed in the history of Jesus of Nazareth—in which he invites his hearers/readers to participate. As Paul recognizes, the validity of this theological, ethical, and experiential orientation ultimately rests neither in the preacher's ability to "make it so" nor in the audience's potentially favorable opinion of the speaker, but rather in the saving action of God. For all that the apostle is desperately trying to do to defend his reputation and retain his stake in the future of the Corinthian church, the ultimate purpose of his opening entreaty is that of every Christian preacher: to invite the audience to reinterpret their own circumstances in light of the vision of God set forth in the death and resurrection of Christ.

2

Triumph and Captivity, Sacrifice and Sufficiency (2:14–17)

Borrowing the imagery of a Roman military parade, Paul reckons with the cost of calling Jesus "Lord." The human impossibility of announcing death and life on God's terms, the unspeakable scandal of crucifixion, and the fact that many of his contemporaries have chosen compromise and accommodation instead, all cause the apostle to wonder whether he is up to the task of Christian proclamation, and impel him to rely more fully on Christ. Paul challenges us to consider our own motives for preaching and the price it will exact, calling for a kind of godly sincerity that refuses to tone down either the ugliness of the cross or the glory of the resurrection. Yet he is convinced that the gospel—and the call to declare it—is God's idea, not ours; that because Christ ushers us into the divine presence we should be more conscious of preaching for God than for our human hearers; and that the most essential qualification for such a ministry is not eloquence, intelligence, or aptitude, but a profound awareness of being inextricably bound both to Jesus's death and to his vindication.

God and Empire

> But thanks be to God, who in Christ always leads us in triumphal proces-
> sion, and through us spreads in every place the fragrance that comes from
> knowing him. For we are the aroma of Christ to God among those who are
> being saved and among those who are perishing; to the one a fragrance from
> death to death, to the other a fragrance from life to life. Who is sufficient
> for these things? For we are not peddlers of God's word like so many; but
> in Christ we speak as persons of sincerity, as persons sent from God and
> standing in his presence.
>
> 2 Corinthians 2:14–17

Having struggled to defend himself against the charge of inconsistency
occasioned by his change in travel plans, Paul now returns to the theological explanation of his ministry with which he began this letter to the
Corinthian church. In the first eleven verses of Second Corinthians, Paul
set out to interpret the Christian experience of affliction and consolation
by implicit reference to the crucifixion and resurrection of Jesus. Here,
toward the end of chapter two, Paul once more focuses on Christ, this time
employing the image of a Roman military parade: "But thanks be to God,
who in Christ always leads us in triumphal procession." The image occasions Paul's first explicit explanation of the ministry of proclamation.

Although modern victory parades frequently honor sports teams,
their most enduring historical function has been military.[1] The origin
of this practice apparently lies with the Romans, for whom triumphal
processions were closely connected with both emperor worship and the
divinization of victorious generals. For a civilization that worshiped its
national deities while acknowledging the gods of other nations, victory
on the battlefield was of more than military significance. It implied that
Roman gods and goddesses were superior to those of other nations. The
deities had triumphed, not mortals alone (compare the taunt, in an earlier

---

1. For instance, New York City held ticker-tape parades to celebrate the Yankees'
1998, 1999, and 2000 World Series baseball victories; Sydney, Australia, hosted parades
in April of 2000 for members of the Australian armed forces who had served in East
Timor, and in October of that year for the Australian Olympic team. Washington
and New York held parades to celebrate the "triumph" of American and coalition
forces during the 1991 Gulf War, and one of Russia's most important annual holi-
days, Victory Day, on May 9, features military parades celebrating the Soviet defeat
of German forces in the Second World War.

era, of one of Sennacherib's officers: 2 Kings 18:33–35; Isa. 36:18–20). Moreover, since the Romans understood such triumphs to have been granted under the general tutelage of the emperor, as well as through the leadership of their military commanders, these individuals could share the praise due to the divine patrons they served.

It was therefore customary to celebrate significant military victory with a triumphal procession, commencing at the city gate (itself a symbol of Roman supremacy) and leading through the main thoroughfare of the city.[2] Perhaps the most famous such procession (at least for those with an interest in New Testament history) took place in Rome some years after this letter was written, following Titus's calamitous victory over Jerusalem and the rebels of Judea. Josephus describes the ensuing victory parade in detail in Book 7 of *The Jewish War*, where he begins by complaining that the magnitude and magnificence of the spectacle far exceed his ability to describe them.[3] Words fail him in his account of the wealth, finery, splendor, and artistry displayed: "Masses of silver and gold and ivory in every shape known to the craftsman's art could be seen, not as if carried in procession but like a flowing river." There were, of course, statues of the victorious Roman gods, and images of winged "Victory"; animals of all sorts, in robes and ribbons; loot from the Jerusalem Temple, including an enormous gold Menorah, the Torah scrolls, and a table of solid gold weighing hundreds of pounds. Actual ships (commemorating a naval engagement on the Sea of Galilee) were carried in procession. But what caused the most astonishment, says Josephus—and the most anxiety— were a series of enormous traveling stages on which the finest sculptors and artists in the empire had depicted the progress of the Jewish War, lest anyone be in doubt as to the reason for celebration. Causing particular alarm was the fact that the stages were three and sometimes four stories tall and wobbled precariously through the streets. Scene after scene portrayed the devastation of the Jewish nation, the defeat of one city after another, and the destruction of Jerusalem. "Placed on each stage," says

2. For a full treatment, see H. S. Versnel, *Triumphus: An Inquiry into the Origin, Development and Meaning of the Roman Triumph* (Leiden: Brill, 1970). T. E. Schmidt ("Mark 15:16–32: The Crucifixion Narrative and the Roman Triumphal Procession," *NTS* 41 [1995], 3–4) notes the gradual appropriation of this ceremony as the exclusive domain of the emperor.

3. The following quotations are taken from Josephus, *The Jewish War* 7.116–57 (tr. G. A. Williamson [Harmondsworth: Penguin, 1970], 370–73).

Josephus, "was the commander of a captured town just as he had been when captured."

Captives were among the main attractions. The victorious general, Titus, had put seven hundred Jewish defenders on display, selected "for their exceptional stature and physique." The victors were robed in scarlet and gold, but even the captives were costumed, so that "under their elaborate and beautiful garments any disfigurement due to physical sufferings was hidden from view." In this parade, battalions of Roman soldiers led the way, followed by the loot and spectacle, then the prisoners. Last of all rode the Emperor Vespasian on horseback, together with his sons Titus and Domitian, all dressed in crimson robes. The whole city of Rome, says Josephus, came out to watch. He says there was standing room only, with "barely enough room left for the procession itself to pass."

Although the events that Josephus describes postdate the Corinthian correspondence by nearly twenty years, Paul's readers would have been familiar both with such ceremonies and with the theological implications of his reference. But what does Paul mean by this cryptic reference in his letter to the Corinthian church? The answer is less than certain, as recourse to any ancient or modern commentary on the passage quickly demonstrates. For a start, we should note that Paul intends it as universal in scope, as to both time and place: "But thanks be to God," he says, "who in Christ *always* leads us in triumphal procession and through us spreads *in every place* the fragrance that comes from knowing him" (or "from the knowledge of him," RSV). As used here, the key verb *thriambeuein* essentially means "to display as the spoils of victory," implying that Christ has conquered and enslaved those who follow him, displays them as evidence of his victory, and leads them to death.[4] For slavery and death were the grim alternatives awaiting enemy soldiers at the conclusion of any "triumph" in which they were unfortunate enough to be paraded through Roman streets. In just such a vein, Paul can depict himself and his companions as "the rubbish of the world, the dregs of all things":

4. Scott Hafemann, *Suffering and the Spirit: An Exegetical Study of II Cor. 2:14–3:3 within the Context of the Corinthian Correspondence* (WUNT 2.19; Tübingen: J. C. B. Mohr, 1986), 22–35; followed by, e.g., Thrall, 1:194–95; Matera, 70–73; *pace* Furnish 174–75. Paul's only other use of this verb is in Col. 2:13–15, where he describes the "principalities and powers," meaning all the spiritual forces that oppose God, as having been captured in Christ's victory parade.

For I think that God has exhibited us apostles as last of all, as though sentenced to death, because we have become a spectacle to the world, to angels and to mortals. . . . We have become like the rubbish of the world, the dregs of all things, to this very day.

1 Corinthians 4:9, 13b

As Matera notes, "Paul himself is deeply aware that he was God's enemy (1 Cor. 15:9) and that he is now under a divine obligation to preach the gospel" (Matera, 72). He describes himself as "a slave to all" (1 Cor. 9:19) because he is first and foremost a "slave of Christ" (1 Cor. 7:22), preaching the gospel, he says, "not of my own will" but by virtue of the responsibility God has entrusted to him (1 Cor. 9:17).

The apostle goes on to develop both positive and negative implications of his chosen imagery:

For we are the aroma of Christ to God among those who are being saved and among those who are perishing; to the one a fragrance from death to death, to the other a fragrance from life to life.

2 Corinthians 2:15–16a

To whom is he referring? Paul frequently speaks in these chapters of "we" and "us" by way of contrast with his Corinthian audience.[5] More specifically, the Pauline "we" and "us" often specify those who proclaim the Christian message, as in 1:19 (literally, "Jesus Christ, proclaimed by us among you; by myself, Silvanus, and Timothy"), and especially 2:17, "For *we* are not peddlers of God's word . . . *we* speak . . . as persons sent from God" (cf. also 1:12, 24; 4:5, etc.). In all likelihood, then, this is the intended sense here: throughout 2:14–16 and on into verse 17, Paul is referring to himself, Silvanus, and Timothy, all of whom have proclaimed the Christian message in Corinth.[6] God, he insists, has captured preachers of the gospel such as himself and his companions, leads them in his victory parade, and through them spreads the life-giving, death-portending odor (that is, knowledge) of the crucified Messiah.

5. E.g., 2 Cor. 1:6, "If *we* are being afflicted, it is for *your* consolation and salvation; if *we* are being consoled, it is for *your* consolation, which *you* experience when *you* patiently endure the same sufferings that *we* are also suffering"; cf. 1:8–10, 12, 14, 24.

6. Alternatively, Paul's "we" may be a rhetorical plural by which he refers to himself alone (so Thrall 1:195–96 and the discussion cited there).

79

Triumphal processions evidently included the use of perfume and/ or incense. For the Roman soldiers, as well as for the crowds along the parade route, the smell would have signaled victory and the manifest supremacy of Rome's armies. For the defeated soldiers and their captive commanders, by contrast, the pungent clouds were yet another sign that they were on their way to death.[7] Particularly in the case of incense, associated with cultic sacrifice in both Jewish and pagan practice, the thought was that God, or the gods, found the odor pleasing (cf. Gen. 8:21; Exod. 29:18, etc.). The use of specifically sacrificial language in 2 Corinthians 2:15 (*euōdia*, odor of sacrifice) suggests that the apostles and their proclamation of Christ are the odor given off by the crucifixion (Eph. 5:2 describes the crucifixion as "a fragrant offering and sacrifice to God"). This aptly conveys Paul's sense that the "smell" conveyed by preachers of the gospel is more than merely passive, as if their reputations alone were tainted by virtue of association with Christ. On the contrary, even as believers offer up their lives in imitation of Jesus, as "a living sacrifice, holy and acceptable to God" (Rom. 12:1), so the apostles' active proclamation of the Christian message also reeks of death. Like the pungent scent of incense clinging to garments, preachers convey a sense of Christ by virtue of their characteristic task, which is preaching itself.[8]

In this respect, Paul and his companions differ from the believers to whom they write, not in kind but in degree. As we saw earlier, Paul understands all Christian discipleship in terms of identification with the death and resurrection of Jesus. Just as it was God's will for the Son to be abased and exalted, so this is the basic pattern of God's will in the life of Jesus's followers. Likewise, Paul has already explained how suffering and consolation are essential to specifically apostolic identification with the crucifixion and resurrection of Jesus. This is the consequence of having been "co-crucified with Christ" (Gal. 2:19), being so closely identified with the death of Jesus as to serve as a sign of its degradation and sacrificial intent:

7. T. E. Schmidt, "Mark 15:16–32: The Crucifixion Narrative and the Roman Triumphal Procession," *NTS* 41 (1995): 5n15.

8. "Paul's apostolic role of '*being led to death*' *en tō Christō* in order to reveal the knowledge of God in 2:14–16a cannot be separated from his call to *preach the word of God en Christō* in 2:17" (Hafemann, *Suffering and the Spirit*, 52 [emphasis original]).

> For I think that God has exhibited us apostles as last of all, as though sentenced to death, because we have become a spectacle to the world, to angels and to mortals. . . . We have become like the rubbish of the world, the dregs of all things, to this very day.
>
> 1 Corinthians 4:9, 13b

In 2 Corinthians, Paul's description of apostolic ministry will refer to both "life" and "death," although with a firm emphasis on the latter:

> We are afflicted in every way, but not crushed; perplexed, but not driven to despair; persecuted, but not forsaken; struck down, but not destroyed; always carrying in the body the death of Jesus, so that the life of Jesus may also be made visible in our bodies. For while we live, we are always being given up to death for Jesus' sake, so that the life of Jesus may be made visible in our mortal flesh. So death is at work in us, but life in you.
>
> 2 Corinthians 4:8–12

Here, the "death" experienced by apostles contrasts strongly with the "life" that has overtaken their hearers. Likely this is because Paul's recent afflictions remain vivid in his memory, as well as because—paradoxically—such an emphasis suits his struggle to regain the allegiance of his disaffected congregants. Far from denying their negative estimation of him, Paul makes it the basis for his self-justification. He freely admits that he has indeed been captured, humiliated, and enslaved. But rather than allowing his worth to be determined by the standards of contemporary society, Paul claims that this is God's doing: "thanks be to *God* who . . . leads us in triumphal procession."[9] Only by virtue of having been soundly "defeated" by God—included in a humiliation like that of Jesus—is Paul subsequently included in the *Triumphus* of this resurrected "Lord." Thus, contrary to his detractors' scornful estimation of him, the humiliation that he suffers is an affirmation rather than a denial of divine favor, a necessary prelude to glory rather than its negation.

On any account, Paul presents a daunting vision of Christian discipleship in general and of Christian proclamation in particular. Yet it is fitting for one who has undergone such a radical redirection of piety and

9. Cf. Paul Marshall, "A Metaphor of Social Shame: *THRIAMBEUEIN* in 2 Cor. 2:14," *NovT* 25 (1983): 302–17, emphasizing honor and shame ("the social metaphor of strength and weakness," 316) as social equivalents of death and resurrection.

theological conviction. At least in his case, the paradigm fits the circumstances of his conversion on the road to Damascus. Even so, significant implications remain for those whose call to faith and ministry is cast in less dramatic terms. However harsh or demanding it may appear, Paul's description belongs to an already extensive tradition of theological reflection on the significance of calling Jesus *Kyrios*, "Lord." To acknowledge Jesus as "Lord" entails for Paul immersion in and imitation of the circumstances by which Jesus came to be known by this supreme title. It is a question of engaging and embodying a lived theology of Christlikeness, and of cruciformity in particular. To be a disciple (and proclaimer) of *Jesus* as "Lord" means submitting after the manner of Jesus to the yet-greater will of Jesus's God. As Jesus, in submission to his Father, is declared "Lord," so disciples, in conscious imitation of Jesus, submit to both. In this sense, the attribution of a theological title ("Lord") implies a distinct hermeneutic and spirituality (the interpretation of human experience in light of that Lord), issues in a concrete set of practices (in this case, preaching and conscious self-abasement), and leads to a profound shift in personal, social, and political allegiances (since there is only "one Lord," Eph. 4:5). In this manner, Paul argues, disciples and preachers alike reflect their own submission to the same divine power that raised Jesus from death and thereby declared him worthy of the title.

If Paul's choice of metaphors illustrates the spirituality of apostolic Christian proclamation by reference to Roman practice (he and his companions have been captured by Christ and put on display; they are the smell of Christ's sacrifice), it also suggests some possible directions for preaching itself. How this is so may be inferred from the preaching of Mark, since a series of recent studies have demonstrated the significance of Roman imperial language, including references to the triumphal procession, within the earliest canonical gospel. Mark's opening line, "The beginning of the good news of Jesus Christ, the Son of God" (Mark 1:1), as well as the centurion's confession from the foot of the cross, "Truly this man was God's Son!" (Mark 15:39), echo the exact language of Roman state religion. Following the precedent set by Julius Caesar, Roman emperors were acclaimed—usually posthumously!—as divine or semi-divine; Julius's adopted son and nephew Octavian (later known as Augustus) took the title *Caesar divi filius* ("Caesar son of god") as a strategy to secure his own claim to office. Particularly in the East, numerous inscriptions refer to Augustus and various successors by such titles as "Savior," "Lord," and "god," while Augustus's accession in particular was hailed as "the beginning of good news for the whole world."[10] In addition, many details of Jesus's treatment prior to crucifixion—in particular the ceremonial robe and crown, the mockery of the soldiers, and the procession to Golgotha—appear to reflect the conventions of an imperial triumph.[11] The reason for this narrative strategy is as much political as it is theological: writing in a period of turmoil throughout the Roman Empire when imperial claims of divinity are being taken to new extremes, Mark wants his readers to be in no doubt as to the identity of the only true "Savior" and "Son of God"—not Caesar, but Jesus of Nazareth.[12]

Of course (like the previous illustration from Josephus), the evidence of Mark likely postdates Second Corinthians by at least fifteen years. Nonetheless, the point of comparison is that we see Paul already engaging the political ideology of his day to express key features of Jesus's Messianic identity. Impelled from without by changes in cultural outlook and from within by a pietist preference for personal experience, many segments of Western Protestantism have by contrast long since abandoned the field of political engagement. Social activism is still widely valued as an extension of Jesus's own concern for those in need. But specifically political activism has largely been reduced to the role of special pleading on behalf of a minority interest group. With very few exceptions, Protestants seem content to work within prevailing political structures, without attempting to critique the political system itself.

The difference between this relative acquiescence and Paul's own outlook could hardly be more pronounced. From the entirely ludicrous vantage point of championing an apparently asinine and untenable religious philosophy, Paul chooses to take on the reigning political ideology of

10. E.g., Kim, "Anarthrous *huios theou* in Mark 15, 39 and the Roman Imperial Cult," *Bib* 79 (1998): 225–38; Craig A. Evans, "Mark's Incipit and the Priene Calendar Inscription: From Jewish Gospel to Greco-Roman Gospel," *Journal of Greco-Roman Judaism and Christianity* 1 (2000): 67–81; J. R. Harrison, "Paul and Imperial Gospel at Thessaloniki," *JSNT* 25 (2002): 78–95, esp. 87n66; and, more generally, John Ferguson, *The Religions of the Roman Empire* (AGRL; Ithaca: Cornell University Press, 1970), 88–98.

11. Schmidt, "Mark 15:16–32," passim; cf. Evans, "Mark's Incipit," 71–73.

12. Evans, "Mark's Incipit," 79–81, and further, Craig A. Evans, "The Beginning of the Good News and the Fulfillment of Scripture in the Gospel of Mark," in Stanley E. Porter, ed., *Hearing the Old Testament in the New Testament* (Grand Rapids: Eerdmans, 2006), 83–103.

his day, boldly insisting that the crucified and humiliated insurrectionist he preaches is mightier than the Roman emperor and his armies. He declares Jesus of Nazareth—not Claudius or Nero—to be Savior, Son of God, and Lord, implying by that claim that the *triumphus* of the crucified Messiah draws even the might of Rome into its train. It would be difficult to conceive of a more compelling mandate for subsequent preachers and teachers to subject the political structures of their own day to the countermanding dominion of the risen Christ.

As a contemporary example of theological audacity in the political arena, and despite overuse of this incident as a sermon illustration, this is precisely the point made by the motto hung from the windows of the United Methodist Church in Ječná Street, Prague (Czechoslovakia), on November 27, 1989, in support of a mass demonstration demanding the fall of the Soviet-backed Communist government. The sign read: "Zvítezil Beránek nás"—"The Lamb Has Won." While the timing of the gesture was opportune, it was made all the more poignant and powerful by the fact that the motto had not been coined for the occasion. It was in fact inscribed, together with a picture of the Lamb with the cross, on a cloth that had been draped over the church's sanctuary rail during communion services throughout long years of official government opposition.[13] As with Paul, the congregants had confessed the victory of the Lamb even while an apparent preponderance of evidence pointed strongly in the opposite direction.

Perhaps Paul's own lack of timidity in this regard stems from an awareness that he has already "suffered the loss of all things," regarding them as worthless precisely because of "the surpassing value of knowing Christ Jesus [his] Lord" (Phil. 3:8). Western political ideologies of the third millennium are (at least for their own citizens) perhaps less autocratic than those of imperial Rome, and the Western church considerably better situated in terms of its social, political, and financial standing. Yet it is remarkable that this situation seems to have produced

13. Dr. Vilém Schneeberger, Prague (personal communication, March 6, 2004). Yet more significantly, the motto is derived from the confession of the Unitas Fratrum, or Bohemian/Moravian Brethren, themselves long persecuted: *Vicit agnus noster, eum sequamur* ("Our Lamb has won, let us follow him"). The story is reported in more general terms by H. Eddie Fox, "A New World Pentecost," in Joe Hale, ed., *Proceedings of the Sixteenth World Methodist Conference, Singapore, July 24–31, 1991* (Lake Junaluska, NC: World Methodist Council, 1992), 93–94.

less rather than greater boldness when it comes to the implications of confessing Jesus as "Lord." Conservative American Protestants in particular (who claim to take the Lordship of Christ more seriously than most) typically see little distinction between allegiance to the state and allegiance to the church. Confusion between the demands of "God and empire" is the common experience of Christian citizens in powerful nation-states: examples (and exceptions) from nineteenth- and twentieth-century Russia, Germany, and Great Britain come immediately to mind. Inability to offer social and political critique, on the other hand, suggests that the church in question has not reckoned fully with the implications of its own confession, or, worse, that it has chosen to ignore the radical personal, social, and political consequences of proclaiming Jesus as "Lord."

Apostleship and the Cost of Proclamation

If we compare our own proclamation with that of the apostle Paul, the first observation to be made is that preachers of the third millennium, ascending their pulpits in places such as Brisbane, Karachi, and South Bend, Indiana, are not apostles in the most directly Pauline sense. Paul is painfully aware of his own abnormal qualifications for the title, for he says of his commissioning, "Last of all, *as to one untimely born,* [Christ] appeared also to me" (1 Cor. 15:8). While he must style himself "the least of the apostles" (1 Cor. 15:9), there is an important sense in which he is also the "last" of the apostles, if we take this term to mean those whom the risen Christ directly commissioned for the initial proclamation of the gospel. In a passage such as 1 Corinthians 15:7, Paul *may* be willing to extend the term "apostle" outside the original eleven or twelve plus himself.[14] Nonetheless, it is perhaps best if we understand Paul's exposition of apostolic proclamation as applying to later preachers and preaching only by extension or analogy. At the very least we can insist that although both the commissioning of subsequent preachers and the context of their proclamation have changed significantly, the essential

14. See discussions in Fee, *The First Epistle to the Corinthians,* (NICNT; Grand Rapids: Eerdmans, 1987), 731–32; Ernest Best, *A Commentary on the First and Second Epistles to the Thessalonians* (BNTC; London: Adam and Charles Black, 1979), 100; cf. Rom. 16:7; Phil. 2:25.

christological content and method of preaching nonetheless remain the same. On these grounds, then, we are justified in seeking foundations and guidelines for preaching ministries of a later day in Paul's defense of his own apostolic ministry.

Far from extolling the glories and virtues of Christian proclamation, Paul starkly emphasizes its challenge and cost. On the one hand is the responsibility of proclaiming God's offer of life to those who are eager to receive it. The enormity of such responsibility consists in the fact that God, not the preacher, is the source of this life. By implication, only by knowing and being in communion with the Giver is one able to speak with integrity of the gift. Otherwise preaching is liable to be little more than words. Nonetheless, this is the easier of the two aspects of preaching, for it amounts to offering life (on God's behalf) to those who know themselves to be dead. Far more difficult, on the other hand, is the profound awkwardness of proclaiming death to those who believe themselves to be alive. Paul here returns to a theme that had occupied him in his earlier correspondence with the Corinthian church:

> For the message about the cross is foolishness to those who are perishing, but to us who are being saved it is the power of God. . . . For Jews demand signs and Greeks desire wisdom, but we proclaim Christ crucified, a stumbling block to Jews and foolishness to Gentiles. . . .
>
> 1 Corinthians 1:18, 22–23

As Gordon Fee comments,

> It is hard for those in the christianized West, where the cross for almost nineteen centuries has been the primary symbol of the faith, to appreciate how utterly mad the message of a God who got himself crucified by his enemies must have seemed to the first-century Greek or Roman. But it is precisely the depth of this scandal and folly that we *must* appreciate if we are to understand both why the Corinthians were moving away from it . . . and why it was well over a century before the cross appears among Christians as a symbol of their faith.[15]

15. Fee, *First Epistle*, 76 (emphasis original). Cf. the fuller treatment by Martin Hengel, *Crucifixion in the Ancient World and the Folly of the Message of the Cross*, tr. John Bowden (Philadelphia: Fortress, 1977). Unless otherwise indicated, the citations in the ensuing discussion are from Gerald G. O'Collins, "Crucifixion," *ABD* 1:1207–10.

There were, generally speaking, three forms or degrees of capital punishment in the Roman world. The quickest and least shameful kind of execution was *decollatio*, decapitation, although as an alternative to the loss of one's head (if an arena and spectators were handy), one could be thrown to wild animals instead (*damnatio ad bestias*). In the case of the early Christians, this meant being served up to hungry lions. A second, more severe form of execution was to be burned alive: covered in tar and set alight. The Roman historian Tacitus (ca. AD 55–120) describes how in about the year 64, the Emperor Nero, seeking to deflect suspicion that he was to blame for devastating fires in the city of Rome, had Christians "burned to serve as lamps by night" in his gardens (as well as crucifying some and having others torn apart by wild dogs: *Annals* 15:44).

Yet to Roman eyes, *crematio* (burning) was not the worst or most shameful way to die. For those they considered the lowest of the low, or the very worst offenders, they reserved crucifixion. This special form of death served, for instance, to deter the many slaves who worked either in Rome or on the vast Italian estates from disobedience or rebellion, to terrify the defenders of a besieged city, or to degrade and punish them after their inevitable defeat. Roman citizens, and especially members of the upper classes, normally had the right to be executed in a more dignified manner than this. Only for high treason, crimes against the state, or desertion in time of war, could a Roman citizen be put to death in this way. In the case of the Roman Christians, Nero subjected his victims to all three forms of execution. His cruel ingenuity shows itself in the fact that he had some first crucified, then set alight, combining two agonizing humiliations into one.

Crucifixion was a form of death that people of good taste preferred not to mention in polite company, and because it was not a fit topic for discussion, few Roman writers have much to say about it.[16] But Cicero, who lived about a century before the time of Christ (106–43 BC), calls it "that most cruel and disgusting penalty," the most extreme form of punishment fit only for slaves (*In C. Verrem* 2.5.165, 168). Elsewhere he writes:

> How grievous a thing it is to be disgraced by a public court; how grievous to suffer a fine, how grievous to suffer banishment; and yet in the midst of any such disaster we retain some degree of liberty. Even if we are threatened

16. Hengel, *Crucifixion*, 37–38.

with death, we may die free men. But the executioner, the veiling of the head, and the very word "cross" should be far removed not only from the person of a Roman citizen but from his thoughts, his eyes and his ears. For it is not only the actual occurrence of these things or the endurance of them, but liability to them, the expectation, indeed the very mention of them, that is unworthy of a Roman citizen and a free man.

Pro C. Rabiro Perd. 5.16[17]

Seneca argues that even suicide is preferable to days of agony on a cross:

Can anyone be found who would prefer wasting away in pain, dying limb by limb, or letting out his life drop by drop, rather than expiring once for all? Can any man be found willing to be fastened to the accursed tree, long sickly, already deformed, swelling with ugly weals on shoulders and chest, and drawing the breath of life amid long-drawn-out agony? He would have many excuses for dying even before mounting the cross.

Moral Epistles 101

This dreadful and terrifying reputation explains Paul's modest assertion that the crucifixion constitutes "a stumbling block to Jews and foolishness to Gentiles" (1 Cor. 1:23b), as well as his claim that those who proclaim Christ represent the aroma of life only to those who are being saved, but the very stink of death to those who are perishing. It also explains what he means by insisting that "God chose what is low and despised in the world, things that are not, to reduce to nothing things that are, so that no one might boast in the presence of God" (1 Cor. 1:28–29). Indeed, there is independent attestation to the accuracy of his assessment. Pliny the Younger (AD 63–ca. 113) describes Christianity as "a perverse, extravagant superstition [*superstitionem pravam et immodicam*]" (*Epistles* 10.96.8), and from Rome of the second century AD comes the well-known graffito of a supplicant bowing before a crucified man with the head of a donkey, accompanied by the mocking inscription, "Alexamenos worships God."[18] It is worth recalling that the name first given by the Antiochenes to followers of Jesus—*Christianoi* (Acts

17. Quoted in Hengel, *Crucifixion*, 42.
18. "The cartoon is probably what it seems; a comic denigration by some pagan wag of the new cult of dupes, a mockery of the asses for whom, as the learned Celsus complained also in the second century, Christianity seemed attractive because it was

11:26)—was intended as derisive: "Christ-lets," "little Christs." Hengel summarizes the matter as follows:

> to believe that the one pre-existent Son of the one true God, the mediator at the creation and the redeemer of the world, had appeared in very recent times in out-of-the-way Galilee as a member of the obscure people of the Jews, and even worse, had died the death of a common criminal on the cross, could only be regarded as a sign of madness. The real gods of Greece and Rome could be distinguished from mortal men by the very fact that they were *immortal*—they had absolutely nothing in common with the cross as a sign of shame (*aischunes* in Hebrews 12:2), the infamous stake (*infamis stipes*), the "barren" (*infelix lignum*) or "criminal wood" (*panourgikon xulon*), the "terrible cross" (*maxima mala crux*) of the slaves of Plautus, and thus of the one who, in the words of Celsus, was "bound in the most ignominious fashion" and "executed in a shameful way."[19]

The point of this extended historical recitation is to observe, first, that hesitation over the apparent asininity of the Christian gospel is hardly new. In our own day the sticking points may be its seemingly perverse glorification of suffering and weakness, its embarrassingly exclusive truth claims, its affront to human independence and self-realization, its challenge to claims of economic or political domination, or the perceived metaphysical impossibility of resurrection:

> In a world that wants to turn us into the spiritual equivalents of personal trainers, "We preach Christ crucified" will still sound like foolishness. It may be a stumbling block to the Jews, foolishness to the Greeks and terminally old-fashioned to the Canadians. It might even be—horror of

---

a religion for weaklings" (Patrick Grant, *Literature of Mysticism in Western Tradition* [London: Macmillan, 1983], 109).

19. Hengel, *Crucifixion*, 6–7. In similar terms, Walter L. Reed ("Spoken to Us by His Son: A Dialogics of the New Testament," in *Dialogues of the Word: The Bible as Literature According to Bakhtin* [Oxford: Oxford University Press, 1993], 79) characterizes the Christian gospel as "blasphemous in its Jewish context, ludicrous in the Greco-Roman setting, and heterogeneous within its own canonical boundaries." From a North American perspective, something of the religious and political dimensions of Jesus's crucifixion—and therefore also its shock value for pious Roman subjects—can be appreciated if we imagine God choosing to personally vindicate, even beatify, an Islamist rebel who had been tortured to death for jihadist preaching against Western interests.

horrors—damaging to our self-esteem. Frankly, a lot of people will prefer to hear tales of power and success—dressed up, to be sure, with a few spiritual trimmings. Do not imagine that preaching Christ crucified will be easier in Canada than in Corinth.[20]

A review of the evidence suggests that the message of the cross has always seemed like folly, impervious to common sense. Preachers of every age have had to choose between theological courage, on the one hand, and the convenient prevarication of intellectual, moral, or social accommodation, on the other. We cannot underestimate how genuinely humiliating it must have been for Paul (immensely proud of both his Roman citizenship and his Jewish ancestry) to preach a message of salvation that sounded (at best) ineffectual to the one audience and stupid to the other. "Who," he asks, with no small understatement, "is sufficient for these things?" (2 Cor. 2:16b).

Peddling the Word

In its state of relative material affluence and correlative spiritual poverty, the contemporary Western church seems at times unequal to either the cruciform and death-portending, or the resurrectional, life-proclaiming aspect of its preaching task. No doubt at least partly in response to the overly negative stereotypes of a judgmental and wrathful God preached by some in past generations, contemporary preaching frequently emphasizes a loving, accepting, affirming God, to the near-universal neglect of the high social, ethical, and material demands and deep personal cost of Christian discipleship. By the same token, any reference to divine displeasure, or to judgment in particular (not to mention the doctrine of hell, implying final exclusion from God's presence), is left to "fundamentalists" and others who know no better. Perhaps these are not proper equivalents to the scandal of crucifixion. But given the decline of the church as a social institution in the past half century, occasioned or accompanied by an exodus of many congregants, Western churches have frequently resorted to marketing the positive aspects of Christian faith, hoping to lure new (or former) members

20. Stephen C. Farris, "A Wise Sort of Foolishness (1 Corinthians 1:18–31)," in Michael P. Knowles, ed., *The Folly of Preaching: Preachers and Proclamation from the Gladstone Festival* (Grand Rapids: Eerdmans, 2007), 161.

with promises of spiritual benefit. But as with any marketing strategy, this approach requires a corresponding de-emphasis on anything likely to be perceived as negative or counterproductive to church growth. Competing in a crowded marketplace, we have reduced the Christian gospel to an instrument for achieving self-realization and personal fulfillment.

Along these lines, Mark Ellingsen notes the influence of the Western psychologized consciousness on our concept of Christian discipleship and ministry:

> Western culture has been markedly influenced by the therapeutic relationship as paradigmatic for individual and cultural models of "healthy" existence. This widespread attitude in turn is believed to have nurtured a tendency to view all institutions, even religion, as human creations designed to facilitate our self-fulfilment.

In other words, the perceived function of the church is to foster personal emotional and psychological wholeness among its members. Ellingsen continues:

> If Christian faith is presented as somehow correlated with an aspect of contemporary human experience . . . then in Western psychologized culture, Christian faith will likely be heard as mere psychological wish-fulfillment. For if Christianity's claims must always be correlated with contemporary human experience in order that they be God's Word, then the Word of God can never be said to stand unambiguously over against and criticize contemporary experience.[21]

To add to our difficulty, or perhaps as a symptom of it, the message of the Western church is often cast in terms that are functionally Unitarian.[22] We may preach about the need for obedience to or the possibility of a relationship with "God." Yet this "God" is neither the acutely personal "Father" of Jesus nor the awe-inspiring "Yahweh" of Israel's historical experience, but some considerably tamer and more comfortingly neutral entity. Nor is the route to this God one of self-abasement and spiritual death, in the footsteps of Jesus. Jesus is set forth as a man of exemplary piety, but not

21. Mark Ellingsen, *The Integrity of Biblical Narrative: Story in Theology and Proclamation* (Minneapolis: Augsburg Fortress, 1990), 26–27.
22. This is the assessment of James B. Torrance, *Worship, Community, and the Triune God of Grace* (Downers Grove, IL: InterVarsity, 1996), 20, 24–30, and passim.

as the sole and essential means by which we may dare approach a holy, sovereign God. Frequently absent is the classic Christian declaration of Christ's having redeemed complete human failure, and with it any mention of the orthodox understanding that ordinary human beings such as ourselves, left free to fulfill our personal and collective potential, typically respond by nailing God's Messiah to the cross. As the Yiddish proverb has it, "If God lived on earth, people would break His windows."

But even more problematic than the rush to avoid alienating prospective congregants with the troubling details of a cruciform spirituality is the fact that economic prosperity has left many segments of the Western church spiritually impoverished. Just as affliction has the potential to inspire devotion, so affluence and relative stability tend to undermine it. We are not alone in this, however. The same principle is evident in the history of Israel, perhaps nowhere more so than in the repeated cycles of spiritual "boom and bust" narrated in the Book of Judges. Whenever the Israelites cry out to be saved from their enemies, God sends a deliverer; but no sooner do peace and prosperity return than the people revert to a more relaxed theological posture. Only renewed affliction alerts them to their spiritual need.

In our own situation, it would seem that we have intentionally avoided or conveniently neglected both the truly "negative" and the truly "positive" aspects of classic Christian proclamation, with the unfortunate result that having eliminated anything that might offend our "target audience," we have simultaneously lost much of what might otherwise have offered them real theological hope. Our contemporary situation recalls the oft-repeated story of Thomas Aquinas (ca. 1225–74), the great medieval theologian, encountering Pope Innocent IV (in office 1243–54).[23] Noting the extent of papal wealth, the pontiff is said to have remarked (alluding to Acts 3:6), "You see, Thomas, the church can no longer say, as when it first began, 'Silver and gold have I none,'" to which Aquinas calmly replied, "That is to be admitted, holy Father; yet neither as at first can we say to the lame man, 'Stand up, walk, be whole.'"

23. The story is related by the Flemish Jesuit Cornelius à Lapide (1567–1637) in his commentary on the Book of Acts (*Commentaria in Acta Apostolorum, Epistolas Canonicas, et Apocalypsin* [Antwerp, 1627], 101; author's translation). G. K. Chesterton (*St. Thomas Aquinas* [London: Hodder and Stoughton, 1933], 43) erroneously attributes the exchange to St. Dominic Guzman, founder of the Dominican order, and (presumably) Pope Innocent III.

The example of Paul, by contrast, suggests that we may be saved from spiritual poverty only by a generous abundance of personal affliction and material want. Not accidentally, these exact conditions—however profoundly unjust—have accounted historically for the spiritual vibrancy of the African-American church. While spiritual benefit by no means justifies oppression, and affliction is not something that pastors or congregations actively seek, long experience (from Paul onward) suggests adversity to be a reality that—in one degree or another—preachers in particular often encounter. It would appear, therefore, again on the basis of the circumstances Paul has recounted, that the primary challenge to a preacher's sense of personal adequacy comes not only from the seeming incomprehensibility of the Christian gospel, but also from the persistently difficult circumstances in which he or she typically endeavors to proclaim its message.

Yet by asking, "Who is equal to such a task?" (2 Cor. 2:16 NIV), Paul implies not that preachers ought to feel adequate, but that they by definition do not and cannot. Again, the crucial theological insight that has emerged out of his own crushing experience of affliction is that it is precisely the recognition of his own *in*adequacy for the task that leads him to depend not on himself, but on the God who alone raised Jesus from the dead. This is an experiential theology, one in which a conceptual framework (crucifixion and resurrection) has merged with and given light to the concrete circumstances of discipleship. Theological conviction and personal experience now appear in the same light, as the preacher testifies that only the power of God is sufficient to reverse and redeem the death of God's Messiah, persistent personal adversity, and the sense of inadequacy for proclamation to which both conviction and experience give rise. In the well-chosen words of Karl Barth,

> As regards preachers themselves, the conformity of preaching to ministry means that they realize how impossible their action is, but that they may still look beyond its uncertainty and focus on the fact of revelation. This will give them confidence that the revealed will of God which is at work in their action will cover their weakness and corruptness, and that they are promised a righteousness which they themselves can never give to what they do. Knowing the forgiveness of sins, they may do their work in simple obedience, no longer, then, as a venture, but in the belief that God has commanded it.[24]

24. Karl Barth, *Homiletics*, tr. Geoffrey W. Bromiley and Donald E. Daniels (Louisville: Westminster John Knox, 1991), 69–70; cf. 88: "A sermon is always the work

The implication of Paul's argument is that many in his own day have also turned aside from the personal, spiritual, and theological rigors of the task. For, he insists, "we are not peddlers of God's word *like so many*" (NRSV), or, in the NIV (which brings out more clearly the sense of base financial motives), "we do not peddle the word of God for profit" (2 Cor. 2:17a). Whether he believes them to be motivated simply by love of money or by lack of theological vision as well, Paul takes a slap at certain of his contemporaries (probably the "super-apostles" who are competing for the loyalty of the congregation), accusing them of mercenary motives (cf. Phil. 1:15–17). The key word here is *kapēleuein*, meaning to hawk or peddle something in order to make money. Used in the marketplace for a wine merchant who waters down his product in order to make a bit more money, it came to be applied to teachers who water down the truth in order to serve their own interests.[25] In the face of those who have raised questions about Paul's own motives, he is insistent that he has not flinched or sold out so as to make his words more palatable to hearers with no appetite for the real thing, but has held to the Christian message in all of its unwelcome awkwardness. His own troubled autobiography provides proof of his point: having been beaten, battered, starved, shipwrecked, and rejected for the sake of the gospel that he preaches, he can hardly be accused of watering anything down for the sake of self-interest.

Nonetheless, the need to defend himself prompts a succinct yet profound summary of the theological basis for Christian proclamation. Here the structure of the passage is all-important, for it demonstrates the progression of Paul's thought. A literal rendering of 2 Corinthians 2:17 provides some sense of the structure and parallel vocabulary of the original:

For we are not,

---

of sinners who have neither the ability nor the will for it but whom God has commanded to do it."

25. So Dio Chrysostom, *Discourses* 8.9, 31.37; and especially Lucian of Samosata (ca. AD 120–80), *Hermotimus* 59, in which "philosophers are likened to merchants (kapēloi) who adulterate (dolōsantes) their product for sordid gain" (Savage, *Power Through Weakness: Paul's Understanding of the Christian Ministry in 2 Corinthians* [SNTSMS 86; Cambridge: Cambridge University Press, 1996], 157n63, cf. n61). The same form that Paul uses (kapēleuontes) appears already with this sense in Plato, *Protagoras* 313d. Cf. the extensive discussion in Thrall, 1:212–15.

1. *as* so many, peddlers of the Word of God,
2. but *as*
   a. from sincerity,
3. but *as*
   a. from God
   b. in the presence of God
   c. in Christ
   we speak.[26]

Four prepositional clauses modify the concluding verb, together defining the act of Christian proclamation. The first of these focuses on the preacher's reputation in relation to a human audience, while the next three focus on God. The distinction between the two sets is signaled by the unexpected repetition of the transitional clause, "but as [*all' hōs*]." Each element is sufficiently rich and important as to warrant treatment on its own terms.

"Out of Sincerity": Forthrightness and Transparency

The apostle's first claim is that his proclamation is motivated by, and thus proceeds from, "sincerity," *eilikrineia*. The basic sense of this word is that of purity or "unmixedness"; Paul uses the corresponding noun with this exact sense in a previous letter, where the Passover tradition of cleansing one's house of leaven serves as a metaphor for moral purity:

> Therefore, let us celebrate the festival, not with the old yeast, the yeast of malice and evil, but with the unleavened bread of *sincerity* and truth.
>
> 1 Corinthians 5:8

26. The parallels are somewhat clearer in Greek:

(Negatively) *ou gar esmen*
1. *hōs hoi polloi kapēleuontes ton logon tou theou,*
2. (Positively) *all' hōs*
   a. *ex eilikrineias,*
3. *all' hōs*
   a. *ek theou*
   b. *katenanti theou*
   c. *en Christō*
laloumen.

Likewise in the first chapter of 2 Corinthians, as we saw earlier, Paul boasts (paradoxically) of the high moral principles that govern his own ministry:

> This is our boast, the testimony of our conscience: we have behaved in the world with frankness (or "uprightness," *haplotēs*)[27] and godly sincerity (literally, "the sincerity [*eilikrineia*] of God"), not by earthly wisdom but by the grace of God . . .
>
> 2 Corinthians 1:12

Paul had spelled out the significance of this principle more fully in an earlier defense of his apostolic ministry to the church at Thessalonika:

> For our appeal does not spring from deceit or impure motives or trickery, but just as we have been approved by God to be entrusted with the message of the gospel, even so we speak, not to please mortals, but to please God who tests our hearts. As you know and as God is our witness, we never came with words of flattery or with a pretext for greed; nor did we seek praise from mortals, whether from you or from others . . .
>
> 1 Thessalonians 2:3–6[28]

Paul's argument in 2 Corinthians 1:12 is the first of several instances in which the apostle appeals for his readers to verify from their own experience that his conduct has been blameless both before them and in the sight of God. Much as he is concerned to reassert his apostolic authority and regain their allegiance, however, Paul understands that he is primarily responsible to God. Thus it is fear of God, rather than fear of causing offense, that keeps him from manipulating his hearers or enticing from them any personal affirmation or material gain.

In one sense, his relative unconcern for the sensibilities and opinions of his hearers makes Paul a hard act to follow, notwithstanding the fact

27. Although an important textual variant reads *hagiotēs*, "holiness," the context favors reading *haplotēs*, "uprightness." See *TCGNT in loc.*

28. Literally: "For our appeal is neither *from* error nor *from* impurity nor *in* [by] deception, but *as* approved by God . . . *thus* we speak, not *as* pleasing people . . ." (*ouk ek planēs . . . oude en dolō, alla kathōs . . . houtōs laloumen, ouk hōs . . .*). On this passage see Best, *Thessalonians*, 93–98; Gorman, *Cruciformity*, 192–95; John William Beaudean, Jr., *Paul's Theology of Preaching* (NABPR Dissertation Series 6; Macon: Mercer University Press, 1988), 46–50.

that few of us face anything like the difficulties Paul has experienced. Thus his claim not to have modified or soft-pedaled his message, either to gain the respect of his hearers or to avoid persecution, appears all the more remarkable. As he insists later on in 2 Corinthians, to some extent merely summarizing the content of 1:12 and 2:17,

> Rather, we have renounced secret and shameful ways; we do not use deception, nor do we distort the word of God. On the contrary, by setting forth the truth plainly we commend ourselves to everyone's conscience in the sight of God.
>
> 2 Corinthians 4:2 TNIV

More than a simple claim of being plainspoken and forthright (although that sense is of course included), Paul's words assume their fullest sense in light of the persistent threat of persecution shared by writer and audience alike, as well as Paul's own experience of unrelenting hardship and affliction. Despite the temptation to minimize the negative or unpopular aspects of the gospel, not the least for reasons of self-preservation, Paul refuses to do so, ultimately valuing God's approval far above any contemporary social estimation of his stature or worth.

The dichotomy that Paul here establishes implies a rather jaundiced view of human nature, for it suggests that the preacher is caught between serving altogether ignoble human concerns, on the one hand, or those of God, on the other. The temptation, it would appear, is either to give the audience what it is predisposed to hear or to tailor one's message so as to serve one's own needs, whether to avoid rejection or to directly advance one's social and material interests. Yet surely it is possible for us to serve both our own interests and those of our hearers in a more positive fashion, as Paul elsewhere claims to do. Nor need the alternatives always be quite as stark as those that Paul proposes. Nonetheless, the principle at stake is that, for Paul, sincerity in proclamation—fidelity to the gospel itself—is a quality exercised first in relation to God, and only then in regard to one's audience.

My own observations of contemporary preachers and preaching suggest that while relatively few feel threatened by persecution or outright rejection, the need and desire for ministerial success nonetheless exercises a powerful effect on sermons and their delivery. The perceived threat may take one of at least three basic forms. First, there is the fear that too negative or demanding a message (especially in the form of ethical censure or moral direction) will offend hearers and thus reduce financial support, or else it may offend the board, council, or other influential members of one's congregation. This threat is felt particularly keenly by those serving under a congregational system of governance, according to which preachers can be summarily dismissed at the pleasure of the church board. Only those who preach under such conditions can appreciate how difficult it can be to choose between one's salary (and the immediate well-being of one's family) and a small sacrifice of content or emphasis out of concern for congregational sensibilities.

In a related vein, second, preachers fear alienating congregations theologically by expressing views at variance with their hearers' presuppositions and prior convictions. Almost proverbial, for instance, is the nervousness displayed in some mainline denominations (my own included) at too frequent, passionate, or personal a mention of the name of Jesus. Conversely, the challenge to forthrightness in more theologically conservative or pietistic congregations is, third, the tendency to paint the Christian life (the preacher's own life in particular) in brighter colors than the facts support. Small blessings are vaunted as major miracles, doubt and temptation are largely downplayed, and the Christian life is depicted as an unending string of refreshing victories. I vividly recall watching a well-known evangelist publicly challenge and "correct" the testimony of a recent convert who said that she had found the life of Christian discipleship to be difficult. Such situations altogether capture the sense of the verb *kapēleuein*, which implies the tailoring of one's message, and in particular soft-pedaling the difficult parts, for the sake of popular appeal, personal gain, or simple self-preservation.

Paul, on the other hand, makes no secret of his many trials, although (as we have also seen) he consistently seeks to counterbalance affliction with consolation:

> We are afflicted in every way, but *not* crushed; perplexed, but *not* driven to despair; persecuted, but *not* forsaken; struck down, but *not* destroyed; always carrying in the body the death of Jesus, so that the life of Jesus may also be made visible in our bodies.
>
> 2 Corinthians 4:8–10

Godly honesty—"sincerity"—demands that he report the whole of his experience. What has been implicit now comes to fuller expression, as

Paul more clearly indicates that what motivates such forthrightness is not primarily concern for the opinions of his hearers, but a sense of obligation before God.

"From God": Divine Initiative

Christian proclamation is conducted not only *ex eilikrineias*, "out of sincerity," but also—using the same preposition in a different sense—*ek theou*, "from God," in 2 Corinthians 2:17. Here as elsewhere in Paul's letters, the phrase *ek theou* expresses a specific contrast to solely human origins.[29] This simple prepositional phrase articulates a profound, all-encompassing theological orientation and outlook. It asserts that preaching, like ministry as a whole, is in essence *theologically* passive, however much mental or physical exertion it may require of its practitioners. It operates on the same principle as the grain in Jesus's parable of the seed that grows secretly (Mark 4:26–29). For all that peasant farming entails in back-breaking labor and unremitting vigilance, the ability to bear fruit lies already within the seed. The earth produces of itself, and therefore, to borrow Paul's agricultural metaphor, "neither the one who plants nor the one who waters is anything, but only God who gives the growth" (1 Cor. 3:7). Similarly, preaching is a matter neither of human initiative nor of human accomplishment, but simply a response to God, in at least two regards. First, and fundamentally, Christian proclamation originates in the broadest sense with the saving initiative of God throughout history, above all as focused in the ministry of Jesus the Messiah: "while we still were sinners," Paul insists, "Christ died for us" (Rom. 5:8). Indeed, creation and redemption alike are expressions of divine initiative in its most absolute form (as Paul affirms in 1 Cor. 11:12: "All things come from God").

Second, and more immediately, Paul claims that both his ministry in general and the specific endeavors that he now undertakes are divinely

---

29. Cf. Rom. 2:29b: "Such a person receives praise *not* from others but *from God*"; 1 Cor. 2:12a: "Now we have received *not* the spirit of the world, but the Spirit that is *from God* . . ."; 2 Cor. 3:5: "*Not* that we are competent . . . to claim anything as coming from us; our competence is *from God*"; 2 Cor. 5:1b: "We have a building *from God*, a house *not* made with hands"; Phil. 3:9: "*Not* having a righteousness of my own . . . but . . . the righteousness *from God* based on faith," etc.

initiated or directed. He has already appealed to the divine origin of his calling in an earlier episode of self-explanation and self-defense:

> An obligation is laid on me, and woe to me if I do not proclaim the gospel! For if I do this of my own will, I have a reward; but if not of my own will, I am entrusted with a commission.
>
> 1 Corinthians 9:16–17

The same holds true for all gifts and ministries (1 Cor. 2:12; 7:7). And this is Paul's answer in the present instance to those who accuse him of being unreliable and inconsistent: he explains that he has simply taken advantage of a God-given opportunity. "When I came to Troas to proclaim the good news of Christ, a door was opened for me in [*or*: by] the Lord [*en kyriō*]" (2 Cor. 2:12; cf. Acts 16:6–10).

Although in 2 Corinthians 2:17 the phrase *ek theou* by itself is somewhat cryptic, two other passages in 2 Corinthians spell out its implications more fully. The first of these appears almost immediately following, as Paul hastens to explain his intent:

> Such is the confidence that we have through Christ toward God. Not that we are competent [*or*: adequate, sufficient] of ourselves to claim anything as coming from us; our competence [*or*: adequacy, sufficiency] is *from God*, who has made us competent [adequate, sufficient] to be ministers of a new covenant, not in a written code but in the Spirit.
>
> 2 Corinthians 3:4–6a RSV

As the language indicates, this is a direct response to his earlier rhetorical question, "Who is sufficient for these things?" (2 Cor. 2:16b). He is simultaneously inadequate and adequate: inadequate because of the overwhelming theological and pastoral responsibilities that such ministry entails, and adequate because he is merely responding to divine initiative and a specific divine commissioning conveyed by the Spirit of God.

An even fuller explanation of the entire range of divine initiative, focusing on the pivotal role of Christ, comes two chapters later as Paul sums up the purpose of apostolic ministry:

> So if anyone is in Christ, there is a new creation. . . . All this is *from God*, who reconciled us to himself through Christ, and has given us the ministry

of reconciliation; that is, in Christ God was reconciling the world to himself
. . . and entrusting the message of reconciliation to us.

2 Corinthians 5:17–19

In this passage, the saving work of Christ recapitulates the original gift of creation, and the ministry of proclamation in turn directly mirrors God's reconciliation of the cosmos "to himself." The link between creation, redemption, and proclamation is sustained by the unifying claim that "all this is from God": all three in sequence proceed from and reflect the same saving grace.

This would suggest that the essential characteristic of Christian preaching is its reflection of christological purpose, and that the essential qualification for such preaching lies not primarily in personal experience, vocational inclination, training, or even apostolic commissioning per se, but rather in the preacher's willingness to yield to and be shaped by the will of God. Experience, aptitude, and commissioning remain highly relevant, as does the acquisition of appropriate professional competencies. But all these are secondary to, flow from, and are shaped by the saving divine purpose expressed in Christ. This is, after all, a core feature of discipleship as a whole, according to the prayer that Jesus taught: "Father in heaven . . . *Your* kingdom come. *Your* will be done . . ." (Matt. 6:9–10). What distinguishes Christian proclamation is its intent to go beyond simply receiving and being subject to God's saving will, but becoming so fully conformed to that will as to be made part of its execution on behalf of others. It is in this sense that Paul can speak of being obligated by or bound to the will of another, and of having been entrusted with a commission.

Admittedly, Paul returns to the theme of boasting with sufficient frequency that we may suspect him of having wrestled with the temptation of pride, even though the primary targets of his rhetoric are the self-vaunting and self-satisfaction of others.[30] But however imperfect an example of the principle he may himself provide, Paul is unequivocal that the combination of human inadequacy and divine sufficiency exclude pride in or boasting of anything more than what the grace of Christ has accomplished (1 Cor.

---

30. Of the 56 instances of the word group *kauchasthai / enkauchasthai / kauchēsis / kauchēma* in Paul's letters, 39 (almost 70%) occur in the Corinthian correspondence. On boasting within this congregation, see in particular 1 Cor. 1:26–31; 3:21; 4:6–7; 5:6; 2 Cor. 10:12–18 (and further, Savage, *Power Through Weakness*, 54–64).

1:26–31; 2 Cor. 10:12–18). Accordingly, the simple clause *ek theou*, "from God," governs not just the content of and justification for Christian preaching, but also the manner of its delivery and the attitude of its practitioners. If, indeed, "all things come from God" (2 Cor. 11:12), then Christian preaching—Christian preachers—can claim little credit for their own success. Paul sums up this operational principle with a paraphrase from Jeremiah 9:24: "Let the one who boasts, boast in the Lord" (2 Cor. 10:17). By happy coincidence, the postmodern aversion to the cult of personality finds ready support (if not a perfect example) in the apostle Paul.

"Before God": In the Divine Presence

The third prepositional clause, *katenanti theou*, is undoubtedly the most complex, for it involves issues that have formed a storm center for Pauline scholarship throughout much of the past century. The assertion appears simple enough: that Paul and those like him proclaim the Christian message "before" or "in the presence of" God. This is likewise Paul's later explanation—echoing the present passage verbatim—for his self-defense before the Corinthian church: "Have you been thinking all along that we have been defending ourselves *before you*? We are speaking in Christ *before God* [*katenanti theou en Christō laloumen*]" (2 Cor. 12:19).[31] Perhaps, in Paul's mind, the present situation is a good illustration of the general principle, even though self-defense is hardly the equivalent of apostolic proclamation. Still, the same issues are at stake, for by questioning specific aspects of his conduct, Paul's detractors challenge the integrity of his ministry as a whole. Here it is helpful to recall once more Paul's insistence, speaking for himself and his apostolic companions, that "by the open statement of the truth we commend ourselves to the conscience of everyone in the sight of God [*enōpion tou theou*]" (2 Cor. 4:2). This implies not only that he and his fellow preachers conduct their ministry in the sight of an all-seeing God (which is what keeps them honest), but also that their hearers are in the same divine presence, which should keep them no less honest and circumspect. Paul elsewhere offers the same justification for his conduct both in regard to the collection of alms for the Jerusalem saints ("We intend to do what is right not only in the Lord's

---

31. Cf. Hafemann, *Suffering and the Spirit*, 170–71.

sight [enōpion kyriou] but also in the sight of others," 2 Cor. 8:21), and in response to his opponents in Galatia ("In what I am writing to you, before God [enōpion tou theou], I do not lie!" Gal. 1:20).

In theological terms, the cryptic wording of 2 Corinthians 2:17 (and 12:19) expresses a realized eschatology. That is to say, preaching is a human activity carried out not only at the behest of God (ek theou), but also—even here and now, prior to death and final judgment—in the full presence of God (katenanti theou). While he is profoundly conscious of his responsibilities toward his congregants and of the need to convince them of his integrity, Paul understands himself to be primarily accountable for his conduct to the God in whose presence he speaks and they, with him, listen. Accordingly, while pastoral sensitivity is nonnegotiable for any and all preachers, it nonetheless takes second place to accountability before God. Nor should this imply a sense of burden or onerous obligation on the preacher, for that would be to forget the principle of grace and divine initiative that gives rise to proclamation in the first place. If one preaches "in the presence of God," then it is well to remember that this is above all an *enabling* presence. God, in other words, makes preaching possible by the gift of Christ who is the content of proclamation, as well as by drawing the preacher constantly into the divine presence as a reminder both of the origin and of the ultimate focus of the message of salvation. As preachers know themselves (as a matter of theological conviction) to be in the presence of God, so they testify to this Christ-caused reality, and by the same token alert their hearers to the same eschatological experience, proclaiming Jesus as the one through whom present reconciliation and enduring communion with God are made possible.

This does not deny, as we acknowledged earlier, the fragmentary and imperfect nature of Christian experience. Christian preachers (at least while they remain in the flesh) cannot claim to be in full possession of redemption, for salvation is not fully appropriated prior to physical death. The tangible sense of God's presence experienced, for example, by Brother Lawrence of the Resurrection (ca. 1611–91) is remarkable precisely because it is so infrequently or inconsistently the experience of most.[32] Paul is not altogether shy about reporting mystical experiences (e.g., 2 Cor. 12:1–4). But what he refers to in this passage does not imply a constant, conscious awareness of dialogue with God, for being "in the presence of

32. Brother Lawrence of the Resurrection, *The Practice of the Presence of God*, tr. John J. Delaney (Garden City, NY: Image, 1977).

God" is a theological conviction before it is a directly experiential one. That is, God's awareness of him takes precedence over his awareness of God. Just as Moses can be said to speak "face to face" with God and yet be forbidden the full sight of that face (Exod. 33:11, 20), and Paul can speak of beholding God's glory yet preclude the possibility of seeing God "face to face" in this life (2 Cor. 4:6; 1 Cor. 13:12), so preachers can testify faithfully that they act in God's presence while yet sensibly experiencing it only intermittently, incompletely, and sometimes not at all.

Such convictions regarding the eschatological setting of Christian proclamation account for the manner in which the writer of the Pastoral Epistles (whether Paul or a Paulinist)[33] exhorts Timothy to remain faithful in pastoring and preaching to the flock under his care. Second Timothy 4:1–2 is frequently cited in the church's commissioning of its own preachers and teachers:

> In the presence of God and of Christ Jesus [enōpion tou theou kai Christou Iēsou], who is to judge the living and the dead, and in view of his appearing and his kingdom, I solemnly urge you: proclaim the message; be persistent whether the time is favorable or unfavorable; convince, rebuke, and encourage, with the utmost patience in teaching.

Here the balance between realized and unrealized eschatology is explicitly stated, as the writer invokes the immediate presence of one who is yet to return as judge. Preachers and congregations alike understand that, having been reconciled to God, they now live in God's very presence, and must govern their actions accordingly. In particular, to speak "in the presence of God" is to acknowledge that the preacher is *not* God, but merely one who is in conversation with God, one whose human words are conditioned and relativized by their divine as well as their human audiences.

"In Christ": Christian Identity

In light of the parallels between creation, redemption, and proclamation, as well as the premise that preachers and hearers alike are drawn

---

33. For a recent survey of this question, affirming Pauline authorship, see Luke Timothy Johnson, *The First and Second Letters to Timothy: A New Translation with Introduction and Commentary* (AB 35A; New York: Doubleday, 2001), 55–99.

redemptively into the presence of God, it becomes clear that the ministry of preaching is not in principle different from the experience of salvation itself. If anything, proclamation is an extension and intensification of God's saving purpose, in which the same redemption or religious transformation that the speaker (presumably) has experienced and continues to experience is now extended, through that person, to others as well. Both are reflections of the same divine-human encounter. Again, proclamation is thus distinguished from salvation not in kind but in focus and, perhaps, degree or manner of expression. The gravity of this observation can hardly be overstated. For in addition to the requirement that preachers be attentive to the personal and social needs of the congregation, and that they be skilled in various communicative techniques, there is the more fundamental and nonnegotiable prerequisite that preachers be individuals of mature discipleship and Christian experience. It is, of course, a fallacy to imagine that one can speak with authority only of what one has personally experienced. Yet the all-encompassing, intense, and highly demanding character of Christian pilgrimage demands full personal engagement on the part of those who proclaim its message. Although few might wish to imitate his experiences too closely, the example of Paul underscores this point, with 2 Corinthians having opened on a note of lived theology.

The apostle makes the same point here by designating as the fourth (and perhaps most important) characteristic of Christian preaching its conduct *en Christō*, "in Christ." The brevity of this phrase belies its considerable importance for Pauline theology: its significance in 2 Corinthians 2:17 can be fully appreciated only within the larger context of its use throughout Paul's letters. Paul never speaks of "Christians," "disciples," or "followers of the Way" (as does Luke, for example); only rarely does he refer to "believers." The only such designation that occurs with any frequency (about 30 times) is "the saints." Most of the time, however, Paul adopts a more functional designation of Christian identity: to be a believer is, for Paul, to be "in Christ."[34]

34. Paul's unique and original formula has spawned a range of attempted descriptions—"mythical"; "mystical-locative"; "spatial"; "instrumental"; "sacramental," etc.—and some have despaired altogether of providing a definition (e.g., BDF §219[4]: "The phrase *en christō* [*kyriō*], which is copiously appended by Paul to the most varied concepts, utterly defies definite interpretation"). Analyses of this term and the history of its interpretation are offered by, *inter alia*, Ernest Best, *One Body in Christ: A Study of the Relationship of the Church to Christ in the Epistles*

To begin with, "in Christ" language describes the work, accomplishment, or significance of the Messiah himself. Thus, says Paul, "*in Christ God was reconciling the world to himself, not counting their trespasses against them*" (2 Cor. 5:19); or, in the classic description of salvation provided by Romans 3:23–24, ". . . all have sinned and fall short of the glory of God; they are now justified by his grace as a gift, through the redemption that is *in Christ Jesus*." More often, however, "in Christ" language describes the state or identity of believers in relation to Christ, as recipients of the salvation that he offers. This includes the past, present, and future aspects of God's work in them:

> I give thanks to my God always for you because of the grace of God that has been given you *in Christ Jesus*.
>
> 1 Corinthians 1:4

> But thanks be to God, who *in Christ* always leads us in triumphal procession.
>
> 2 Corinthians 2:14

> As all die in Adam, so all will be made alive *in Christ*.
>
> 1 Corinthians 15:22

This single term encompasses the range of Christ's accomplishment, from its decisive inauguration to its present implications and its ultimate, eschatological fulfillment. Thus Paul can tell his congregants, again with laconic brevity, *ei tis en Christō, kainē ktisis*, literally, "If anyone [is] *in Christ*, [a] new creation!" (2 Cor. 5:17), or, with equivalent economy of expression, "*ex autou de hymeis este en Christō Iesou*" (1 Cor. 1:30), "from Him you are in Christ Jesus." We will come no closer than this to

---

of the Apostle Paul (London: SPCK, 1955), and Michel Bouttier, *En Christ* (Études d'histoire et de philosophie religieuses 54; Paris: Presses universitaires de France, 1962); a brief summary and bibliographic survey is offered by Markus Barth, *Ephesians 1–3: A New Translation with Introduction and Commentary* (AB 34; Garden City, NY: Doubleday, 1974), 69–71, 409–10. Gorman (*Cruciformity: Paul's Narrative Spirituality of the Cross* [Grand Rapids: Eerdmans, 2001], 36–37) makes the important point that, according to this formula, "Spirituality for Paul is not private but communal . . . Being 'in Christ' refers to the experience not merely of the individual but of the community."

the bare essentials of Paul's thought on the matter, for here he expresses the correlation of Christ and Christian in its simplest form: we are "in Christ" or "in the Lord." This is Paul's way of indicating that by virtue both of the Lord's initiative and of their own response, believers have come to share his identity, his life, and his new humanity.[35] The subject and object of this saving identification appear interchangeable: just as believers are "in Christ," so Christ is "in" them (2 Cor. 13:5); just as Paul speaks "in Christ" (2 Cor. 2:17; 12:19), so Christ, says Paul, "is speaking in me" (2 Cor. 13:3). Indeed, Paul understands the whole of his ministry to be "in Christ," so that he can speak of his "ways" (1 Cor. 4:17), his "work" (1 Cor. 9:1), even of his "apostleship" (1 Cor. 9:2) as being "in the Lord." Considering the whole of his work to be guided by the risen Christ, he is able to say of his ministry in Troas that there "a door was opened for me *in the Lord*" (2 Cor. 2:12).

The closing verses of 2 Corinthians chapter 2 incorporate two such expressions. Paul's use of the "in Christ" formula in 2:14, as well as elsewhere in his letters, sheds light on the more cryptic reference in 2:17: "*in Christ* we speak before God with sincerity, as those sent from God" (TNIV). The earlier passage, as we saw previously, focuses on all that God has accomplished through Christ: "But thanks be to God, who *in Christ* always leads us in triumphal procession, and through us spreads in every place the fragrance that comes from knowing him." Yet Paul's careful wording balances divine accomplishment with an emphasis on the recipients of grace ("God ... leads *us* in triumphal procession"), as well as on God's employment of human instruments for proclaiming the gospel ("*through us* [God] spreads in every place the fragrance that comes from knowing him"). In other words, Paul's use here and in 2:17 of the "in Christ" formula suggests that Christ's accomplishment, Christian identity, and Christian ministry are all inextricably linked. Christian proclamation is an expression of Christian salvation, which is in turn an expression of Christ's saving work.

Having been captured by Christ, then, Paul finds himself dragged along in a procession—both an identity and a ministry—not of his making. Rather than being subjected to the coercive might of Rome (although

---

35. The alternative to being "in Christ" is thus to be (in terms of identity) "in Adam" (1 Cor. 15:22) and (functionally) "in your sins" (1 Cor. 15:17), the result of which, Paul avers, is certain death.

that too will transpire before long), he has been seized by the Son of God. But whereas defeat and capture would normally have led to slavery and death, Christ's "triumph" leads to a paradoxically liberating slavery and the gift of "eternal life" (Rom. 6:23). At least three major consequences proceed from this dynamic. First, Paul's "capture" by Christ implies—as we have been saying all along—that the foremost qualification for Christian proclamation is not eloquence, intelligence, or professional aptitude, but rather mature Christian spirituality. Only to the extent that Paul understands himself to be "in Christ," interpreting the circumstances of his life in relation to Christ, does he presume to speak *of* Christ. The same, it need hardly be said, obtains for all who proclaim the Christian message. Skill in exegesis or communication can do no more than build on the more basic requirement that preachers know—and know intimately—the Lord of whom they speak.

Parenthetically, we may compare this to the spirituality of John's gospel, in which Jesus admonishes his disciples, "Apart from me you can do nothing" (John 15:5). In that passage, the metaphor of a vine and its branches conveys the same sense of divine initiative and theologically passive or receptive ministry as Paul's metaphor of having been conquered and made to proclaim the victory of another:

> "I am the true vine. . . . Abide in me as I abide in you. Just as the branch cannot bear fruit by itself unless it abides in the vine, neither can you unless you abide in me."
>
> John 15:1, 4

Second, if Paul's "in Christ" language alerts us to the inner dynamic of Jesus-centered spirituality that forms the core motivation for preaching, it also affirms that the *content* of Christian proclamation is likewise characterized by Messianic confession. For preaching to be conducted "in Christ" implies a concrete theological commitment rooted in the church's historical proclamation of Jesus of Nazareth as the Jewish Messiah. This calls for courage and depth of conviction on the part of today's preachers, who conduct their ministries in a christologically skeptical age and—for some at least—in a christologically skeptical church. To preach "in Christ" is to preach on the basis of nonnegotiable christological commitments, so that preaching both arises from and contributes to christological confession. Preaching that fails to take the messianic identity of Jesus as its fundamental starting point cannot properly be designated "Christian." Like Paul's use of the "in Christ" formula, preaching may include historical reference, the announcement of salvation, moral exhortation, and more, but all of these are validated only by the intentional movement of the sermon from or toward the specific messianic identity of Jesus of Nazareth. Or perhaps we may say that they are validated by the preacher's hope of inspiring the hearers to move in a similar direction.

Third, the political dimensions of Paul's language continue to intrude on our thinking. Whereas in the Western consciousness, "religion" is a matter of private conviction, rather than "public truth,"[36] Paul takes on the powers that be with daring assertions of Christ's supremacy, even—especially—in matters of nationalist ideology and the cultural, political, military, and economic domination that this entails. The importance of this observation for the Western, and especially the North American church—often so oblivious to the claims of empire as to see no conflict between the Christian gospel and national self-interest—can hardly be overestimated. This is not simply a matter of affirming that faith and works go hand-in-hand, or that churches that emphasize personal faith should also be characterized by their commitment to social justice. Rather, the implication of Paul's theologically bold language is that the public proclamation of Jesus as Savior and Lord intentionally subjects all such claims on our allegiance to the claims of Christ, especially where the church's message has been co-opted within one's culture or subverted by the state.[37] To preach "Christ crucified and risen" unexpectedly confirms the adage that "politics and religion don't mix"—but if we are to follow Paul's example, this is because politics and everything else in life must yield to the resurrected Jesus, not the other way around.

36. The works of Lesslie Newbigin provide an excellent introduction to this feature of post-Enlightenment Western thinking; see, e.g., *Foolishness to the Greeks: The Gospel and Western Culture* (Grand Rapids: Eerdmans, 1986), esp. 16–20, 75–79; and *The Gospel in a Pluralist Society*, 27–38.

37. Two recent, provocative examples of such critique are Richard Horsley and James Tracy, ed., *Christmas Unwrapped: Consumerism, Christ, and Culture* (Harrisburg, PA: Trinity Press International, 2001), and Brian J. Walsh and Sylvia C. Keesmaat, *Colossians Remixed: Subverting the Empire* (Downers Grove, IL: InterVarsity, 2004).

In Christ, We Speak

At the end of 2 Corinthians 2:17 comes the verb, although translation into English typically sets it at the head of the sentence. As the climax of Paul's thought, this entire set of theological qualifiers is finally referred to the distinctive act of Christian speech: "Out of sincerity, as from God, in the presence of God, [and] in Christ, *we speak.*" Here and elsewhere Paul intends, by the otherwise ordinary verb *lalein*, not human speech in general but Christian proclamation in particular. This verb occurs sixty times in the extended Pauline corpus (including the Pastorals), of which twenty are in the first person, and (remarkably) all but two of these in First and Second Corinthians. This detail alone points to Paul's use of these letters as an occasion for reflecting on the purpose and significance of his own speech. The fact that the congregation has called his message into question forces him to be more explicit about foundations and manner of apostolic proclamation. Particularly in the Corinthian correspondence, the first-person forms of *lalein* refer (with 1 Cor. 13:1b being the sole exception) to Paul's articulation of divine wisdom (1 Cor. 2:6, 7, 13), his authority in relation to scripture (1 Cor. 9:8; cf. 14:21; Rom. 7:1), speaking "in tongues" (1 Cor. 13:1a; 14:6, 18, 21), moral exhortation (15:34), and explicitly Christian proclamation (2 Cor. 2:17; 4:13; 12:19; cf. 1 Thess. 2:4). Indeed, so self-conscious is Paul about the power of apostolic utterance that he feels it necessary to indicate when he is *not* appealing to the Lord's authority (so 2 Cor. 11:17, 23).

Although preachers may be tempted to claim similar authorization, Paul's own pivotal and historically unrepeatable status must be acknowledged. The Christian canon is now closed, and the simple fact the pastor wishes to speak is insufficient grounds for the congregation to listen! But this is all the more reason—for those whose own preaching depends in large theological measure on that of Paul—to attend to the sources of his authority. Even if the consequences of our preaching are unlikely to be as far-reaching, its essential theological foundations remain unchanged. Christological confession as the anchor of Christian identity and ministry, realized eschatology, unconstrainable divine initiative, and the obligation to forthrightness whatever the cost—these together sum up the theological, confessional, and social dimensions of preaching. Preachers preach, in short, less because of who they are than because of who Christ is, and who they become in Christ.

Far from suggesting self-aggrandizement, personal gain, or social affirmation, Paul's account of the preaching life thus emphasizes the human impossibility of proclaiming the scandal of the cross. The difficulty and cost of such a ministry match the counterintuitive, counter-cultural nature of the message and the bitter-sweet, death-and-life challenge that it conveys. The more fully we understand what Paul had in mind, the more we will join him in pondering, "Who is equal to such a task?" (2 Cor. 2:16 NIV). Yet rather than causing despair or defeat, this question leads Paul, and us with him, to consider the grace and enabling power of God. Somewhat unexpectedly, the apostle now turns to consider the question of Christian confidence.

3

Confidence and Conviction
(3:1–18)

Where can a preacher find confidence to speak? Paul's answer is many-layered and complex. Such confidence, he says, derives from the fact that Christ has revealed the truth about God more fully even than Moses, from the knowledge that the mystery of God's purposes has now been laid open for everyone to see, and—above all—from the conviction that to contemplate Christ brings profound change to the beholder. Just as Jesus mirrors the nature of God, so knowing Jesus causes us to reflect Christ's own nature, and even to share in the glory that God has given him. The preacher's confidence comes from knowing—paradoxically—that he or she is not required to bring about such change, but that Christ can and does (even if the results, as at Corinth, appear uneven or incomplete). For an age obsessed with personal freedom, personal appearance, and (at least for a privileged few) personal "glory," Paul offers a compelling account of the true source of human transformation, and of the preacher's role in declaring that such apparently selfish aims are, in fact, what God desires to accomplish in us through Christ.

> Are we beginning to commend ourselves again? Surely we do not need, as some do, letters of recommendation to you or from you, do we? You yourselves are our letter, written on our hearts, to be known and read by

all; and you show that you are a letter of Christ, prepared [or: delivered] by us, written not with ink but with the Spirit of the living God, not on tablets of stone but on tablets of human hearts. Such is the confidence that we have through Christ toward God. Not that we are competent of ourselves to claim anything as coming from us; our competence is from God, who has made us competent to be ministers of a new covenant, not of letter but of spirit; for the letter kills, but the Spirit gives life.

2 Corinthians 3:1–6

Adequacy and Inadequacy: The Validation of Preaching

To this point, Paul's apologia has reflected on the will and purpose of God in Christ in relation to his own life and calling as an apostle. Here, by contrast, his focus shifts. Paul now proposes that the "sufficiency" or "adequacy" of the preacher, and thus the validation of Christian proclamation, becomes evident in the experience of the hearers themselves.

Paul's rhetorical question—"Are we beginning to commend ourselves again?"—proves unexpectedly revealing. Although Paul had earlier boasted about his sincerity (2 Cor.1:12), this is his first explicit mention of commendation or approval, from which we may deduce that some in the congregation have accused him of self-aggrandizement.[1] Perhaps other apostles have produced letters of recommendation, or have flattered congregants by asking them to provide such letters, leading to the expectation that Paul will do the same (Matera, 76). Indeed, Paul elsewhere vacillates between commending himself "to the conscience of everyone in the sight of God" (2 Cor. 4:2; so also 6:4; 12:11) and refusing to imitate the "super-apostles" in doing so (2 Cor. 5:12; 10:12, 18). Here, however, he insists that the "proof" of his ministry, or rather the proof that the Spirit of God is at work through him, is plainly visible in the lives of his detractors. For his detractors would not be in a position to criticize him—that is, they would not be members of the congregation in the first place—were it not for his founding ministry among them: "You yourselves are our letter," he says, "Written on our hearts, to be known and read by all; and

---

1. This may also explain why the language of recommendation is so prominent in this epistle: the key verb, *synistanein* (transitively, "to recommend or approve"), occurs nine times in 2 Corinthians alone, out of a total sixteen in the entire New Testament.

113

you show that you are a letter of Christ, prepared by us" (3:2–3a). This implies that it is not enough for preachers simply to claim divine approval for their ministries, even though Paul frequently does as much himself, and even though this is an important aspect of his apologia. Ultimately, ministerial validation (as Paul understands it) emerges rather from the dynamic interplay of God, preacher, and congregation, each of whom proves inseparable from the others, and each of whose "voices" must emerge in the proclamation and hearing of the gospel.

To begin with, Paul freely acknowledges that he cannot stand alone: "Not that we are competent," he admits, "to claim *anything* as coming from ourselves; our competence is from God" (2 Cor. 3:5 NRSV, alt.). In a move that seems rhetorically disarming, Paul effectively concedes the accusations of his detractors—that he is inadequate for the task at hand. But the experience of suffering in Asia Minor has taught him that rather than disqualifying him, the acknowledgment of inadequacy and failure (whether in his own mind or in the view of those who disparage him) actually qualifies him for ministry. If human weakness and divine commissioning are the first two qualifications for the "confidence" Paul claims "through Christ toward God" (3:4), the third, no less essential element of ministerial justification is the simple fact that Paul's preaching has proven effective in practice. Notwithstanding the current state of discord between preacher and congregation, Paul can irrefutably claim that his ministry has borne fruit in Corinth.

Paul's reasoning in this passage is deliciously subtle. Unraveling its nuances begins with a simple question: Who is writing whom? For a start, Paul is obviously writing to the Corinthians: they have his letter(s) in hand. Does he need letters from others to Corinth, he asks, or from Corinth recommending him to others (3:1)? The grammar of the original indicates that he does not think either to be necessary. No, he says, they themselves are a letter that commends him to any who may question his credentials, "to be known and read by all" (3:2). How, then, can the congregants question his qualification when they themselves are proof of it?[2]

Yet Paul does not claim to be the actual writer of this human epistle. In the case of the papyrus letter that they have before them, he may be its

---

2. This is similar to Paul's reasoning for the veracity of the resurrection in 1 Cor. 15:12 (so Beaudean, *Paul's Theology of Preaching* [NABPR Dissertation Series 6; Macon: Mercer University Press, 1988], 134–35).

author, but another (the amanuensis) has written down his words, and still another (likely Titus or his unnamed companion, 2 Cor. 8:6; 12:18) has borne the physical document to its intended recipients. Just so, he reasons, Christ is the author of the Corinthians, the Holy Spirit the equivalent of ink and pen, and the writing surface neither papyrus nor stone but tender human hearts. Paul and Timothy (1:1), or perhaps Paul, Silvanus, and Timothy (those who together first preached the gospel in Corinth, 1:19), are simply letter carriers who have discharged their responsibility by delivering the message entrusted to them: "You show that you are a letter of Christ, delivered by us, written not with ink but with the Spirit of the living God" (3:3).[3] In other words, the complex chain of events by which the physical letter they are now reading (or, more accurately, hearing read) has come to them allows the congregants to grasp the complexity of the process that has formed their new community, as well as the contributions of each of its human and divine participants. Far from asserting his own abilities, Paul effectively dodges congregational criticism by insisting that power and "effectiveness" have never been his to claim. True, the congregants are his "workmanship," but only "in the Lord" (1 Cor. 9:1 RSV).

We may pause momentarily to reflect on this point. Paul, apostle to the Gentiles, founder of numerous churches and author of as many as 13 of the 27 books in the New Testament, is reluctant to take credit for his apparent accomplishments. He blurts out that he has worked harder than any of the apostles, but quickly adds a qualification: "though it was not I, but the grace of God that is with me" (1 Cor. 15:10 NRSV). How, then, may we account for the pride of office that seems to accompany at least some prominent preachers in our own day? Perhaps it is reasonable to conclude either that they are taking credit for more than they should (because their effectiveness is a gift of Christ) or, conversely, that they are right to take credit for what is only their own. In contrast to either example, Paul's profound humility is occasioned by the extent of his own past offenses, the depth of his present affliction, and the recognition of whose name and commission he bears. In any event, he says, the simplest proof of preaching is the fruit that it bears.

3. The verb in question, *diakonein*, has a wide range of meanings, as can be seen from the various ways in which it is translated: "you are a letter of Christ, *prepared* by us" (NRSV); "the *result* of our ministry" (NIV); "given to us to *deliver*" (NEB); "*delivered* by us" (RSV).

For those of Jewish background, as well as for readers who are otherwise familiar with Christian exegetical practice, Paul's reasoning may seem even more compelling. In broad terms, he alludes to the stone tablets received by Moses on Sinai (Exod. 24:12; 31:18, etc.), contrasting these with the more pliable human material on which the Spirit is now said to record God's will. But Paul also has in mind key biblical prophecies that point to the renewal of Torah and covenant:

> The days are surely coming, says the LORD, when I will make a new covenant with the house of Israel and the house of Judah. . . . I will put my law within them, and I will write it *on their hearts*; and I will be their God, and they shall be my people.
>
> Jeremiah 31:31, 33b

> I will give them one heart, and put a new spirit within them; I will remove the heart of stone from their flesh and give them a heart of flesh, so that they may follow my statutes and keep my ordinances and obey them . . .
> A new heart I will give you, and a new spirit I will put within you; and I will remove from your body the heart of stone and give you a heart of flesh.
>
> Ezekiel 11:19–20a; 36:26[4]

These ancient promises are even now being fulfilled among both Jews and Gentiles in ancient Corinth, just as Paul has declared in the course of his preaching. That Corinthian *Gentiles* should now have come to share in the blessings of Israel provides a compelling affirmation of Paul's ministry in their midst.

An essential feature of Paul's apologetic *and homiletic* strategy is thus to demonstrate ways in which his hearers themselves constitute the fulfillment of God's purpose. His preaching is inextricably linked to and its efficacy validated in the religious experiences of his audience. This being so, it is evident that preachers must attend to evidence of God at work in their congregants even while they listen for God's voice from the more traditional biblical and theological sources. Only such pastoral and theological attentiveness to the writing of the Spirit on human hearts will allow the preacher to declare to the congregation, as did Paul, "You yourselves are our letter . . . to be known and read by all; . . . you

---

4. Cf. Furnish, 183; Thrall 1:226–27.

are a letter of Christ . . . written not with ink but with the Spirit of the living God."

But in what, precisely, consists the ministerial validation Paul claims? His reference is not to conversion alone, as if the simple presence of a Christian community in Corinth proves that Paul's preaching really "works." This is doubtless implied. But the reference is more specific, to a divine purpose "written . . . on tablets *of human hearts*."[5] In Paul's thought, the "heart" is not only the central organ of the body; it is also the focus of the inner life, the seat of emotions, thought, reflection, and will.[6] As the locale in which the Spirit works (2 Cor. 1:22) and the place where God's saving illumination shines (2 Cor. 4:6), it represents the inner means by which believers both understand the gospel and determine to follow it. What Paul appeals to, in other words, is more than Christian identity per se, but the fact that the Corinthian believers feel themselves so proudly able to live the life of faith, even to the point of criticizing one of those who first announced it to them. As Hafemann observes, "Paul is not merely pointing to the fact that the eschatological promise to Ezekiel is now being fulfilled. He is also asserting that it is being fulfilled through his *own* ministry, since Paul is the one through whom the Spirit came to the Corinthians."[7]

On the other hand, the allusion to a new covenant further qualifies the task of the preacher. If, in fact, it is the Spirit of God who enables trust and moral transformation within one's hearers, then, again, these are not results for which the preacher can take credit. Nor, by the same token, are they results that a preacher should feel constrained to produce. To the extent that it is undergirded by the inner enablement of which Jeremiah and Ezekiel spoke, preaching is first an act of trust directed toward God

---

5. In 2 Cor. 3:2, the manuscript evidence is divided between "written on *your* hearts" (referring to the congregants) and "written on *our* hearts" (a reference to Paul and his companions). Although the latter reading is better attested, 3:3 indicates that the "hearts" of the hearers are also in view: "*You* are a letter of Christ . . . written . . . on tablets of human hearts." Cf. *TCGNT, in loc.*

6. J. Behm, "*kardia*, etc.," *TDNT* 3:611–13; cf. the helpful summary of Joseph A. Fitzmyer, *Romans: A New Translation with Introduction and Commentary* (AB 33; New York: Doubleday, 1993), 127–28.

7. Hafemann, *Suffering and the Spirit: An Exegetical Study of II Cor. 2:14–3:3 within the Context of the Corinthian Correspondence*, (WUNT 2.19; Tübingen: J.C.B. Mohr, 1986), 215 (emphasis original), although his assessment of Paul as the eschatological "Spirit-giver" (217) is perhaps overstated.

before it can be an act of persuasion directed to its human audience. Here too it is evident that the ministry of preaching operates by the same principles as, and is an extension of, the dynamic of faith that undergirds cruciform discipleship in general.

Yet while it affirms their Christian identity, Paul's response does not constitute a blanket validation of his opponents' point of view. Paul concedes his human weakness and insufficiency, but only so as to emphasize the sufficiency of his divine commissioning. Likewise he affirms the work of the Holy Spirit in the lives of his hearers, if only to imply that he cannot be entirely ineffectual—since the congregation represents the fruit of his labors! But this affirmation is general rather than individual: endorsing the Christian identity and motivation of the congregation as a whole still leaves him free to refute criticism offered by particular members. As applied to subsequent contexts and congregations, this line of reasoning implies that preachers under fire are not constrained to silence by the Christian sincerity of their detractors: Paul seems to have no difficulty in seeing his detractors as simultaneously "Spirit-filled" and utterly mistaken in their convictions. Of course, he has an advantage that may not be available to other beleaguered preachers: most of those to whom he writes have been converted under his ministry. The pastor who inherits a settled congregation, whose members were either converted under the ministry of another or who are Christian by nurture or culture, cannot make the same claim. Nonetheless, the implications of Paul's argument are far-reaching, namely that the preaching of the Christian gospel is bound to bear fruit, and that the "validation" of such a ministry must ultimately be visible in the collective life of its recipients. Preacher and congregation, in short, are theologically interdependent with regard to one another, and in the process jointly dependent on God.

"Resurrection" as a Heuristic Category for Homiletical "Success"

This broad premise entails several more specific implications, each of which seems relevant beyond the situation for which Paul originally articulated them. The first is that "success" in the pulpit (as with ministerial success generally) is neither humanly quantifiable nor entirely subject to human control. Preachers know this only too well from personal experience: the sermon over which one has labored long and honed to verbal perfection proves to be an inexplicably awkward flop, whereas the ten-minute "homilette" thrown together at the last minute in anxiety and haste proves to be both moving and memorable. Yet when the preacher attempts to do the same thing the following week, entering the pulpit with a minimum of preparation and maximal hope of divine intervention, the only measurable result is embarrassment all around. This is what makes preaching so infuriating: not that one can never "get it right," but that the process of "getting it right" often seems arbitrary. To say this is not to obviate the importance of good exegesis, culturally relevant illustrations, logical structure, and persuasive rhetoric. Paul himself employs these to the extent of his abilities. But he is wise enough to know that the effectiveness of his preaching in bringing about conviction, conversion, or spiritual consolation is not dependent on these factors alone. It is not that Paul eschews effective communication skills, but that he knows them not to be the final measure of his ministry:

> When I came to you, brothers and sisters, I did not come proclaiming the mystery of God to you in lofty words or wisdom. For I decided to know nothing among you except Jesus Christ, and him crucified. . . . My speech and my proclamation were not with plausible words of wisdom, but with a demonstration of the Spirit and of power, so that your faith might rest not on human wisdom but on the power of God.
>
> 1 Corinthians 2:1–2, 4–5

Although from an earlier letter, this statement too represents an extension of the general principle whereby the apostle understands his life and ministry to reflect the paradigm of Jesus's death and resurrection, relying for affirmation or effectiveness on "God who raises the dead" (2 Cor. 1:9) rather than on human factors alone. We have already explored the way in which preaching about a crucified and risen Messiah would have seemed nonsensical to Jew and Gentile alike. Paul's argument, therefore, is simply that the *method* of Christian proclamation depends as much on the principle of divine intervention as does its content.

Because Christian proclamation appeals both conceptually and pragmatically to what Paul calls "the power of God," "success" in preaching is, ultimately, neither arbitrary nor capricious (however much it might appear so in particular instances). Accordingly, aspiring preachers might do well to return to traditional disciplines of prayer, contemplation, and spiritual devotion that (ironically) tend to get neglected as we hurry through the latest book on effective communication or struggle to master the newest homiletic technique.[8] Paul's argument does not, of course, imply that spiritual discipline will of itself bring about the desired result; rather, such practices are exercises in spiritual humility and dependence on something greater and more powerful than homiletical skill alone. In Paul's view, then, the process of preparing and delivering sermons is, at its best, an exercise of the same spiritual principles that one enjoins upon one's listeners and that constitute the essence of the Christian message: that God graciously acts to reverse human weakness, inability, and loss, restoring and remaking those who depend on God to act in their circumstances as in the case of Jesus. Preaching is, in any event, an exercise in spirituality, but Paul enjoins us to make it an act of cruciform spirituality in particular.

The Imperfection of Preaching

The second implication of Paul's position is that the effects of even the best preaching are neither uniform nor perfect. So much is this so that Paul himself complains of "daily pressure because of . . . anxiety for all the churches" that he has founded (2 Cor. 11:28; cf. Acts 20:31). His anxiety arises at least in part from a lively awareness of their potential for error. Whatever results Paul can observe among his converts in terms of spiritual growth and transformation are visible only in the aggregate: any number of counterexamples are obvious on an individual level, in Corinth and elsewhere (cf. Gal. 3:1–5; Phil. 4:2, etc.). Thus the principle of active dependence on the life-giving power of God extends well beyond the preaching moment, and into the continuing life of the church. Jesus offered a radical form of this premise in the parable of the weeds among the wheat (Matt. 13:24–30, 37–42), insisting that sin, evil, and evildoers must remain inextricably entangled with the life of God's people prior to the end of time! Paul's own analysis is less drastic: although he flatly condemns those whose preaching reveals base motives (2 Cor. 10:12; 11:12–15) and suggests that factional infighting serves to distinguish

8. The work of Richard Foster (especially *Streams of Living Water: The Great Traditions of the Christian Faith* [New York: HarperSanFrancisco, 1998]) and his Renovaré initiative (www.renovare.org) offer comprehensive practical assistance in this regard.

those who are "genuine" or "approved" from those who are not (1 Cor. 11:19), not even in the most extreme case (the immoral man of 1 Cor. 5:1–5) does he call into question the basic Christian allegiance of detractors among his converts at Corinth.[9] That judgment, he suggests, is not his to make, but one that only the Corinthians can arrive at (1 Cor. 6:1–6; 2 Cor. 13:5). Even then, he suggests, lack of Christian allegiance would indicate failure on his part, not theirs (2 Cor. 13:5–7).

In sum, his preaching is effective because God makes it effectual, although failure on his part remains a real possibility. Even where his ministry indeed bears fruit, parts of the ripening crop (while genuine) may nonetheless prove to be blemished or immature: the evidence of Paul's own letters indicates that some sections of "God's field" (1 Cor. 3:9) require constant vigilance, ongoing correction, and taxing pastoral care. Were his ministry uniformly successful, Paul might be tempted to take the credit; the fact that it is not points beyond him to the God who alone is the source of transformation.

Whether envisaging success or failure, this line of reasoning raises an important question: if the results of even the most faithful apostolic preaching are at best uneven or liable to misinterpretation, what degree or kind of change can preachers look for as an indication that their own ministries are faithful and effective? Fortunately, Paul is clear, third, on this point also.

The Face of Moses and the Face of Christ: Preaching for Change

In order to understand Paul's explanation of the "results" of faithful preaching, we must first explore his complex analogy from Moses, the Law, and Mount Sinai (2 Cor. 3:7–18). In this regard, Paul begins with the theological assumption that Israel and the church are communities formed around distinct covenants, each of which reveals God's will. From this point, his reasoning proceeds *a fortiori*: if the written terms of the previous covenant, a covenant that condemns those who fail to obey it (Deut. 27:26), was attended with such glory that Moses's face shone and the people could not look on him, how much more so must

9. The "false apostles" whom Paul condemns categorically in 2 Cor. 11:12–15 do not constitute a counterargument to this assertion, since they are evidently not Pauline converts.

a covenant that enables obedience, with the Spirit inscribing life on the hearts of believers, be attended by glory? Indeed, he argues, the superiority of God's new and permanent dispensation surely means that this new glory must be all the greater than what went before, as presaged by the fact that Moses's shining face soon reverted to normal (2 Cor. 3:7–11). According to the biblical text, Moses wore a veil in an effort to calm the holy terror that the sight of him occasioned (Exod. 34:30–35); Paul, by contrast, proposes that the purpose of the veil was to obscure the fading illumination of Moses's face (2 Cor. 3:13).

This leads to a second contrast: whereas, he says, the heart (*kardia*, 3:15) of anyone who adheres to the Mosaic covenant has a veil over it that obscures thought (3:14) and—by implication—volition, turning to Christ removes any such obscurity or misunderstanding. That is, even as the Israelites could only gaze on the veiled glory of Moses's face, so at present they see only the veiled truth of the Mosaic covenant, rather than the full glory of the gospel (Matera, 92–95). But insofar as God's Spirit conveys spiritual understanding and substantially liberates the human will from its state of moral paralysis, so the working of the Spirit now effects spiritual transformation:

> Now the Lord is the Spirit, and where the Spirit of the Lord is, there is freedom. And we, who with unveiled faces all *reflect the Lord's glory*, are being transformed into his likeness with ever-increasing glory, which comes from the Lord, who is the Spirit.
>
> 2 Corinthians 3:17–18 NIV

Although the NIV translation of Paul's Greek seems straightforward enough, some indication of its complexity emerges by comparison with the NRSV, which renders the italicized phrase, "And all of us, with unveiled faces, *seeing the glory of the Lord as though reflected in a mirror*, are being transformed . . ." The key verb, *katoptrizesthai*, can mean either "to gaze on something indirectly, as in a mirrored reflection," or "to reflect back (like a mirror) light from some other source" (cf. L&N 14.52, 24.44). Which of these did Paul intend? Did he mean that believers contemplate and are transfigured by the glory of God reflected in the face of Jesus; or that the proclamation of the Christian gospel reflects God's glory, and its hearers are thereby transformed; or that believers themselves reflect the divine glory conveyed to them by the Spirit? A number of indications favor the first of these interpretations. Christ himself is "the image of God," says Paul a few verses later (2 Cor. 4:4), in whose face God's glory shines (4:6c). Just as God declared, "Let there be light" at the beginning of creation (although Paul paraphrases the statement as "Let light shine out of darkness"), so now, in a new act of creation (cf. 5:17), God has caused light to shine in the "hearts" of believers, bringing to light there a knowledge of the true divine nature revealed by Christ (2 Cor. 4:6ab). Moreover, as Matera (97) observes with regard to the role of the believer, "the notion of transformation seems to require the sense of contemplation, since it is easier to understand how one is transformed by contemplating God's glory than by reflecting it."

The highly condensed argumentation of 2 Corinthians 3:18 becomes somewhat easier to understand once we clarify its grammatical structure, as follows (so Furnish, 238–39):

We all,
   a. with unveiled faces,
   b. beholding as in a mirror the glory of the Lord

Are being transformed
   a. into the same image
   b. from glory to glory
   c. as from the Lord, the Spirit.

From this it will be seen that the subject of the sentence, "we all," is quali-fied by two descriptive clauses, and the process of "being transformed" by three more. Paul's purpose is to describe (although indirectly) the consequences of Christian proclamation, because this is the subject to which he returns in the verse immediately following: "*Therefore*, since it is by God's mercy that we are engaged *in this ministry* . . ." (4:1). Thus whether the preaching of the Christian message shines the glory of Christ onto believers, or believers reflect the divine glory that is announced to them, in the Spirit, by apostolic proclamation, Paul is concerned to show that the ministry of preaching ultimately results in the glorious transfor-mation of its hearers. If the question under consideration is what change or spiritual effect indicates the efficacy of preaching, Paul's answer can be broken down into the following observations, which roughly follow the order of the five dependent clauses in 2 Corinthians 3:18: apostolic preaching conveys knowledge of God, discloses divine glory, presents Christ as God's true "image," discloses God's purpose of conforming humanity to that image, explains this transformation as participation in divine glory, and attributes all such change to the work of the Holy Spirit. We will now deal with each of these issues in turn.

a. Unveiled Faces

Although we have already briefly discussed Paul's rather polemical contrast between the "veiled" understanding of those who look to Moses and the Mosaic covenant, and the "unveiled" regard of Christian believers, this theme emerges elsewhere in slightly different form. Paul understands that the fullness of God's purpose for humanity has now been revealed. As he explained in an earlier letter, "we preach Christ crucified" (1 Cor. 1:23; cf. 2:2), the paradoxical weakness and implausibility of which represents "the mystery [*mystērion*] of God" (2:1),[10] a "secret [*en mystēriō*] and hidden wisdom of God, which God decreed before the ages for our glorification" (2:7 RSV). That is, the declaration of divine purpose is now an "open secret," manifest and revealed to all who can get past the stumbling block of the cross. Although the passage is generally held to be a post-Pauline addition, the doxology that concludes the letter to the Romans speaks of the gospel and of Paul's own "proclamation of Jesus Christ" as "the revelation of the mystery that was kept secret for long ages but is now disclosed, and through the prophetic writings is made known to all the Gentiles, according to the command of the eternal God" (Rom. 16:25–26).[11] This idea comes to its fullest expression in the letters to the Ephesians and Colossians, most succinctly so in Colossians 1:25–28, where the apostle describes his mandate as one of making fully known "the mystery that has been hidden throughout the ages and generations but has now been revealed to his saints." The substance and essence of this open secret is, he says, "Christ in you, the hope of glory."

10. So NRSV, although part of the textual tradition reads *martyrion*, "testimony," a reading adopted by the NIV. See further, *TCGNT, in loc.*

11. On this passage and the question of its origins, see, e.g., C. E. B. Cranfield, *The Epistle to the Romans* (ICC; Edinburgh: T & T Clark, 1975, 1979), 1:5–8, 2:808–12; Fitzmyer, *Romans: A New Translation with Introduction and Commentary* (AB 33; New York: Doubleday, 1993), 753–55.

Notwithstanding the venerable theological tradition that speaks of a *deus absconditus*, or "hidden god," who ultimately lies beyond the categories of human language and experience, Paul's position in 2 Corinthians is that, in Christ, both the nature and purposes of God are laid open precisely to those from whom such knowledge had hitherto been withheld. Jewish Christians in particular would have recognized the irony: whereas to Israel had always belonged "the adoption, the glory, the covenants, the giving of the law, the worship, and the promises" of God (Rom. 9:4)—to the exclusion of Gentiles—now the tables had been turned. As part of God's "mystery," much of Israel rather than the Gentile nations is at least temporarily prevented from receiving divine revelation (so Rom. 11:25). Accordingly, preaching on the Pauline model cannot claim ignorance of God's ways. On the contrary, Pauline proclamation proceeds on the assumption that God's saving purpose—indeed, God's very character—has now been made plain.

The application of such knowledge in particular cases is undoubtedly problematic. Yet especially in classic areas of difficulty—for instance, theodicy and innocent suffering—the Christian gospel and the cruciform spirituality it engenders remain relevant. Paul claims nothing less than that human suffering and tribulation find meaning in light of Jesus's own, even more unjust death. This, he says, is God's ultimate purpose in Christ. Innocent suffering, however random, evil, and meaningless it may otherwise be, will ultimately be reversed after the manner of Jesus's own resurrection, with the end result being "that the creation itself will be set free from its bondage to decay and will obtain the freedom of the glory of the children of God" (Rom. 8:21). Rather than confessing agnosticism or incomprehension, the task of Christian preaching is thus to bring the many agonies, doubts, and uncertainties of human existence into the light of *Jesus's* death and resurrection, in hope and expectation that, ultimately, all of creation will share in a transformation like his. Preaching locates itself, "with unveiled face," *within* the revealed *mystērion* of which Paul writes, rather than standing outside it, as though unable to fathom the "mystery" (in its conventional sense) of God's ways. Faithful apostolic proclamation, then, seeks to bring clarity to the position of the hearer as one included within the divine purpose, to whom God's will and God's ways have already been made clear via the paradox of the cross. This is what Paul has in mind for the Colossian and Laodicean believers, whom he desires to "have all the riches of assured understanding and . . . the knowledge of God's mystery, that is, *Christ himself*, in whom are hidden all the treasures of wisdom and knowledge" (Col. 2:2–3).

Paul's wording is specific on this point: "*And all of us . . .* seeing the glory of the Lord . . . are being transformed" (2 Cor. 3:18). This means that preachers—notwithstanding Paul's own visionary experiences (2 Cor. 12:2–4)—can claim no special knowledge or spiritual insight to which their hearers do not also have access. There is no hierarchy of illumination in Pauline theology, for the *mystērion* of the cross and resurrection is available to all. But this does not obviate the role of proclamation with regard either to believers or to nonbelievers (so Rom. 10:14–17); on the contrary, the task of preaching is to make known to all what God has made available to all.

b. Beholding the Glory of the Lord

Christ transforms believers—and, at least potentially, humanity as a whole—by drawing us into the very presence, and confronting us with the reality, of Israel's God. This is what Paul refers to as "the glory of the Lord," reflected in the face of Christ and beheld in turn by believers. With the phrase *katenanti theou* of 2 Corinthians 2:17 and 12:19, Paul has already indicated that from the perspective of the preacher, apostolic proclamation takes place "before the face" of God. Here he further explains how being in God's transforming presence is a privilege enjoyed by all of Christ's followers.

Comparison with Moses, which is implicit throughout this passage, provides an important clue to Paul's intended meaning.[12] In the Book of Exodus, the "glory [LXX *doxa*] of the Lord" that first appeared in the cloud accompanying the Israelites (Exod. 16:10) descends on Mount Sinai. Moses is taken into the cloud for forty days and nights (Exod. 24:16–18), then following his nation's brief apostasy prays that he might once more see God's glory for himself (33:18–22). God accedes to this request by revealing the fullness of the divine name (34:5–7). When Moses descends a second time from Mount Sinai, the Septuagint specifies that his face has

12. Regarding the relevance of this argument for non-Jewish congregants, says Savage (*Power Through Weakness: Paul's Understanding of the Christian Ministry in 2 Corinthians* [SNTSMS 86; Cambridge: Cambridge University Press, 1996], 106; cf. 107–9), "it is important to note that Moses was not only by far the most widely known Jewish figure in Graeco-Roman antiquity, he was also the most respected."

been "glorified" (*dedoxastai, dedoxasmenē*; Exod. 34:29–30). In the tradition with which Paul is familiar, the presence and sight of God's glory are reflected in Moses's external appearance, however brief or impermanent that change may have been. But if Moses once beheld "the glory of the Lord," Paul insists, how much more so do those to whom God has now granted "the light of the knowledge of the glory of God in the face of Jesus Christ"; if Moses's external countenance was illuminated, how much more so those into whose "hearts" God's light now shines (2 Cor. 4:6).

But what is the practical relevance of God's glory and presence for contemporary Christian proclamation? To begin with, they imply that preaching announces a definitive divine-human reconciliation that opens the way to communion with God. Comparison with Moses implies that unlike the prophet, those who approach God through Jesus now dwell permanently in God's presence (a notion that is also foundational to the Gospel of John). Whereas in his earlier letters Paul had envisaged this primarily as a privilege reserved for the end of human history (1 Thess. 4:17; 2 Cor. 4:14), he subsequently adopts a more "realized" eschatology, perhaps the clearest expression of which is found in Colossians 3:1, 3:

> So if you have been raised with Christ, seek the things that are above, where Christ is, seated at the right hand of God. . . . for you have died, and your life is hidden with Christ in God.

Although, as Colossians 3:4 observes, the dimensions of this new life are not yet fully manifest, the spatial metaphor of things "above" and "below" captures the dual circumstances of the believer. Still firmly located in the physical world with all of its trials and limitations, believers nonetheless have full access to the heavenly realm, toward which their gaze is constantly directed.

More specifically, open contemplation of "the glory of the Lord" (that is, of God rather than Jesus) implies that believers are granted a full awareness of God's nature and character—as first disclosed on Sinai to Moses and now revealed more completely in the person of the divine Son. More significantly, the object of their contemplation is neither passive nor inert, but vital and dynamic: the "glory"—that is, the force and reality—of God is such that it impinges radically on the beholder.[13] This

13. Cf. Fitzmyer (*Romans*, 283): God's glory refers to "the radiant external manifestation of his presence in the Tabernacle or Temple, [the] *kĕbôd YHWH*. . . . In

means that the focus, content, and consequences of apostolic preaching are "theological" in the proper sense of the word, concentrating on the full disclosure of the gracious and saving character of God.

So to summarize the implications of our analysis thus far, apostolic preaching conforms to the revelatory character of the Christian message in at least three ways. First, Paul proclaims the *content* of the gospel as a matter of divine self-disclosure, the revelation to Gentile and Jew of a saving purpose which had previously been hidden from the one and partly obscure to the other. Second, insofar as preaching is carried out "in the presence of God" and announces that Christ has opened the way into that presence, lived experience of God provides the *context* for preaching. Third, God's self-revelation in Christ determines the universal *scope* of preaching. That is, if the limited revelation of the first covenant (to Israel alone) has now been supplanted by the universally accessible revelation of the covenant of Christ, so it must include not only Jew and Gentile (as in Corinth), but also citizen and slave, male and female alike (cf. 1 Cor. 12:13; Rom. 10:12–13; Gal. 3:28, etc.). Apostolic proclamation, because it presents a crucified and transfigured Messiah to the whole world, includes all humanity in its address, thereby subverting the social, ethnic, economic, and political boundaries that would otherwise determine our identity (cf. Eph. 2:13–22). In short, God's revealed "glory" is the cause of preaching, provides its focus, and determines its effects.

c. As in a Mirror

If we have interpreted the verb *katoptrizesthai* correctly (that is, "to reflect as in a mirror"), it conveys the sense that believers do not look upon God directly, but see the "glory" that is characteristic of God mirrored in the face and image of Jesus. Thus while "glory" is properly predicated of God (1 Cor. 10:31; 2 Cor. 4:6, 15, and frequently), it may also, by extension, be referred to Jesus. That Paul has this extended reference in view here is indicated by 2 Corinthians 4:4 ("the god of

---

Hebrew *kābôd* basically denoted the weight of esteem or honor that a king or important person enjoyed (1 Kings 3:13). This concept was extended to Yahweh and to what made him impressive to human beings, the force of his self-manifestation and the radiant splendor of his presence."

this world has blinded the minds of the unbelievers, to keep them from seeing the light of the gospel of *the glory of Christ*, who is the image [*eikōn*] of God") and 2 Corinthians 4:6 ("God . . . has shone in our hearts to give the light of the knowledge of the glory of God *in the face of Jesus Christ*"; cf. 1 Cor. 2:8; Phil. 4:19; 2 Thess. 1:9). Although it places considerable exegetical weight on a single ambiguous verb, the homiletical implications of such an interpretation are twofold. First, conceptually, if Christ is the "mirror" of God's glory, then apostolic preaching is not only theological in the general sense, but unswervingly christological in its claim that Jesus of Nazareth most clearly reflects the reality both of Israel's God and of humanity created in the image of God. This may represent an awkward or unwelcome claim in the atmosphere of theological relativism that pervades much preaching in mainline churches of the West, but it is unavoidable nonetheless. Indeed, a close reading of the two verses just cited indicates that both formulations imply the work of preaching in particular, for Paul speaks of "the light of the *gospel* of the glory of Christ" (2 Cor. 4:4) and "the *knowledge* of the glory of God in the face of Jesus Christ" (2 Cor. 4:6) as essential aspects of apostolic proclamation. Only by christologically explicit preaching, it would seem, are such "light" and "knowledge" conveyed to their intended human audience.

Second, that the Corinthian believers are said to gaze on and/or reflect God's mirror image reveals how closely Paul is in touch with the cultural situation of his audience. For in terms of material culture, "Corinth . . . was long renowned for the unsurpassed brilliance of the bronze and bronze products—including mirrors—that it produced."[14] It is not unlikely that Paul's choice of metaphors has been influenced by this fact. As to the thought world of his audience, Corinthians of Jewish background were already familiar with the idea of humanity having been created in the "image [LXX: *eikōn*] of God" (Gen. 1:26–27), which is basic to both the christology and the theological anthropology of this passage. Likewise for those familiar with Greco-Roman culture, says Furnish,

14. Furnish, 239. Paul's claim in 1 Cor. 13:12 ("in a mirror, dimly") does not contradict the present argument, since that passage intends a different point, contrasting present knowledge with future fulfillment and implying that "where the *imperfection* of a mirrored image is in mind, [it] must be expressly noted" (ibid.; emphasis added).

A widespread idea in the Hellenistic age—for example, among the mystery religions—was that the beholding of a god or goddess could have a transformative effect on the worshiper.[15]

At the same time, Paul's theology has anti-imperial overtones: statues of the (semi-divine) Roman emperor and his family were found "in even the tiniest communities," and Roman subjects intentionally sought to model themselves—their hairstyles and clothing, for example—according to these images.[16] Neither set of ideas is identical or precisely contemporaneous with what Paul seeks to convey, but there is sufficient similarity to suggest that his ideas would have been immediately recognizable even for Gentiles with little knowledge of Jewish concepts. The point is already obvious without the added benefit of a compelling Pauline illustration, but not even the radically christological focus of apostolic preaching eliminates the need for cultural relevance as an essential feature of effective communication.

d. Transformed into the Same Image

Resemblance to or identity with Christ is not necessarily the immediate *goal* of preaching, because it is not something that human activity is inherently capable of accomplishing. Nonetheless, as a work of the Spirit that accompanies preaching, it is the ultimate *consequence* of apostolic proclamation. According to Paul, faithful preaching turns the gaze of the beholder toward Christ, and it is the glory of God reflected by Christ that brings about spiritual "transformation." But of what does such transformation and new identity consist? The infrequency with which the vocabulary of 2 Corinthians 3:18 occurs elsewhere in Paul's writing (specifically, the

15. Furnish (420) cites the *Metamorphoses* of Apuleius (from the mid-second century AD; its fictive narrator, Lucius, is a Corinthian) and instructions from the late-first to third century AD *Corpus Hermeticum,* for a devotee to turn the eyes of his heart toward "the image of God," so as to be drawn upward and transformed "into an immortal body." For an introduction to the *Corpus Hermeticum,* see Brian P. Copenhaver, *Hermetica: The Greek Corpus Hermeticum and the Latin Asclepius in a New English Translation, with Notes and Introduction* (Cambridge: Cambridge University Press, 1992). The texts to which Furnish refers are found on pp. 17 (IV, 11*b*), 31 (X, 6), and 49–50 (XIII, 3).

16. See Paul Zanker, *The Power of Images in the Age of Augustus*, tr. Alan Shapiro (Ann Arbor: University of Michigan Press, 1988), 292–95.

verb *metamorphousthai* and its cognates) makes his thought on this point relatively easy to trace.

Whereas 2 Corinthians 3:18 speaks in general terms of beholders being "transformed" into the image of Christ, and Romans 8:29 refers to believers as "predestined to be conformed [*summorphous*] to the image of [God's] Son," Romans 12:1–2 exhorts its readers more specifically:

> Present your bodies as a living sacrifice, holy and acceptable to God, which is your spiritual worship. Do not be conformed to this world, but *be transformed* [*metamorphousthē*] by the renewing of your minds, so that you may discern what is the will of God—what is good and acceptable and perfect.

That is, their transformation toward conformity with Christ takes place in the "renewal" of their minds—their understanding and conceptual outlook.[17] But it should not escape our notice that in the following verses, Paul immediately spells out the practical implications of this change in outlook.[18] Members of the Christian community are to reject the hierarchies of value that otherwise determine their place in Greco-Roman society, for they "are one body in Christ, and individually members one of another" (Rom. 12:5, RSV); they employ their gifts in love for the common good and "outdo one another in showing [rather than receiving] honor (12:6–10); they forgo vengeance, blessing their persecutors instead (12:14, 19–20), seeking to "live peaceably with all" (12:18) and to "overcome evil with good" (12:21). To be sure, exhortations to moral virtue are widespread in the Hellenistic world,[19] but what stands out here is the fact that these virtues are the outworking of the believers' identification with Christ. Paul's oft-quoted exhortation to the Philippians says, "Your attitude should be the same as that of Christ Jesus, who, being in the form [*morphē*] of God . . . made himself nothing, taking the form [*morphē*] of a slave" (Phil. 2:5–7 NIV mg., alt.). Conversely, it is their

---

17. Cf. Col. 3:10: "[You] have clothed yourselves with the new self, which is being renewed in knowledge [*epignōsis*] according to the image of its creator," with "knowledge" here referring to the divine character manifested by Jesus—"compassion, kindness, humility, meekness, and patience" (Col. 3:12).

18. I am grateful to Sylvia Keesmaat for pointing out the concrete dimensions of Paul's thought in this passage.

19. See John T. Fitzgerald, "Virtue/Vice Lists," *ABD* 6:857–59.

unexpected lack of conformity to Christ that causes Paul to lament over the Galatian believers, "My little children, for whom I am again in the pain of childbirth until Christ is formed [*morphōthē*] in you" (Gal. 4:19). At the risk of over-harmonizing the various texts, it would appear that the "transformation" of which Paul speaks entails (at least for the present) a renewal of understanding that issues in conformity to the moral character of Jesus and proper discernment of the will of God.

Notwithstanding the association in 2 Corinthians 3:18 (and Phil. 3:21) of Christ's image with "glory," these other descriptions of transformation focus on less obviously metaphysical notions of humility and servility. The fullness of shared glory, however, lies yet in the future, when the believers' imitation of Jesus's crucifixion and vindication becomes complete. Thus Philippians 3:10 speaks of being "conformed [*summorphizomenos*]" to Jesus's death by means of suffering as a pre-condition for resurrection, when Jesus "will transform [*metaschēmatisei*] the body of our humiliation that it may be conformed [*summorphon*] to the body of his glory" (Phil. 3:21).

While such passages typically urge moral action, they also consistently—and paradoxically—employ the passive voice in key verbs,[20] so as to imply divine rather than human agency as the primary means of actual change. What, then, is the relationship between "turning to the Lord" (2 Cor. 3:16) and "being transformed" (3:18)? Likewise in Romans 12, how can Paul urge the believers both to "present [their] bodies" (an active command) and to "be transformed" (in the passive voice)? In the second example, the human and divine agency, human and divine responsibility, come together in the idea of "sacrifice," which is Paul's term for the way in which believers present themselves physically to God. For it is in offering precisely the part of themselves that (as with Jesus) is most subject to degradation, suffering, and death that they become subject in turn to the gracious, saving will of God. As Paul discovered anew in Asia Minor, believers imitate the sacrifice of Christ by yielding their own desperate frailty and mortality to "God who raises the dead." They are "transformed into the same image" as they come to

---

20. E.g. "those whom he foreknew he also predestined to *be conformed* to the image of his Son" (Rom. 8:29); "*be transformed* by the renewing of your minds" (Rom. 12:2); "all of us . . . are *being transformed* into the same image" (2 Cor. 3:18); "until Christ *is formed* in you" (Gal. 4:19).

resemble the one who died and was raised by the power of God. Indeed all believers, and not only those who suffer tribulation, eventually imitate Christ in this manner, for, says Paul, their bodies are "sown in dishonor, [but] raised in glory"; they are "sown in weakness, [but] raised in power" (1 Cor. 15:43). Accordingly, the promise in 2 Corinthians 3:18 of transformation into the image of Christ *in glory* should not be interpreted independently of what Paul has already said in 1:8–10 and 2:15–16 concerning his own abasement and conformity to Christ. The one whom the Corinthians behold and by whose reflected glory they are transfigured is none other than the one with whom they, like Paul, are also "co-crucified" (Gal. 2:19).

Although they are in written rather than oral form, these passages may be taken as generally representative of the moral (or "paranetic") and instructional ("catechetical") content of Paul's preaching. Whether in person or by the public reading of his letters, he exhorts his hearers to be conformed to Christ, both to conduct themselves according to the model of Christ and to yield themselves (so Rom. 6:19) to the transformative reality of Christ that is at once within and beyond them. In this manner, apostolic preaching testifies simultaneously to human moral responsibility and to the limitations of that endeavor. Paul exhorts his hearers to be conformed to Christ while confessing their common inability to bring about the fullness of such conformity. Preaching, insofar as it proclaims with Paul that we are *"being changed* into his image," testifies to the sole adequacy of God in Christ to effect the regeneration— indeed, "resurrection"—of the preacher, the preacher's message, and the preacher's audience alike. Nor is preaching the only form that such testimony may take, for there will be many means—from prayer and contemplation to community life and works of charity—whereby believers may "behold the glory of the Lord" and be incrementally changed by it.

While Paul seems to intend "glory" primarily as a visual metaphor for divine reality, indications both ancient and modern suggest the possibility of something closer to physical illumination. Although it may simply be a literary motif (intended to recall Moses on Sinai), Matthew's account of the transfiguration includes the detail that Jesus's face "shone like the sun" (Matt. 17:2; similarly Luke 9:29). Likewise the face of Stephen, the first martyr, is said to have shone like that of an angel (Acts 6:15). The apocryphal second-century work known as the *Acts of Paul* describes the apostle in much the same terms, as "full of grace, for at times he looked like a man, and at times he had the face of an angel."[21]

Anecdotally, I attended a missions conference in December of 1976 at the University of Illinois at Urbana-Champaign. While browsing in the bookstore I was startled to see, walking past me, a diminutive woman whose face seemed literally to emanate light. Later I was even more startled to recognize this same woman on stage, telling the 16,000 conference delegates how in 1964, as a medical missionary to the Congo, she had been raped by soldiers during that country's post-colonial civil war. To our silent and horrified astonishment, Helen Roseveare testified to the vividness of God's presence in the midst of her overwhelming pain and degradation, an experience she described as "being crucified that Christ may live wholly in me."[22] Although no one, least of all Paul, would suppose that such an outcome justifies suffering or makes it any less devastating, the apostle's own trials evidently brought him into close communion with Christ. If the tragic example of Helen Roseveare provides any indication, such transformative spiritual intimacy may occasionally manifest itself in what can only be described as "glory," shining in the face of the sufferer.

We may be grateful that unlike their counterparts elsewhere in the world, few Western believers share the sufferings of Christ to such a degree. For this reason, the idea of being transformed into his image may not seem accessible, relevant, or even particularly attractive. Yet Paul's choice of vocabulary provides some welcome assistance in this regard. As it happens, the noun *morphē* can mean anything from "visual appearance, outward form" to "essential nature or character, consistent with appearance" (L&N 58.2, 15). Likewise the corresponding verb, *metamorphousthai*, can mean either "to change the essential form or nature of

21. Cited by F. F. Bruce, *Commentary on the Book of the Acts: The English Text with Introduction, Exposition, and Notes* (NICNT; Grand Rapids: Eerdmans, 1979), 136n29. Further examples, primarily from traditions of the Eastern church, are cited by Kallistos Ware, "St. Maximos of Kapsokalyvia and Fourteenth-Century Athonite Hesychasm," in Julian Chrysostomides, ed., *Kathegetria. Essays Presented to Joan Hussey for her 80th Birthday* (Camberley, Surrey: Porphyrogenitus, 1988), 422–23.

22. Helen Roseveare's address is published as "The Cost of Declaring His Glory," in David M. Howard, ed., *Declare His Glory Among the Nations* (Downers Grove, IL: InterVarsity, 1977), 203–11. The quotation is from p. 211. It must be stressed once again that the fact of victims finding justification *amid* suffering does not imply the justification *of* suffering. On the contrary, the relevance of Jesus's crucifixion is that it represents God's identification with victims, rather than oppressors.

something" or "to take on a different physical form or appearance" (L&N 13.53, 58.16). Such language does not carry the profound suspicion regarding outward appearances that bedevils our own sense of perception. Even so, Paul's vocabulary raises the question of what kind of change Christ accomplishes in believers, and whether it is truly substantial, or merely "skin-deep."

At least in Western culture, the re-fashioning of personal appearance is an ever-present concern. This is implied not only in the vocabulary of "makeup" (i.e., cosmetics) and the "makeover," but also in the notions of "models" or "modeling," and of "fashion" itself. Each of these terms originates with or incorporates a verb having the sense of "to construct" or "to form."[23] Our desire to create new identities and images for ourselves is thus reflected in the language that we use. Similarly, whereas the entertainment industry in general is dominated by "stars" whose interests and appearance we eagerly emulate, television and film in particular offer a paradigm for multiple identities and the possibly of change. For a postmodern culture in which personal identity is not fixed, but infinitely negotiable,[24] "actors" (or, more provocatively, "idols") represent for us the ability to try on a variety of roles or scripts. We are invited to participate by proxy or by projection (literally and figuratively) in the imaginative role-playing of our favorite actors.[25]

By contrast, Christ offers both glory ("stardom"!) and the profound inversion of personal glory. He offers the possibility of a personal identity that is no longer unstable, but both authentic to human nature and beyond any role that we might otherwise achieve. To be "transformed into his image" is a process neither of self-making nor of merely superficial change, but of submitting to the life-giving creativity of another. Playing on different senses of the word, we may think of this as moving beyond

23. Somewhat more obscurely, it may be instructive to note the etymological link between the words "figure" (that is, bodily shape), "feign," "feint," "fiction," and "figment," all derived from the Latin *fingere*, to fashion or form.

24. The negotiable instability of personal identity (which they designate the "nomadic self") as a feature of postmodernism is discussed by Middleton and Walsh, *Truth is Stranger Than it Used to Be: Biblical Faith in a Postmodern Age* (Downers Grove, IL: InterVarsity, 1995), 46–62, esp. 56: "In answer to the . . . question, Who are you? the postmodern self replies, 'My name is Legion, for we are many.'"

25. The themes of serial identity and identity by proxy are brilliantly explored, for example, in Woody Allen's films *Zelig* (1983) and *The Purple Rose of Cairo* (1985), respectively.

mere "acting" to "becoming" and "being" in the image of Christ. To extend the metaphor of theater yet further, Christian transformation, announced by apostolic preaching, invites hearers to serve as understudies to one who is simultaneously Author and primary Actor in the human drama. We are invited to assume the identity and destiny of Jesus, to imitate his actions and attitudes, and in the process of doing so to share his suffering as well as his all-transforming consolation.

What might this mean in practice? For a society obsessed with personal appearance, body weight, and physical—especially sexual—performance, conformity to the image of Jesus offers the possibility of accepting our human frailty as a necessary condition of creaturely existence; of deriving our sense of worth and identity from something more than adornment, sexual self-expression, or physical attributes alone; perhaps even of free-dom from the pervasive fear and denial of death that lies just below the surface of Western culture. It offers hope to those like my students, male and female alike, hardly any of whom are able to say that they are truly content with their bodies or their physical appearance.

e. From Glory to Glory

However much he may elsewhere describe the goal of the Christian life in terms of covenantal, relational, or ethical qualities (compassion, kindness, humility, etc.), Paul's shorthand for the transformation of human existence is "glory," perhaps because that term most succinctly expresses the numinous and transcendent divine reality that believers share with Christ. Paul seems confident that glory has indeed taken root in at least some of his hearers, for he commends the two unnamed brothers who ac-company Titus as "messengers of the churches, the glory of Christ" (2 Cor. 8:23). According to Matera (199), this description "is best understood as an expression of praise for the service that these men are rendering to the churches. By what they are doing, they render glory to Christ and manifest that glory to others." Yet Paul may also intend something more personal and substantial. In 1 Corinthians 11:7 [NIV], man is said to be "the image and glory of God" and woman the "glory" of man. Although the passage's hierarchy of gender is as much theologically as sociologically problematic, Paul seems to be referring to those who are "in Christ" and have begun to reflect the glory of their Lord by virtue of mystical union with him. This suggests that Titus's fellow envoys are likewise distinguished not only by their function as messengers but also by the transformative work of Christ in their lives. While they undoubtedly bring "glory" to Christ by the faith and faithfulness of their lives, Christ also brings "glory" to them. Even so, Paul understands such glory to be more characteristic of a future state: "This slight momentary affliction is preparing us for an eternal weight of glory beyond all measure" (2 Cor. 4:17). As he explains to the believers in Rome, Christ serves as proof "that the creation itself *will be* set free from its bondage to decay and *will* obtain the freedom of the glory of the children of God" (Rom. 8:21).

This careful balancing of present and future, of current tribulation and glory yet to come, best explains the phrase "from glory to glory" in 2 Corinthians 3:18, or, as the NRSV paraphrases, "[we] are being transformed into the same image *from one degree of glory to another*." Paul's apostolic proclamation of the glory that attends those who gaze on Christ is no more triumphalist than is his earlier description of the counter-imperial Christian "triumph." On the contrary, it acknowledges that change is gradual rather than sudden, and partial rather than complete (cf. 1 Cor. 13:12). Both his own profound suffering and the aggravating contentiousness of the Corinthian saints (or, they would counter, Paul's own flaws and failings) furnish ample proof that sanctification and "glorification" are neither instantaneous nor absolute. Once again, although it is unwise to place too much exegetical weight on a single phrase, the theological modesty of this approach warrants a similar caution on the part of those who proclaim Christ's glory to later congregations. At least in his own preaching, Paul is able to acknowledge both the stark imperfection of current circumstances and the glorious hope that spurs him on, together with the church of Christ, "from one degree of glory to another."

f. As from the Lord, the Spirit

Paul consistently implies that preaching plays a modest, at best subsidiary role in the process of glorification: "For this purpose," he explains to the Thessalonians, "[God] called you through our proclamation of the good news, so that you may obtain the glory of our Lord Jesus Christ" (2 Thess. 2:14). A careful reading of this phrase suggests that proclamation of the Christian message represents a call *to* glory, but not the means *of* glory. As we observed earlier, that hearers gain a share in Christ's glory may be an eventual consequence of preaching, but it is not a direct result, since glorification is effected by the Spirit alone. Although this is not the place to explore Paul's doctrine of the Holy Spirit as the agent and instrument of human transformation, due emphasis on pneumatology places preaching in its proper perspective.

The (perhaps unexpected) corollary of the assertion that only the Spirit can facilitate spiritual change is not that preaching is thereby rendered insignificant, but that preaching is thereby rescued from the possibility of insignificance. Whereas Paul may declare himself to be no more than a commissioned messenger, a mere delivery boy (2 Cor. 3:3), the message he brings is one of divinely authored salvation. However humanly puny it may at times appear, whether due to Paul's own lack of impressive rhetoric or the nervous self-consciousness of the first-time homilist, preaching participates by virtue of the Spirit's action in the *Missio Dei*, the divine announcement of human redemption decisively proclaimed in the person of Jesus. Declaring God's purpose of salvation via the death and resurrection of Jesus cannot be a merely human activity to the extent that its validation rests with the work of the Holy Spirit. Although the preacher's voice cannot be confused with the voice of God, much less replace it, and although only the human voice may be immediately audible, apostolic proclamation depends on the claim that God continues to speak, indeed that this divine "speaking" is what makes human speech about God both possible and effective.

There is a sense, therefore, in which preachers need not be concerned about the "effectiveness" of their preaching, for whatever "effect" lies within their control (that is, the power of rhetoric or the influence of personality on a congregation) falls far short of the ability to bring about salvation or sanctification. Preaching is thus, as much for the preacher as for the audience, an act of faith. It is a gesture of overt dependence on God to accomplish what the faithful themselves cannot. It is, as much for us as for Paul, a participation in Christ's death and resurrection, a coming to the end of one's own sufficiency so as to rely utterly on the sufficiency—or grace—of God.

If the work of preaching is authenticated, given power and substance by the intervention of God's Spirit, then a prime consequence of such preaching is "freedom," for, says Paul, "where the Spirit of the Lord is, there is freedom" (2 Cor. 3:17). In the immediate context, this must mean freedom from spiritual incomprehension regarding the nature of God's requirements (the "veil" of 3:15–16), and freedom also from the condemnation and death that arise out of God's righteous requirement of human obedience (3:6–9). If we may extrapolate further, Paul seems to suggest that proclaiming the Christian gospel, which is the message of Jesus's death and resurrection, brings about an entirely new understanding of God's relationship with humanity, now characterized not by an impossible demand but by a gracious offer that restores full *koinōnia*, fellowship, through the mediation of Jesus (1 Cor. 1:9).

This reading of "freedom" in the present context is in line with its significance elsewhere in the Pauline corpus: the freedom that Christ brings is freedom from bondage to the forces of sin, condemnation, and consequent exclusion from God's kingdom (see esp. Rom. 8:2, "the law of the Spirit of life in Christ Jesus has set you free from the law of sin and of death"; Gal. 5:1, "For freedom Christ has set us free," etc.).[26] Particularly suggestive is Ernst Käsemann's proposal (recalling Lochman's comments, noted earlier) that Paul has in view here the Hellenistic doctrine of *ananke*, the cosmic, divinized principle of inexorable "Necessity" that holds humanity in bondage to death:

> Hellenism already regarded the world and humanity as the arena and the object of the struggle between flesh and spirit, already held existence to be determined by its bondage to one or the other of these two powers. . . . But Paul knows the Lord, who does not reign as Necessity, but, according to 2 Corinthians 3.18 [*sic*], dispenses freedom: the freedom to decide between obedience and disobedience.[27]

Preaching, then, announces the availability of emancipation—in Christ—from slavery to impersonal destiny and death. Granted, Western audiences of the third millennium might not immediately think of their lives as controlled by impersonal cosmic fate, but the fear of death remains very real, many people experience addictions or other personal difficulties that seem beyond their control, and the enduring popularity of horoscopes, fortune-telling, chakras, and the like hints at belief that cosmic forces indeed exercise a certain dominion over human destiny.[28]

26. See further discussion in Thrall, 1:275–76; Barrett, 123–24 (referring to Käsemann); see following note.

27. Ernst Käsemann, *Essays on New Testament Themes*, tr. W. J. Montague (Philadelphia: Fortress, 1982), 119; further explanation of the Hellenistic concept of *ananke* is offered by W. Grundmann, "*anankazō*, etc.," *TDNT* 1:344-45.

28. Although his categories have a decidedly modernist ring, George Hunter (*How to Reach Secular People* [Nashville: Abingdon, 1992], 52–53) acutely observes that

This being said, the proclamation of "freedom" is nonetheless para-doxical. On the one hand, the Christian gospel promises to set its hearers free from their enslavement to "necessity," and to the fear of nothingness and physical death, enabling them to make truly free moral choices (as Paul explains at length in Rom. 7:15–8:17). Yet the route by which such freedom may be achieved travels unavoidably by way of the cross, via assimilation into an alternative death, namely that of Jesus. Inherent in Christian proclamation is thus an acknowledgment that "death" of one sort or another is unavoidable, even if hearers are now free to choose which they prefer! Preaching that is faithful to the gospel must be faithful to both sides of this paradox, proclaiming the distinctly Christian definition of both "death" and "life" in explicit contrast to whatever other definitions are offered by popular culture and belief. Thus Paul can insist—with no small irony—that the reason he preaches the liberating gospel "free of charge" is that obligation or "necessity," *anankē*, has been laid on him (1 Cor. 9:16)!

Because Christian discipleship includes significant social and political dimensions, the agency of the Holy Spirit points toward both inward and outward transformation as the ultimate outcome of apostolic preaching. Preachers have a theological duty to expose injustice and urge high ethical standards on their congregations, and Paul does as much in each of his letters. But moral and social responsibility on the part of the church is the consequence and counterpart, rather than the cause, of inward regeneration. Thus the immediate object of the Spirit's work is, as we saw earlier, the human "heart" and "mind" (1 Cor. 2:16: "We have the mind of Christ"; cf. Rom. 12:2), with their capacity for "thought" (*to noēma*: 2 Cor. 4:4; Phil. 4:7, etc.) and "knowledge" (*epignōsis*: Phil. 1:9; Col. 1:9–10; 3:10, etc.). Paul is not simply interested in changing the external circumstances of his hearers' lives, and would have been profoundly conscious of the inability of most of his hearers to bring about social change outside the boundaries of their small community. Precisely because of their weakness and social insignificance, he is confident that only a transformation in understanding and outlook will be sufficient to anchor and empower any subsequent alteration in conduct or circumstances.

"Secular people experience forces in history as 'out of control'" (i.e., that there is no purpose or plan to the process of history), even as they "experience forces in personality as 'out of control'" (in the form of addictions, dependent relationships, etc.).

During one of his annual Ash Wednesday addresses to students and guests at Regis College, Toronto, in the early 1980s, Catholic theologian Henri Nouwen made a similar point. In response to the concerns of a questioner exhausted by the demands of social justice ministry and discouraged by the fragility and impermanence of social reform, Nouwen commented that an individual's external circumstances, however much improved by Christian intervention, may later revert to their original state of discord or oppression. Yet helping people to find anchorage in God, he said, offers an unvarying source of consolation, strength, and motivation for further endeavor, as much for those ministering as for those to whom they minister.

We asked at the outset what kind of change or spiritual effect might indicate the efficacy or "adequacy" of preaching. Careful examination of 2 Corinthians 3:18 leads to the paradoxical conclusion that producing a particular spiritual "effect" is not, in fact, the immediate purpose or goal of apostolic proclamation. Granted, from a human point of view, preaching is both intentionally theological (concentrating on the full disclosure of God's saving character) and explicitly christological (in its claim that Jesus of Nazareth enacts the saving purpose of God). It envisages the transformation of its hearers into the image of Christ, both exhorting them to ethical conformity with Christ and re-interpreting their existence according to the heuristic categories of sacrificial death and divinely accomplished resurrection. It anticipates and participates in the creation of a new society within the community of believers. Yet preaching confesses its own inability to bring about such ends, and admits that any change in the direction of "glory" is likely to be fragmentary and imperfect. As the preacher's own act of faith, preaching itself expresses a cruciform spirituality, relying for validation on divine agency in the person of the Holy Spirit. In this consists the "glory" of preaching itself, which makes itself subject to and thereby participates in God's salvific intent. Preachers and hearers alike may experience that saving purpose and the empowering agency of the Spirit in terms of inner "freedom," a new understanding of their circumstances and identity, and/or gradual moral conformity to Christ in both personal and social areas of endeavor. To the extent that lives otherwise continually characterized by weakness and "death" become marked by God's power of resurrection, believers may be said to resemble Christ, or, in the terms that Paul prefers, to reflect the "glory" of God, since these are results that only God can bring about.

141

Hope and Boldness

One further aspect of Paul's comparison between the revelations mediated by Moses and Jesus is particularly relevant to the task of preaching, although its explanation has had to await the exposition of the passage as a whole. "Since, then," Paul says, "we have such a hope, we act with great *boldness* [*pollē parrēsia chrōmetha*], not like Moses, who put a veil over his face to keep the people of Israel from gazing at the end of the glory . . ." (2 Cor. 3:12–13). According to Numbers 12:3, Moses was exceedingly "humble" or meek (LXX *praüs*, as in Matt. 5:5), "more so than anyone else on the face of the earth"; Paul apparently interprets his eagerness to hide behind a veil as an indication of the same tendency. Moses's reputation provides an opportunity for contrasting the attitude and outlook of one who announces the new covenant in Christ. Not only here but throughout his correspondence, Paul typically uses the language of "boldness" to describe the manner of his own apostolic proclamation.[29] Just as he tells the Roman church that he is "not ashamed of the gospel" (Rom. 1:16), so the positive expression of this sentiment appears in 1 Thessalonians 2:2:

> Though we had already suffered and been shamefully mistreated at Philippi . . . we had courage [or: we were bold, *eparrēsiasametha*] in our God to declare to you the gospel of God in spite of great opposition.

Philippians 1:20 offers a further contrast between "shame" and the "boldness" of proclamation:

> It is my eager expectation and hope that I will not be put to shame in any way, but that by my speaking with all boldness [*parrēsia*], Christ will be exalted now as always in my body, whether by life or by death.

Likewise the letter to the Ephesians concludes with a plea for prayer that clearly expresses the apostle's sense of obligation not to curtail or minimize the difficult, improbable, and demanding message of Christ:

> Pray also for me, so that when I speak, a message may be given to me to make known with *boldness* [*parrēsia*] the mystery of the gospel, for

29. Fuller discussion in Furnish, 230–31.

which I am an ambassador in chains. Pray that I may declare it boldly [*parrēsiasōmai*], as I must speak.

Ephesians 6:19–20; cf. 3:12

In 2 Corinthians, we have seen the apostle insist that he conducts himself "with frankness and godly sincerity" (2 Cor. 1:12; cf. 2:17); the statement in 3:12, "we act with great boldness," may be taken as an alternative expression of the same claim. It is certainly true (so Furnish, 230–31) that Paul is once more responding both to accusations that he has not conducted himself honorably and to the dishonorable conduct of certain other preachers who have taken advantage of the Corinthian church (2 Cor. 2:17; 11:20). But Paul's characterization of his ministry as conducted "with great boldness" is more than polemic or self-defense, for it appeals to a much larger premise, that of Christian "hope." Christian "hope," in turn, serves as a code word for the promise and expectation that the salvation believers now experience in part will one day be theirs in full. This is evident from any number of passages, prominent among them Romans 5:1–5, wherein Paul describes the Christian "hope of sharing the glory of God" (so also Col. 1:27: "Christ in you, the hope of glory"; cf. 1:5: "the hope laid up for you in heaven"). "Hope," he says, looks to all that is not yet part of the Christian experience, all that remains as yet unseen (Rom. 8:24–25). Yet the guarantee of this hope is the present gift of God's Holy Spirit ("hope does not disappoint us, because God's love has been poured into our hearts through the Holy Spirit that has been given to us," Rom. 5:5; so 8:23; 15:13; Gal. 5:5).

All this helps to explain what Paul has in mind in 2 Corinthians 3:12, for he is in the process of describing the "ministry" or "dispensation of the Spirit," attended by glory, that characterizes the new covenant of Christ (3:7–11, 18). He is fully aware that neither he nor his hearers are yet in full possession either of the Spirit or of God's glory, however much their experience of such things may surpass that of Moses, the Israelites, and adherents of the Mosaic covenant. In this passage too, the hope of which he speaks is "hope of sharing the glory of God" more fully, hope that even as believers "are being transformed" into the image of Christ by the ministry of the Spirit, "from one degree of glory to another," so ultimately both hope and glory will come to full fruition "before the judgment seat of Christ" (2 Cor. 5:10). In the meantime, however, Paul is faced with many dangers and pressures not to proclaim the Christian message as

143

he has been mandated to do. What sustains his outspoken "courage" or "boldness"—the term *parrēsia* includes both senses—is Christian "hope," hope that the burdens of present affliction will be far outweighed by the glory still to come. This is all the more important insofar as the most evident and immediate sources of "glory"—then as now—have to do with models and strategies of political or military power, personal self-promotion, and socio-economic hierarchy that run counter to the mandate of the cross. If "the *sufferings* of this present time are not worth comparing with the glory about to be revealed to us" (Rom. 8:18), how much more so is this true of the apparent "glory" of this present age, however pervasive—and oppressive—the latter may currently appear.

Even if Christian hope is oriented to the future, it is nonetheless both experienced and expressed in the present. Paul's personality—to the extent that it can be inferred from the evidence of his letters—suggests that his own sense of "boldness" might easily have been mistaken for boastfulness or arrogance. Likewise there is a danger that "boldness" on the part of any preacher might seem triumphalist, insensitive, or overbearing. Notwithstanding such real dangers, Paul implies that "confidence" (3:4) and "courage" (3:12) in proclamation are based on two experiential factors. The first, as we saw earlier, is the assurance that God has enabled him and his apostolic companions to accomplish something of which they would not otherwise have been capable, which is to be "ministers of a new covenant." This is, to a large extent, a functional argument, an assertion that can be proved or disproved in relation to the concrete, if imperfect results of one's ministry.

The second basis for boldness of proclamation is more theological, more an exercise of spiritual vision. Paul is emboldened by a peculiarly Christian ability to, as it were, see the unseen. Speaking "in Christ" and "in the presence of God" (2:17), enabled by the life-giving ministry of the Holy Spirit (3:6) and "beholding the glory of the Lord" (3:18), he courageously proclaims God's ability to bring life out of death. Confidence in preaching, therefore, is not a function of personality or technique so much as it is a consequence of theological conviction and an expression of a cruciform spirituality. Because of Christ, and in particular because Christ has been raised from an especially brutal death, Paul and other preachers are able to interpret their circumstances, when necessary, against the immediate evidence of their senses. What would otherwise appear both futile and illogical—whether the death of Jesus, the message of the gospel itself, or the frequently adverse

144

circumstances of preacher and audience—gains a new and hope-filled meaning in light of Christ's glorification. As Herbert Edwards declares in his sermon of the same name, "Things are not always what they seem":

> All appears to be over: the broken body is buried. The tomb is securely sealed. The guards are posted. And faith and hope are buried with the corpse. But God, who always reserves the last word unto himself, immobilizes the guards, breaks the seal, removes the stone, relativizes the finality of death, and raises Jesus from the dead. Things are not always what they seem . . .[30]

This should not be taken to imply that preachers themselves need to impose a particular theological interpretation on contemporary events, for the reinterpretation of those events is not ultimately dependent on the preacher's own perception or proclamation (however much these are still part of the equation). On the contrary, just as the preacher is convinced by factors beyond his or her own control (namely, the resurrection of Jesus, the gift of the Spirit, and the experience of being sustained amid tribulation), so the hearers will be convinced by factors beyond the preacher's control. Preachers may be responsible for many things, including but not limited to keeping the church books and organizing Sunday School. And preachers frequently imagine that they are responsible for convincing their hearers of the things of God. If this is true at all, it is so only in the most limited sense. In the end, however, the realization has overtaken Paul that he is not personally responsible for God, the gospel, or the life of Christ in believers, himself included. He does not sustain the life and mission of Christ; the life of Christ sustains him, and the mission of Christ makes his ministry possible. It is the simplest of all insights, but could hardly be more profound.

As Paul had previously explained regarding the ministry of various apostolic emissaries in Corinth (himself included),

> I planted, Apollos watered, but *God* gave the growth. So neither the one who plants nor the one who waters is anything, but only God who gives the growth.
>
> 1 Corinthians 3:6–7

30. Herbert O. Edwards, Sr., "Things Are Not Always What They Seem," in Thomas G. Long and Cornelius Plantinga, Jr., ed., *A Chorus of Witnesses: Model Sermons for Today's Preacher* (Grand Rapids: Eerdmans, 1994), 203.

This leaves the preacher free to rely neither on persuasive rhetoric, appeals to emotion, nor even the ability to make a strong intellectual argument. Or at least the preacher need not rely on these alone, but is free to testify more directly to the work of God in Christ—above all in Jesus's resurrection, but also throughout church history, in the preacher's own experience, and in the spiritual experiences of the hearers—precisely because it is "God who gives the growth." Preachers do little more than echo and respond to God's life-giving, transforming work in each of these areas.

Conversely, Paul seems to imply that lack of theological understanding (or, more precisely, shallowness of spiritual vision) will lead to theological timidity, or lack of conviction and boldness in preaching. That is, those who do *not* contemplate "glory" will find themselves unable to speak boldly or courageously of God's ability to bring life out of death. But here we must be more specific: Paul does not seem to dwell on theological doubt *per se*, although (notwithstanding his own recent crisis of faith) he is hardly tolerant of it elsewhere (e.g., Rom. 14:23). Rather, as we have seen all along, what concerns him are the dual temptations of having one's preaching influenced either by the received standards of social or intellectual propriety or by the dictates of self-interest, whether the accumulation of wealth and power, the quest for approval, or the avoidance of adversity (cf. 2 Cor. 4:2).

By implication, the transition from timidity to confidence and conviction in the pulpit is not likely to be accomplished by assertiveness training or a course in public speaking. For the "hope" of which Paul speaks is a predominantly theological quality, one that is acquired, whether in the study, in prayer, or through the experience of personal crisis, only by appeal to and deeper knowledge of "God who raises the dead." The kind of preaching he has in mind is an exercise in Christian hope, Christian hope is the consequence of Christian vision, and Christian vision arises— at least if Jesus and Paul are to be believed—out of the recognition that we must rely in the first instance on a gracious God who consistently reverses human sin, failure, and simple inability. Once more, this is the essence of a cruciform spirituality. Paul now begins to spell out the role and function of the preacher in greater detail.

4

Not Ourselves
(4:1–15)

At least within the church, the office of the preacher carries with it a certain honor and prestige. Faithful preaching commands respect; truly excellent preaching may bring material reward. But Paul takes the opposite view. As he sees it, preachers provide an example not simply of humility, but of a kind of humiliation and loss that leads them to model radical reliance on Christ. His definition of preaching focuses attention away from the concerns of personality, congregational or denominational identity, or political interest—at least as ends in themselves—and toward the divine mercy that makes ministry possible and puts all such concerns into proper perspective. Paul insists that even as the crucified Jesus and the Risen Lord are one and the same person, so humble dependence and divine affirmation go together. Because Jesus is his model, Paul is not content with "servant leadership," but makes the far more radical claim that he as an apostle and preacher is a "slave" to his rebellious congregation. That is how they treat him, and that is what Christ has made him. But because Christ—not the congregation—is his true Lord, it is Christ who sustains him and makes his ministry flourish. Only intimacy with the Lord Jesus, both crucified *and* risen, can create a preacher like this.

Therefore, since it is by God's mercy that we are engaged in this ministry, we do not lose heart. . . . For we do not proclaim ourselves; we proclaim Jesus Christ as Lord and ourselves as your slaves for Jesus' sake. . . . But we have this treasure in clay jars, so that it may be made clear that this extraordinary power belongs to God and does not come from us. We are afflicted in every way, but not crushed; perplexed, but not driven to despair; persecuted, but not forsaken; struck down, but not destroyed; always carrying in the body the death of Jesus, so that the life of Jesus may also be made visible in our bodies. For while we live, we are always being given up to death for Jesus' sake, so that the life of Jesus may be made visible in our mortal flesh. So death is at work in us, but life in you.

2 Corinthians 4:1, 5, 7–12

Mercy

Having juxtaposed the limited or fading glory of the old covenant with the life-giving glory of the new, Paul now turns to consequences and implications: "Therefore, possessing this ministry by virtue of having received mercy, we do not get discouraged [*enkakoumen*]."[1] Just as Paul previously defended himself on the grounds that his ministerial sufficiency or competence was a gift from God, and that the prospect of sharing God's glory accounted for his courage or boldness, so here he explains his ministry as an expression of divine mercy, from which he derives much comfort in the face of affliction.

His reference to mercy recalls the language of Rom. 12:1, where Paul moves from catechesis to paranesis with the exhortation, "I appeal to you therefore, brothers and sisters, *by the mercies of God*, to present your bodies as a living sacrifice, holy and acceptable to God. . . ." The key phrase "by the mercies of God" serves to summarize the entire theological argument of Romans, which is that a merciful God has intervened to save a

---

1. 2 Cor. 4:1, author's translation, as other verses in this note. This recalls the transitional statements of 3:4 ("Such is the confidence we have through Christ toward God") and 3:12 ("Since we have such a hope, we are very bold"). The next such transition is indicated by the similar vocabulary of 2 Cor. 4:16, "For this reason we are not discouraged [*enkakoumen*]," marking off verses 4:1–15 as a more or less integral unit of thought.

universally estranged humanity.[2] So in 2 Corinthians 4:1, Paul declares the apostolic mandate to be a microcosm of the larger Christian message: "it is by God's *mercy* that we are engaged in this ministry." The mercy that they preach announces the mercy they have been shown. Even the fact of their preaching is an expression of mercy. Only because divine mercy is the source of discipleship and ministry alike, Paul and his fellow apostles "do not lose heart." They are not discouraged by what would otherwise have surely discouraged them.

This sense of encouragement is the very antithesis of the state of mind Paul reported in 2 Corinthians 1:8, which was that he and his companions had earlier "despaired of life itself." On that occasion Paul had found himself unexpectedly rescued and consoled, and so could proclaim God's consolation to others in turn (2 Cor. 1:3–7). Here in 4:1, "mercy" and "encouragement" are simply alternative expressions for this same divine "consolation." In this passage, and notwithstanding the change in vocabulary, Paul applies the lessons of Asia Minor to his understanding of ministry in particular. All the more so if it was the faithful performance of his apostolic mandate that elicited such mortal affliction, Paul's "near-resurrection" experience has validated and affirmed the cruciform character of his discipleship and his ministry alike. This means that the consolation and encouragement on which he relies are at once retrospective (looking back to the resurrection of Jesus), prospective (looking forward to future glory), and immediate (looking to God's saving action in present experience). Having thus summarized the *basis* for his ministry, Paul now moves to explaining the *content* and *manner* of his preaching.

We Do Not Proclaim Ourselves

For the most part, 2 Corinthians 4:2–4 restates previous arguments. Verse 2 ("we refuse to practice cunning or to falsify God's word . . .") recalls Paul's protest of sincerity in 2:17 ("we are not peddlers of God's word like so many," etc.); verse 3 ("our gospel is veiled . . . to those who are perishing") resumes the themes of perishing and veiled understanding

2. So Cranfield, *The Epistle to the Romans* (ICC; Edinburgh: T&T Clark, 1975, 1979), 1:595–96.

from 2:15 and 3:14–16; and the wording of verse 4 ("the light of the gospel of the glory of Christ, who is the image of God") directly repeats the immediately preceding argument from 3:18.[3] But in 2 Corinthians 4:5, "Paul returns to the theme of his apostolic ministry" (Matera, 103), encapsulating the whole of its character and purpose in a single telling phrase:

> For we do not proclaim ourselves; we proclaim Jesus Christ as Lord and ourselves as your slaves for Jesus' sake.

Not least because of its explicit reference to preaching via the verb *kērussein* ("to announce, herald, preach"), this verse provides an unexpectedly rich resource for further exploring Paul's concept of apostolic proclamation.

To begin with, why does Paul find it necessary to deny that he preaches "himself"? Perhaps, as Thrall suggests, the explanation is at least partly that

> He is countering the charge that his evangelistic activity is motivated by the egotistical concern to achieve power over people (1.24; 10.8), or to create a reputation for himself and make financial profit out of it.[4]

Certainly Paul makes this kind of accusation against others who have sought to usurp his authority in the Corinthian church (2 Cor. 2:17; 11:19–20). If nothing else, this implies that the dual problems of simony (undertaking ministry out of a desire for financial gain) and inflated ministerial egos are as old as the church itself. Along the same lines, Furnish proposes (249; *pace* Thrall, 1.312) that the Corinthians have also misunderstood the kind of injunction represented by 1 Corinthians 4:16 and 11:1: "Be imitators of me, as I am of Christ" (cf. 7:7). Presumably they find such instructions self-serving and arrogant, so that Paul must now respond by assuring his congregants, "We do *not* preach about ourselves or for our own sakes."

Paul's intent in having urged the believers to imitate him is just the opposite of what it might seem, as emerges with particular clar-

---

3. Matera (98–99) argues for a more complex chiastic or "ring" pattern in these verses, bracketing 3:7–18.

4. Thrall, 1:313, who includes the observation of Windisch "that this kind of charge was current in philosophical polemic against the sophists" (n852).

ity from the context of the first such exhortation in chapter four of 1 Corinthians:

> To the present hour we are hungry and thirsty, we are poorly clothed and beaten and homeless, and we grow weary from the work of our own hands. When reviled, we bless; when persecuted, we endure; when slandered, we speak kindly. We have become like the rubbish of the world, the dregs of all things, to this very day. I am not writing this to make you ashamed, but to admonish you as my beloved children. For though you might have ten thousand guardians in Christ, you do not have many fathers. Indeed, in Christ Jesus I became your father through the gospel. I appeal to you, then, be imitators of me.
>
> 1 Corinthians 4:11–16

In comparison with the powerful role and elevated social position of the priesthood in both Greco-Roman and Israelite religion, for Paul to describe himself, Apollos, and Cephas as "God's servants, working together" and "stewards of God's mysteries" (1 Cor. 3:9; 4:1) might seem to imply privilege and exaltation. Yet the example of Christ and the conduct of the apostles reverses all such expectation. Therefore, rather than being "puffed up in favor of one against another" (1 Cor. 4:6), the believers should be humble toward one another, even as the litany of afflictions he cites indicates the commensurate humility—indeed, constant humiliation—of apostles such as he.

In this respect the Corinthian church might take note of the Thessalonian believers, whose own suffering mirrors that of Christ and Paul and, in turn, provides a pattern for others to imitate:

> You became imitators of us and of the Lord, for in spite of persecution you received the word with joy inspired by the Holy Spirit, so that you became an example to all the believers in Macedonia and in Achaia.
>
> 1 Thessalonians 1:6–7[5]

This, then, is the reasoning behind Paul's injunctions to imitation: if Paul is the "father" of the Corinthian believers and they his "beloved children," surely they too ought to conduct themselves as does he. Far from being

---

5. Further explored in Beaudean, *Paul's Theology of Preaching* (NABPR Dissertation Series 6; Macon: Mercer University Press, 1988), 38–41.

self-vaunting, Paul's appeal for imitation counsels humility, altogether inverting the image of apostles (or modern preachers?) as powerful figures who, together with their factions, compete for supremacy.[6]

Similarly in 2 Corinthians 4:5, Paul's "For we preach not ourselves" characterizes his approach to the gospel as a whole—with the conjunctive "for" likely referring back to the foundational premise that apostles such as he "have this ministry by the mercy of God." This assertion is the direct equivalent in corporate terms of Paul's confession in Galatians 2:19–20: "I have been crucified with Christ, and it is no longer I who live, but . . . Christ who lives in me." Whereas that statement expresses a cruciform spirituality in personal terms, 2 Corinthians 4:5 articulates the same principle as it applies to all apostles and preachers of the Christian message, implying that human identity and human agency are brought to nothing by the cross. By definition, says Paul, the message of the cross turns attention away from the proclaimer and toward the one proclaimed.

On a personal level, preaching is therefore not—and notwithstanding the influential opinion of Phillips Brooks—an expression of "personality."[7] Whatever their contribution to human communication may be, its power is ultimately rooted not in psychology, eloquence, "charisma," or one's ability to persuade, but in the empowerment of the Holy Spirit. Admittedly, the title *kērux*, "preacher, herald" (the direct cognate of *kērussein*, "to preach") appears nowhere in Paul's lists of the gifts of the Spirit. But that is because the task of proclamation belongs to "apostles," the charism that Paul ranks first among all bestowed by the Spirit (1 Cor. 12:28–29; cf. Eph. 4:11). Much less is preaching an exercise in, or an activity undertaken for, the purpose of self-promotion or self-fulfillment. This is particularly difficult to grasp when the cult of personality (whether in sports, politics, or the entertainment industry) is so prevalent in our society. Paul's "not ourselves" sets aside the promotion and marketing of personalities that occurs especially in larger churches, where it is little more than an ecclesiastical version of identity projection, hero worship, and our fondness for adulating the "stars" of our own making. Granted, Paul *is* drawing

6. As we will see shortly in our discussion of slavery as a metaphor for leadership, Paul's appeal for them to imitate his humility also subverts the congregants' understanding of the all-important roles of patron and client, respectively.

7. See Phillips Brooks, *Lectures on Preaching Delivered Before the Divinity School of Yale College in January and February, 1877* (New York: Dutton, 1893), 5–8: "Truth through Personality is our description of real preaching" (8).

attention to himself, but he is doing so in a way that confounds the expectations of his congregants, debasing rather than exalting himself in a manner that can be explained only in relation to the counterintuitive example of a crucified Messiah.

With regard to community, "not ourselves" means that neither is Christian proclamation primarily concerned with the promotion or maintenance of church or denomination, notwithstanding the fact that so much of our preaching is denominationally bounded and culturally specific. Like the Incarnation, preaching is of course unavoidably located within a particular language and cultural situation, yet it cannot be accounted for simply on the basis of these human circumstances, any more than its purpose is simply to preserve the language or culture in which it is articulated. Were this the case, we would all be constrained to preach in the languages of Jesus and the early church—whether Latin, Greek, or better yet, Aramaic. In fact, it is the universal scope of the Christian message—its reference to the one who is proclaimed rather than the proclaimers—that sustains particular, culturally bounded expressions of that message, and not *vice versa*. Otherwise, the gospel is reduced to little more than a social ideology, which is precisely what makes cultural Christianity so tepid and unappealing in the present day.

Nor, for the same reason, can the message of the cross be co-opted in support of the *polis*, or state, with its social and political systems that maintain public order. This, as we saw earlier, is already indicated by the theological claim that Jesus, rather than Caesar, is *Kyrios*, "Lord." To the extent that their purpose is to regulate and sustain human community, social systems are not open to the necessity of their own demise; to the extent that they create stability and security by political means, they tend to be self-sustaining and self-protective. Thus they typically resist claims of "lordship" other than their own. Yet Paul's experience of persecution, and above all the fact that not even his precious Roman citizenship has been able to protect him from it, indicates that his "not ourselves" extends also to the sphere of politics and social systems. In addition to heralding a clash of values between church and state,[8] this is a significant observation in light of the way that evangelism and mission are sometimes conducted, with relatively disadvantaged listeners professing Christian faith in the hope of sharing something of the greater affluence or social standing

8. So, further, Gorman, *Cruciformity: Paul's Narrative Spirituality of the Cross* (Grand Rapids: Eerdmans, 2001), 356–60.

of the missioners. In this respect also, to preach "not ourselves" means that conversion focuses steadfastly on the qualities and gifts of the one proclaimed, rather than those of the proclaimers, whatever culture they may represent, and however appealing the latter may seem. It is thus well for preachers to be aware that their own strengths and weaknesses, the various needs of their hearers, and especially the social location out of which they speak, are all capable of significantly distorting the Christian message. However much they are responsible themselves for conducting exegesis, finding illustrations, and delivering a sermon in a particular human language at a particular time and place, their hope and confidence rests in the theological claim that the power of preaching derives not from any of these as such, but from the life-giving, resurrecting intervention of God. As we might say today, "It isn't about us."

It might be tempting to think that preachers need not be concerned with content or presentation on the grounds that homiletic efficacy is a divine responsibility. The issue can be formulated along the lines of Paul's more famous query, "Should we continue in sin . . . that grace may abound?" (Rom. 6:1). Here the question might be put, "Should we neglect sermon preparation, that God may give the growth?" Paul's own example precludes this eventuality, for, he says, "I worked harder than any." He then hastens to add: "Yet it was not I, but the grace of God that is with me" (1 Cor. 15:10). This aptly expresses the paradoxical dynamic: human instrumentality remains indispensable, yet it relies on the enablement of grace. Or as the popular adage has it, "Without God, we cannot; without us, God will not."

Jesus Christ as Lord

As crucifixion presages resurrection, so the renunciation of self in 2 Corinthians 4:5 anticipates the announcement of the gospel's true content. Paul is not renouncing his own role as apostle, or the necessity of human agency (for "how are they to hear without someone to proclaim him?" [Rom. 10:14]). But the order of his syntax follows the logic of the cross, explaining the position of the preacher vis-à-vis the message that he or she proclaims. Just as Christ draws humanity into the nullity of death in order that he and they might become subject to the "new creation" of resurrection, so preachers declare, "Not ourselves!" as a precondition for them and their message becoming subject to the life-giving reality of "Jesus Christ as Lord."

This formula, as most commentators observe, is an expansion of the basic Christian confession, *Kyrios Iēsous*: "Lord Jesus" or "Jesus [is] Lord" (1 Cor. 12:3; cf. Rom. 10:9; so Barrett, 134). By combining a personal name with a simultaneously theological and political title, this most elemental statement of faith identifies Jesus of Nazareth as the exalted "Lord" of both Jewish theocracy and Roman state ideology. The formulation in 2 Corinthians 4:5 is even more complete, incorporating three names or titles. Paul's Greek (*kērussomen ... Iēsoun Christon kyrion*) manages with fewer articles and particles than are required by idiomatic English, as a result of which our translation must insert some explanatory additions: "we preach 'Jesus Christ [as] Lord'" or "we preach '[the] Lord Jesus Christ.'"[9] These three terms often appear together (ten times in 1 Corinthians, six of them in the first chapter; also 2 Corinthians 1:2; 13:13), most commonly with a possessive pronoun: "Jesus Christ *our* Lord" (e.g., 2 Cor. 1:3; 8:9).

The frequency with which these titles coincide should highlight rather than obscure the significance of their juxtaposition. For the kind of preaching that Paul has in mind begins with the crucified rabbi, the historically humiliated Jesus of Nazareth: "We preach *Jesus* . . ." If preaching thus takes as its starting point the theological premise of Incarnation—God's entry into fragility and suffering—it can never be abstracted from the awkward particularities and vicissitudes of human existence. Yet neither is it bound by human limitations, whether personal or political, for it equally confesses the reversal of Jesus's humiliation and the affirmation of his messianic anointing: "We preach Jesus as *the Christ*." Along the same lines, apostolic preaching declares that the supremely abased one has been supremely exalted: "We preach Jesus as Christ and *Lord*." Finally, the combination of "Christ" and "Lord" hints at the reconciliation of Jew and Gentile that Jesus's death and resurrection have now accomplished. The Greek term *Christos* never applies to persons in Hellenistic literature. As an adjective it simply means "spreadable" and, as a noun, "ointment."[10] As a title meaning "the anointed one [of God]," it is unique to the Septuagint, the New Testament, and other literature of the Jewish and Christian communities. The word *kyrios*, on the other hand, notwithstanding its

9. 1 Cor. 12:4 and Rom. 10:9 (literally, "no one is able to say 'Lord Jesus'" and "if you confess 'Lord Jesus' with your mouth") are similarly succinct, suggesting they and 2 Cor. 4:5 all cite established confessional formulae.

10. W. Grundmann, "*Chriō*, etc.," *TDNT* 9:495.

8,500 or so appearances in the Septuagint, has a long history in classical Greek: "That Christians in the Greek-speaking world were well aware of the fact that *kyrios* and *kyria* were commonly used with reference to the various pagan deities, especially of the oriental-Hellenistic religions is, of course, unquestionable."[11] Applying both *Christos* and *Kyrios* to Jesus as theological titles would thus suggest, at least for the mixed Jewish-Gentile audience of ancient Corinth, a certain meeting of worlds, communicating the soteriological relevance of his exaltation to Jew and Gentile alike.

According to Beaudean, the emphatic location and function of the title "Lord" (*Iēsoun Christon kyrion*) implies that Paul "has succeeded in splitting apart the conception of Jesus Christ as Lord from that of the historical Jesus."[12] On the contrary, the combination of "Jesus" and "Christ" already accomplishes the opposite, even as the more basic acclamation *Kyrios Iēsous* obviates any modernist distinction between the "Jesus of history" and the "Christ of faith." As Paul sets it out in 2 Corinthians 4:5, the proper content of apostolic preaching is the full divine-human identity of Jesus: "We preach Jesus: Christ *and* Lord."

Paul's awareness of the theological tensions and paradoxes implied by such a juxtaposition is evident in at least one other description of the preaching task that also employs the cognates *kērussein* ("to preach") and *kērugma* ("proclamation"):[13]

> For since, in the wisdom of God, the world did not know God through wisdom, God decided, through the foolishness of our proclamation [*kērugma*],

---

11. Cranfield, *Romans*, 2.528; cf. W. Foerster, "*Kyrios*, etc.," *TDNT* 3:1047: "the word *kyrios* is used of the Greek gods from the classical era right on into the imperial period, first as an adjective, then increasingly as a noun, and specifically when it is desired to state that the gods can control definite spheres" (although Foerster goes on to argue that its application is frequently governed by non-Greek usage).

12. Beaudean, *Paul's Theology of Preaching*, 150, citing John Schütz, *Paul and the Anatomy of Apostolic Authority* (SNTSMS 26; Cambridge: Cambridge University Press, 1975), 117.

13. Just as the noun *kērugma* can stand without further qualification (e.g., 1 Cor. 2:4; 15:14), so the verb *kērussein* can appear without a direct object (so Rom. 2:21; 10:14–15; 1 Cor. 1:21; 9:27; 15:11). More frequently, however, Paul specifies the content of his preaching: "*the word of faith* that we proclaim" (Rom. 10:8); "Some proclaim *Christ* from envy and rivalry" (Phil. 1:15); "the *gospel* that I proclaim among the Gentiles" (Gal. 2:2); "*the gospel* that . . . has been proclaimed to every creature under heaven" (Col. 1:23); "we proclaimed to you *the gospel of God*" (1 Thess. 2:9).

to save those who believe. For Jews demand signs and Greeks desire wisdom, but we proclaim [*kērussomen*] Christ crucified, a stumbling block to Jews and foolishness to Gentiles.

1 Corinthians 1:21–23

The folly and scandal of the Christian message is nothing other than the disgraceful execution of God's Messiah. More specifically, the "stumbling block" appears to be the fact that some in Corinth want to affirm Jesus's empowerment and glorification *without* the abasement that preceded it. Yet that, for Paul, would be to empty the gospel message of its distinctiveness and invalidate its divine source. The same scandal stands in the background even when the content of the *kērugma* refers more directly to resurrection:

Whether then it was I or they, so we proclaim [*kērussomen*] and so you have come to believe. Now if Christ is proclaimed [*kērussetai*] as raised from the dead, how can some of you say there is no resurrection of the dead? If there is no resurrection of the dead, then Christ has not been raised; and if Christ has not been raised, then our proclamation [*kērugma*] has been in vain and your faith has been in vain.

1 Corinthians 15:11–14

Although this is not Paul's main point, resurrection would be neither relevant nor necessary without the Messiah's prior death, and gains exponentially in significance not just as a supernatural event, but as the reversal of deep shame and abasement. In short, the disgraced "Jesus [of Nazareth]" and the resurrected "Lord" and "Christ" are found to be inextricably one and the same. Thus we notice that Paul does not bother to speak of "*Jesus* crucified," for human death is hardly remarkable.[14] By contrast, the claim to preach "*Christ* crucified" (1 Cor. 1:23) epitomizes in a single phrase the paradox, scandal, and divine surprise of the Christian message.

The unexpected humiliation of apostles and preachers, and the even more surprising reversal represented by resurrection, likewise underlie Paul's defense of his ministry against the "super-apostles" whose presence

---

14. Or more precisely, on the few occasions when Paul does mention the name of Jesus in reference to crucifixion (1 Cor. 2:2; Gal. 3:1; 5:24; 6:14), it is always in combination with the titles "Christ" and/or "Lord."

in Corinth threatens to turn the congregation against him. Although such reconstructions are necessarily speculative, we may infer the nature of their message from the scattered hints that Paul provides.[15] The Corinthians seem offended that Paul has refused to accept monetary compensation for his work (2 Cor. 11:7–9). For his own part, Paul hints darkly that others whom he strategically declines to name are guided by mercenary motives (2:17). He accuses these false apostles of having preyed on the congregation and taken advantage of their hospitality (11:20), which likely included accepting monetary payment. As a separate issue, Paul quotes certain of his detractors as saying, "'His letters are weighty and strong, but his bodily presence is weak, and his speech contemptible'" (2 Cor. 10:10). By contrast there are "some," says Paul, who "commend *themselves*" (2 Cor. 10:12; cf. 11:18), apparently boasting of their Jewish heritage (11:21a–23a), their rhetorical prowess (11:6), and their social standing or "outward appearance" (5:12).[16]

Paul's response to the seemingly impressive credentials of these in-terlopers is unusual: "If I must boast," he says, "I will boast of the things that show my weakness" (2 Cor. 11:30). True, Paul also boasts of his positive qualifications, particularly his Jewish background (11:22–23) and the special revelations that have been accorded him (12:1–6). Yet he repeatedly returns to the refrain that it is his lowliness and weakness that validate his ministry, rather than the opposite: "I myself, Paul, appeal to you by the meekness and gentleness of Christ" (10:1); "Did I commit a sin by abasing myself?" (11:7, RSV); "Who is weak, and I am not weak?" (11:29); "I will boast all the more gladly of my weaknesses, so that the power of Christ may dwell in me" (12:9).[17] This, too, is an expression of his general principle: "We do not proclaim ourselves."

15. For a comprehensive treatment of this issue, see Savage, *Power Through Weakness: Paul's Understanding of the Christian Ministry in 2 Corinthians*, (SNTSMS 86; Cambridge University Press, 1996), 64–99 (other sociocultural analyses are summarized by Furnish, 53–54).

16. Note in particular the language of 11:3, comparing the "cunning [*panourgia*]" of both the serpent in Eden and the deceivers in Corinth (versus Paul's own refusal to "practice cunning [*panourgia*]," 4:2) and expressing fear that the believers are being corrupted or "led astray [*phtharē*]" (versus Paul's claim in 7:2, "we have corrupted [*ephtheiramen*] no one") from their former "uprightness" or "sincerity [*haplotētos*]" of devotion (contrast 1:12, "we have conducted ourselves . . . with uprightness [*haplotēti*]." Cf. Matera, 243.

17. Basing his analysis on the questionable assumption that orality implies public (i.e., open-air) performance, Richard Ward ("Pauline Voice and Presence as Strategic

Paul and his opponents differ not only in these external measures, he alleges, but in the essence of their message as well:

> For if someone comes and proclaims [*kērussei*] another Jesus than the one we proclaimed [*ekēruxamen*], or if you receive a different spirit from the one you received, or a different gospel from the one you accepted, you submit to it readily enough.
>
> 2 Corinthians 11:4

The meaning of "another Jesus . . . a different spirit . . . a different gospel" has been the focus of considerable scholarly discussion, the details of which cannot be reviewed here.[18] Perhaps the best clue to the meaning of the passage as a whole is Paul's reference to "*another* Jesus"—that is, a Jesus other than Jesus of Nazareth in his weakness and humiliation, the Crucified One.[19] For Paul, the simple name *Iēsous* almost always refers to the human Jesus who suffered and became subject to resurrection (so Rom. 8:11; 1 Thess. 4:14), and to the way in which believers should emulate Jesus's suffering and humiliation:

> He humbled himself and became obedient to the point of death—even death on a cross.

Communication," *Semeia* 65 [1994]: 95–107) argues that the performance of 2 Cor. 10–13 would have commended its reception: "the effect of the performance is to reestablish Paul as a potent and powerful voice within the Corinthian community" (106). But this seems contrary to the content of his message: both here and in the letter's earlier chapters, Paul makes a virtue of weakness and humility, avoidance of which would undermine the meaning of the cross. By contrast Jennifer A. Glancy ("Boasting of Beatings [2 Corinthians 11:23–25]," *JBL* 123.1 [2003]: 85–97) explores the significance of Paul's humiliation in a Greco-Roman social context: "Paul does not try to revamp the prevailing *habitus*; he does not call dishonor honor. Rather, he represents his abject mien as cruciform" (134).

18. See the representative treatments of Barrett, 275–77; Furnish, 500–502; and Thrall, 2:667–71. Compare the reference to "another gospel" in Gal. 1:6 (on which see Beaudean, *Paul's Theology of Preaching*, 66–69).

19. That Paul uses the title *Kyrios*, "Lord," 29 times in 2 Corinthians (although some of these refer to God) and *Christos* 47 times, compared with only 19 occurrences of the name "Jesus" (and only once, at 8:9, in the 116 verses between 4:14 and 11:4), suggests that he is consciously choosing the name here. Likewise it is notable that of 181 appearances of the name *Iēsous* in Pauline literature (excluding the Pastorals and Col. 4:10), all but 15 are in combination with one or both of these titles.

> Therefore God also highly exalted him and gave him the name that is above every name, so that *at the name of Jesus* every knee should bend, in heaven and on earth and under the earth, and every tongue should confess that Jesus Christ is Lord, to the glory of God the Father.
>
> Philippians 2:8–11

Here the two-part movement of Jesus's death and exaltation are mirrored by the actions of disciples and preachers alike: self-abasement "at the name of Jesus" precedes confession of him as "Christ" and "Lord."[20] This is Paul's own experience, for, he says, "I carry the marks *of Jesus* branded on my body" (Gal. 6:17). Most explicit of all is 2 Corinthians 4:8–11, in which Paul characterizes apostolic suffering as carrying around "the death of Jesus" (not, that is, of "the Lord" or "the Christ") in one's own body:

> We are afflicted in every way, but not crushed; perplexed, but not driven to despair; persecuted, but not forsaken; struck down, but not destroyed; always carrying in the body the death of Jesus, so that the life of Jesus may also be made visible in our bodies. For while we live, we are always being given up to death for Jesus' sake, so that the life of Jesus may be made visible in our mortal flesh.[21]

All this points decisively to the meaning of 2 Corinthians 11:4: that Paul accuses some of preaching "another *Jesus*" is an ironic contradiction in terms. In fact there is no "other" Jesus: no Jesus, that is, other than the scandalously rejected man of Nazareth, "the crucified Christ who manifests God's power through weakness":

> If, in contrast, the intruding apostles focused attention on their powerful deeds, eloquent speech, and ecstatic experiences, it is unlikely that the cross of the crucified Christ played as central a role in their preaching.[22]

20. On this passage as the summary of Paul's "master narrative," see Gorman, *Cruciformity*, 88–92, 164–69, 278–80.

21. Even the anathema formula of 1 Cor. 12:3 is "*Jesus* be cursed" rather than "the Lord Jesus" or "Jesus Christ," for the latter would represent an impossible contradiction. Cf. W. Foerster, *Iēsous*, *TDNT* 3:287–89 ("The name borne by Jesus is in the first instance an expression of His humanity," 287; and 289 on Pauline usage).

22. Matera, 244. Focusing on the identity of Jesus himself is preferable to the view of Savage (*Power Through Weakness*, 156) that to preach "another Jesus" refers to a message lacking the moral demand of "servant-like humility."

Nor, one might add, can there be any other "spirit" or "gospel": the apparent love of the "super-apostles" for glorification without humiliation represents a betrayal of both the manner and the means by which Jesus has established human salvation, and bidden his followers to share it. Theirs is simply not the gospel that Paul knows, which explains why he brands its exponents as servants of Satan (2 Cor. 11:13–15)! The implication of his polemic is that the lifestyle of the preachers is as eloquent an exposition of their message as any words they might choose to employ. Paul is unequivocal that the message of the cross gives glory to God alone, indeed that it strips its messengers of glory as thoroughly as would death by crucifixion. If there is any glory in preaching, it is the gift of God alone.

Paul's summation of his ministry in 2 Corinthians 4:5 begins by insisting that the declaration "not ourselves" is integral to the Christian message and its proclamation. Paul will reiterate this point at the end of the verse, where he speaks (on behalf of all apostolic preachers) of "ourselves as your slaves *for Jesus' sake*," and here again the unadorned name is hardly accidental. Still, humility and humiliation are not goals or moral virtues in themselves. Their only value is that they provide opportunity for divine reversal. Like his use of the name "Jesus" apart from theological titles, so Paul's references to preaching and proclamation in the passages we have reviewed (1 Cor. 1:21–23; 15:11–14; 2 Cor. 1:17–22; 11:4) focus on the folly and weakness of crucifixion only as preconditions for restoration and transformation by the power of God's resurrection. Accordingly, the "not ourselves" can never be proclaimed apart from the "Jesus Christ as Lord," just as (in keeping with Paul's response to the "super-apostles") the proclamation of divine exaltation must remain rooted in the humiliation that preceded it.

The relevance of these considerations for subsequent practice far exceeds any purely intellectual or creedal concern for Christian orthodoxy: that is, that preachers affirm both the cross and the resurrection, the full humanity and the full divinity of Jesus of Nazareth as Lord and Christ, or that preaching balance Jesus's identification with human circumstances and his glorious transformation of them. These are valid concerns, but they are not all that should engage us. In particular, Paul's assault on preachers who concern themselves with status, appearance, and the material benefits of Christian ministry is painfully relevant to the church of an image-conscious culture that values these goals above almost anything else. Although it applies far more widely, this issue is perhaps best

161

illustrated with reference to television as a medium for communication of the Christian message.

Television, by definition, presents its viewers with an artificial world. Even if the image on the screen is of a church sanctuary or crusade, rather than the meticulous illusion of a television studio, the preacher is not really present to the audience, nor the audience to the preacher. Nor are the viewers in contact with one another. There is no context for such preaching in the life of a faith community. There is no one to touch, to fall out with, or to be accountable to. If there is to be flesh-and-blood forgiveness, and real-life reconciliation, it must take place somewhere else. The message that is presented can be no more than a précis of the real thing, with all the hiccups, interruptions, and false starts carefully edited out. The service of worship or preaching fits miraculously into a thirty- or sixty-minute time slot, unlike the more ragged contours of the real event. There are no babies crying, no out-of-tune pianos or sopranos, and no worries that George the caretaker has again forgotten to replace the light bulb at the pulpit. Even apart from its unavoidably enormous expense, television favors beautiful presenters and successful ministries. The weary struggles of the lonely or impoverished suburban pastor, perennially five minutes late for everything, are never represented. Yet whatever programming does make it on air creates the illusion that the former, rather than the latter, is the average and norm. What is more, people seem to be converted, healed, or made to prosper each week without fail. If nothing else, television is a medium of power and prestige that, by definition, draws attention to its own success:

> but for all its attractiveness, that approach cannot be squared with Paul's theology of preaching. From Paul's point of view, authentic preaching does not draw its strength from itself, nor does it draw attention to itself, but . . . operates exclusively from the strength of God.[23]

It is not that congregational ministry must amount to unvarying drudgery or unremitting failure. Given the privilege of being invited into the sacred moments and issues of human life with the astonishing news of Jesus's compassion and grace, nothing could be farther from the truth. But ministry as a whole is a ragged business, frequently attended

23. Beaudean, *Paul's Theology of Preaching*, 205.

by frustration and uncertainty. Like preaching itself, it sometimes succeeds spectacularly and at other times fails dismally. Paul might even argue that the "failures" are more important than the "successes," because they provide an opportunity for God to triumph where Jesus's servants do not. Cruciform ministry is by definition predicated on the gracious sufficiency of God and the otherwise definitive insufficiency of its human instruments. Yet none of this messy reality ever appears on the television screen. Electronic media have compelling advantages, not least the ability to reach large numbers of people with the message of Christ. But whether in front of cameras or well out of their sight, if ours is to be, in fact, the message of *Jesus* as Lord and Christ, then Paul's many trials, his weaknesses, and even his reputed homeliness counsel profound caution as we minister in an image-conscious, prestige-honoring, and power-positive culture. Paul, for one, seemed very doubtful that there was any way to reconcile the human hunger for success and glory (at least as exemplified by his "super-apostolic" rivals) with the strange route that God had chosen, in Jesus's death and resurrection, to bestow these very objectives as gifts for humanity.

Ourselves as Your Slaves

In the course of his correspondence, Paul refers to himself (and occasionally his companions) by a variety of terms that define the purpose of his ministry as one of rendering service to others. "Think of us in this way," he told the Corinthians in previous correspondence, "as servants [*hupēretas*] of Christ and stewards [*oikonomous*] of God's mysteries" (1 Cor. 4:1). Likewise Paul speaks of apostles as *diakonoi*, "servants," subject to the one they call "Lord": "What then is Apollos? What is Paul? *Servants* through whom you came to believe, as the Lord assigned to each" (1 Cor. 3:5). So too in the present letter he speaks of apostles as "ministers [*diakonous*] of a new covenant" (2 Cor. 3:6) or, alternatively, as "servants [*diakonoi*]" of God (2 Cor. 6:4; cf. Eph. 3:7) or of Christ (2 Cor. 11:23; cf. Col. 1:7).

The terms *hupēretēs*, *oikonomos*, and *diakonos* each convey distinctive emphases. The first of these terms, for example, is employed in the New Testament "to refer to many diverse types of servants, such as attendants to a king, officers of the Sanhedrin, attendants of magistrates, and, especially in the Gospel of John, Jewish Temple guards" (L&N 35.20). In both classical and biblical usage, *hupēretēs* designates one who is subject to and executes the will of another, whether in the military hierarchy, with reference to government bureaucracy, or in the service of the gods.[24] So Paul testifies in his defense before King Agrippa with regard to his conversion and commissioning for ministry:

> Then I asked, "Who are you, Lord?" "I am Jesus whom you are persecuting," the Lord replied. . . . "I have appeared to you to appoint you as a servant [*hupēretēn*] and as a witness of what you have seen of me and what I will show you."
>
> Acts 26:15–16 NIV

Rengstorf offers a helpful comparison:

> The *hupēretēs* is distinguished from the *doulos*, always used for a slave, by the fact that he is free and can in some cases claim a due reward for his services. But the *hupēretēs* also differs from the *diakonos* . . . In the case of the *diakonos* the accent is on the objective advantage his service brings to the one to whom it is rendered. . . . The special feature of [a] *hupēretēs*, however, is that he willingly learns his task and goal from another who is over him in an organic order but without prejudice to his personal dignity and worth.[25]

Likewise an *oikonomos* is a manager, a trustee or administrator, a position of responsibility and—as in the case of Erastus, the *oikonomos* or public treasurer of Corinth (Rom. 16:23)[26]—considerable social standing.

The term *diakonos* introduces a less-welcome element, for "in Greek eyes serving is not very dignified. Ruling and not serving is proper to a man." Particularly in light of its originally more concrete sense of "one who serves tables," *diakonia* is the proper domain of those with lower social standing, of women and servants in particular.[27] Nonetheless, such language is particularly prominent in 2 Corinthians, where Paul writes of apostles having been granted a "*ministry* of reconciliation" (5:18), of the collection for the

---

24. K. H. Rengstorf, "*hupēretēs*, etc.," *TDNT* 8:530–44.

25. Rengstorf, *TDNT* 8:532–33.

26. Cf. F. F. Bruce, *The Epistle of Paul to the Romans* (TNTC; Grand Rapids: Eerdmans, 1963), 280.

27. H. W. Beyer, "*diakoneō*, etc.," *TDNT* 2:82.

Jerusalem churches as a "*ministry* to the saints" (8:4; 9:1, 12–13), and of his own work as a *diakonia*, "service," to the Corinthian church (11:8).[28]

The indignity is all the more glaring in Paul's frequent designation of himself, his fellow apostles, indeed of believers in general as "slaves [*douloi*] of Christ" (Rom. 1:1; 1 Cor. 7:22; Gal. 1:10; Eph. 6:6; Phil. 1:1; Col. 4:12; cf. 2 Tim. 2:24) and slaves of God (Rom. 6:22; Titus 1:1).[29] Particularly in Corinth would this have seemed unusual, as F. W. Beare points out in his commentary on Philippians 1:1:

> When Paul describes himself and Timothy as slaves of Christ Jesus, he is using language which would sound strange and even shocking to Greek ears. Cynics and Stoics would indeed hold that the slave was a man and a brother, and that the wise man is truly free, whatever his civil status; but not even among the philosophers did any Greek speak of his own relation to the divine power which he served as that of a "slave." There is no background in Greek usage for the use of slave as a figure of religious devotion. Nor did the Hebrew think of himself as a "slave" of his God.[30]

The incongruity would ultimately have been as much social as conceptual or ethical, for the image of the Christian "slave" implies far more than mere obedience—even absolute obedience—to Christ as "Lord." To understand how this is so, we must first recall the fact that Greco-Roman societies were considerably more stratified than, say, those of modern North America or Western Europe. Categories of social class and status were determinative of identity, and movement between them the exception rather than the norm. Paul rebukes the Corinthian church in particular for the way in which their adherence to the norms of social stratification has led them to "show contempt for the church of God and humiliate those who have nothing" (1 Cor. 11:22). That is, rather than recognizing that mutual submission to the dictates of Christ leads to a mitigation of social divisions, they have conducted their communal meals in the manner of any other club or guild. In such situations it was typical for those of higher social rank to be served more and superior food and

28. That is, 20 of the 43 Pauline uses of *diakonos*, *diakonia*, and *diakonein* occur in 2 Corinthians.

29. Compare the similar use of the cognate verb *douleuein*: Rom. 12:11; 14:18; 16:18; Gal. 5:13; Eph. 6:7; Col. 3:24; 1 Thess. 1:9.

30. F. W. Beare, *The Epistle to the Philippians* (BNTC; London: Adam and Charles Black, 1959), 50.

drink than those of lower standing, even to the point of intentionally humiliating the less-favored. But what is customary behavior elsewhere in the world of their day earns the Corinthians a sharp reprimand.[31] In short, the Corinthians are evidently conscious of their social differences, and Paul's instructions regarding slave-likeness are likely to have made them more rather than less so.

At least among the lower classes, self-sale into slavery was not unheard of as an indirect means of social advancement (since citizenship was often bestowed on a slave at manumission) and even citizens might be enslaved in cases of grave debt.[32] But consciously aspiring to "downward mobility" was unthinkable. Although his characterization of the early church tends more to satire than to historical accuracy, the pagan Celsus, writing around AD 178, "alleged that the church deliberately excluded educated people because [its] religion was attractive only to 'the foolish, dishonourable, and stupid, and only slaves, women, and little children.'"[33] What is important for our purposes is the implied equivalence of "foolish, dishonourable, and stupid" and "slaves, women, and little children"—with slaves at the head of the list. Yet this is what Paul boldly proclaims himself to be: a "slave" of Christ, and the Corinthians along with him (1 Cor. 7:22). Even more pertinently, to embrace slavery was to fall under the shadow of the cross, for crucifixion was a fate typical of slaves. Sceledrus, a slave in *Miles Gloriosus*, penned by Roman dramatist Titus Maccius Plautus in about 205 BC, laments, "I know the cross will be my grave: that is where my ancestors are, my father, grandfathers, great-grandfathers, great-great-grandfathers."[34]

---

31. Meeks, *The First Urban Christians: The Social World of the Apostle Paul* (New Haven: Yale University Press, 1983), 67–69, citing in particular Theissen, *The Social Setting of Pauline Christianity: Essays on Corinth*, tr. John H. Schütz (Philadelphia: Fortress, 1982), 290–317. In similar fashion, Paul exhorts the Galatian believers, "For you were called to freedom, brothers and sisters; only do not use your freedom as an opportunity for self-indulgence, but through love become slaves to one another" (Gal. 5:13).

32. S. Scott Bartchy, "Slavery (Greco-Roman)," *ABD* 6:67. Such privileges were by no means granted automatically upon manumission, in addition to which the ambitions of freedmen provoked a bitter response from those who resented what they perceived to be an encroachment on their own social prerogatives (so Meeks, *First Urban Christians*, 22). Savage (*Power Through Weakness*, 37–40) provides examples of prominent freedmen in contemporary Corinthian society.

33. Meeks, *First Urban Christians*, 51, citing Irenaeus, *Contra Celsum* 3.44.

34. Quoted in O'Collins, "Crucifixion," *ABD* 1:1208.

In Paul's case, the implied plunge in social status would have been, if possible, even more precipitous, for he was by birth a full Roman citizen. Acts 22:28 provides us a momentary glimpse into the privileges of Roman citizenship, for there Paul is able to escape judicial flogging—that is, examination by torture—on the grounds that he holds citizenship as a birthright (similarly, Acts 16:27). The Roman commander, by contrast, confesses that he had obtained citizenship only by expending a large sum of money, presumably in the form of a bribe. Corinth, we recall, had been re-populated with freed slaves, to whom Rome had granted the precious privilege of citizenship. Indeed, the poet Crinagoras (who flourished ca. 45–25 BC) bemoans the servile fate of this once-noble city, calling its new inhabitants "a crowd of scoundrelly slaves" (cited in Furnish, 7). This newfound status would have been a source of great civic pride and personal comfort, making Paul's proposal seem all the more repugnant, the approximate equivalent of a well-intentioned white preacher suggesting to contemporary African-Americans that they re-embrace slavery as the basis of their own spiritual identity.

Bruce notes that "the possession of Roman citizenship was a high social distinction in the Near East."[35] Paul enjoyed coveted privileges of legal protection and social distinction likely shared by few others in the city's small Christian community. Accordingly, representing himself as a "slave" would have seemed shocking, to say the least. He had admonished the Corinthians, "You were bought with a price; do *not* become slaves of human masters" (1 Cor. 7:23), and (although the wording is ambiguous) seems to have counseled slaves to take advantage of manumission if offered (1 Cor. 7:21).[36] For him to propose a willing descent from the privileged position of Roman citizen to that of a slave—even as a metaphor—would have verged (once again) on idiocy. Yet it was a fitting imitation of Christ's own acquiescence to humiliation: Paul preached a "Lord" who had assumed the place of a slave (Phil. 2:7), one who "though he was rich, yet for your sakes he became poor, so that by his poverty you might become rich" (2 Cor. 8:9).

Perhaps such language could be accounted for on the basis of Jesus's post-resurrection status as exalted "Lord," for despite the tendency

35. F. F. Bruce, "Citizenship," *ABD* 1:1048.
36. On the interpretation of this verse, see Fee, *The First Epistle to the Corinthians* (NICNT; Grand Rapids: Eerdmans, 1987), 316–18.

among Greeks in particular to regard slaves as inherently inferior, the social status of a slave throughout much of the Roman world depended largely on that of the owner.[37] The Corinthians might have understood this to be a religious version of self-sale into slavery as a means of self-betterment (perhaps for the "debt" of sin). But at least in the present passage Paul firmly excludes that option. His formulation is, "We do not proclaim ourselves; we proclaim Jesus Christ as Lord and ourselves as *your* slaves for Jesus' sake" (2 Cor. 4:5). Paul proposes that he, a Roman citizen, is morally bound to serve and benefit those who have been converted under his preaching. He had proposed as much in a previous letter: "For though I am free with respect to all, I have made myself a slave to all, so that I might win more of them" (1 Cor. 9:19). Now he elevates the principle from an incidental observation on the nature of his conduct to the very essence of the Christian message: "We proclaim . . . ourselves as your slaves." In this regard Paul is the very opposite of the "super-apostles," who demand honor and acclaim and seem quick to punish those who fail to offer it. "For you put up with it," he laments, "when someone *makes slaves of you*, or preys upon you, or takes advantage of you, or puts on airs, or gives you a slap in the face" (2 Cor. 11:20). Yet by all the moral and social conventions of Paul's day, it is the conduct of these false apostles that makes sense to the congregants, not the incomprehensible disregard for self-esteem and social propriety displayed by the apostle.

Such considerations assume their proper dimensions once we recognize that Paul is consciously subverting a series of expectations that are central to Roman social custom and political ideology, as well as to the religious concepts that underlie them. As founder and "father" of the congregation, Paul has assumed the all-important role of "patron" to the fledgling community; they, in turn, would have understood themselves as his "clients." As such, their relationship would have been governed by considerations of "reciprocity": he was expected to convey *charis*: "favor" or "beneficence"; they in turn owed him loyalty and honor. In the highly stratified cultures of the Mediterranean world, it was normal for those of lower status or rank to rely on their social superiors to convey honor "by association" and to negotiate on their behalf with other social elites. Favors bestowed in this

37. Bartchy, "Slavery (Greco-Roman)," *ABD* 6:66.

regard deserved favor and allegiance in return.[38] Indeed, their relationship to Christ as "Lord" would have functioned along much the same lines. Religious conversion in the ancient Mediterranean world was not primarily a process of psychological crisis resolution, but involved a change in divine patronage.[39] As their heavenly patron, Jesus would likewise be expected to bless and favor them, just as they owed him honor and obedience as a result. It would have made complete sense for the divine Son (as well as the Spirit) to intercede on their behalf with the supreme God (as Paul explains to Roman believers in Rom. 8:26–27, 34).

Gorman's analysis of social power in the Greco-Roman world is particularly helpful at this point, for it suggests that the Corinthians have not yet grasped the full implications of declaring Jesus to be *Kyrios*, "Lord." Social order in Corinth, as a Roman colony, would have been governed by Roman political ideology. Viewing the Roman emperor as a semi-divine figure not only implied that his reign was sanctioned by the gods, but also established the basic structure and dynamics of Roman society:

> The emperor was at the top of a ladder of Roman power, with his closest associates just beneath him. Below the most powerful lay a hierarchy of power, "a culture of competition based on meritocracy . . . in which admiration, esteem, and recognition were crucial motivating factors." The higher up the ladder people were, the greater honor they were due *and the closer to the divine realm they were believed to be* . . .
>
> In this cultural context, "power" and "glory," or "honor," were associated with high culture and status. Among the means of possessing and displaying power and honor were wealth and abundance; political, social, and military achievements and influence; family heritage and status; friends; impressive physical appearance; learning; and eloquent speech.[40]

Although we are already familiar with social manifestations of power from our earlier study of ancient Corinth, Gorman's analysis adds an

---

38. As an example from contemporary Western culture, the opening scene of Francis Ford Coppola's 1972 film, *The Godfather*, illustrates this principle perfectly.

39. Zeba A. Crook, *Reconceptualising Conversion: Patronage, Loyalty, and Conversion in the Religions of the Ancient Mediterranean* (BZNW 130; Berlin: Walter de Gruyter, 2004).

40. Gorman, *Cruciformity*, 270 (emphasis added), in part paraphrasing Dieter Georgi, *Theocracy in Paul's Praxis and Theology*, tr. David E. Green (Minneapolis: Fortress, 1991), 62–63.

important theological dimension, suggesting that Paul's self-abasement, the status reversal he requires of his converts, and his proclamation of Jesus as "Lord" are of a piece. On the one hand, acknowledging Caesar to be "Lord" commits Roman subjects to an implicitly theological pattern of social interaction in which self-aggrandizement and self-display imply divine approval—and divinely sanctioned power. By contrast, confessing *Jesus* as "Lord" subverts prevailing social and political structures and their theological underpinnings, committing his disciples instead to cruciform self-abasement and status reversal. Insofar as *his* reign has divine approval, piety and godliness are manifested by means of humility rather than social prestige, by honoring others rather than demanding to be honored by them.[41] Like Jesus himself, Paul models the radical sociopolitical implications of Christ's reign, and the contrary worldview of "the kingdom of God" (1 Cor. 15:24, 50, etc.).

Such conflicting expectations explain much of the congregation's perplexity and estrangement from the apostle. Although they have pledged their allegiance to Jesus as "the Lord of glory" (1 Cor. 2:8), this allegedly divine patron turns out to have suffered the humiliating fate of what the poet Crinagoras would have called a "scoundrelly slave." Perhaps Paul's emphasis on divine *charis* has inadvertently compounded the problem: the Corinthians may believe that since Jesus's resurrection has reversed his degradation, the latter was merely anomalous or temporary, and is therefore no longer relevant to discipleship. They and the super-apostles apparently understand Christian faith to entail emancipation via resurrection alone.[42] The fact that Paul also willingly participates in abasement is part of the scandal. He presents himself as the client of an executed criminal insurrectionist, and expects the Corinthians to be his clients when his own conduct is no less contemptible. No small part of Paul's difficulties in Corinth is his failure to act as a patron should.[43] Not only is his deport-

41. Gorman (*Cruciformity*, 300) again cites Georgi to this end: "Paul . . . asserts that since Jesus, humankind is not intrinsically controlled by competition and success, superiority and inferiority, superordination and subordination. Rather, humanity is controlled by the mutual solidarity of a life born out of a common death" (*Theocracy*, 71).

42. So Patte, *Preaching Paul* (Philadelphia: Fortress, 1984), 36.

43. Cf. Marshall, "A Metaphor of Social Shame: *THRIAMBEUEIN* in 2 Cor. 2:14," *NovT* 25 (1983): 313–14: "Recommendation was a common social custom in Graeco-Roman society which initiated reciprocal friendship based on *pistis* or *fides*. It seems

ment inappropriate (in addition to his unimpressive appearance, he has proven unreliable with regard to a promised visit), but—and this by his own admission—he is constantly being humiliated at the hands of others. Not least, he refuses to allow his clients to honor him in the customary manner, preferring the hardships and socially demeaning position of a laborer, a tentmaker (1 Cor. 4:12). As Ronald Hock observes,

> In the social world of a city like Corinth, Paul would have been a weak figure, without power, prestige, [or] privilege. . . . To those of wealth and power, the appearance (*schēma*) of the artisan was that befitting a slave (*douloprepēs*).[44]

How, then, can he remain the congregation's patron, all the more so when other, apparently more dignified and certainly more conventional candidates for this honor are not lacking? Paul's answer is astonishing: he models his conduct on that of his and the Corinthians' true patron, who is the crucified *and* exalted Jesus. In a reversal of their expectations, Paul will be the "slave" of his patronal clients, even as Jesus is the "slave" of all. Paul presents himself (as Beaudean observes with reference to 1 Cor. 9:17–19) as "a slave to Christ, a slave to the gospel, and therefore a slave to all for the gospel's sake."[45] Far from disqualifying him, however, this is what it means to be a true patron of the congregation, after the manner of Jesus. It is no wonder that they find him and his conduct incomprehensible.

Although patron-client relations continue to function as an important social principle in some parts of the world (e.g., agrarian cultures of Latin America, or in Central and Southeast Asia), they are considerably less prevalent in the West. Yet the underlying dynamics of

---

that the Corinthians accused Paul of breaching that relationship by his inconstancy, the antithesis of *pistis*, and 2 Corinthians represents his attempts at reestablishing his relations with them as their parent apostle."

44. Ronald F. Hock, *The Social Context of Paul's Ministry: Tentmaking and Apostleship* (Philadelphia: Fortress, 1980), 60, quoted in part by Stowers, "Social Status, Public Speaking, and Private Teaching: The Circumstances of Paul's Preaching Activity," *NovT* 26 (1984): 71. Hock documents the exhausting, subsistence-level toil of most artisans and tradespeople, as well as the social hostility and contempt they typically endured (34–37), pointing out that several of the hardships Paul lists (e.g., hunger, thirst, cold, nakedness, and fatigue) "were largely due to his life as an artisan" (36; cf. 60).

45. Beaudean, *Paul's Theology of Preaching*, 120–21.

power, affluence, personal honor, and social advancement remain in play. There is always the temptation for Christian leaders to associate with social elites and power brokers, as much in smaller churches as in larger ones. Much hand-wringing among mainline North American churches has been occasioned by a precipitous decline in public respect and social influence throughout the latter half of the twentieth century. Christians are keenly aware that they are now only one special-interest group among many, and long for the restoration of their former (social) "glory." Paul's admonition to the Philippians is as relevant today as in its original setting:

> Do nothing from selfish ambition or conceit, but in humility regard others as better than [i.e., socially superior to] yourselves. Let each of you look not to your own interests, but to the interests of others.
>
> Philippians 2:3–4

In Paul's view, a lived example of personal humility with the renunciation of "power politics" is as integral to the apostolic message of the cross as its verbal proclamation, for the simple reason that Jesus's own life, ministry, and death follow the same pattern.

Yet for all this, Paul is no wimp, and knows how to crack the whip when necessary (2 Cor. 13:2–4 provides one instance). Nor should his example be taken to imply that pastors and preachers are powerless before their congregations. Paul certainly is not. Nonetheless, there is a difference between the widely popular notion of "servant leadership" and what Paul proposes, and that not only because of the vast differences that separate our respective cultural domains. "Servants" to a large extent retain their personal freedoms, rights, and privileges. Within the Christian community, willingness to serve has come to be seen as noble and virtuous in its own right, subtly reflecting honor on those who conduct themselves in this manner. The notion of "servanthood"—if not actual humility—has a certain cachet. Paul, by contrast, makes the abdication of personal rights and bondage to the spiritual welfare of his congregation an integral feature of the gospel that he preaches. "Jesus Christ as Lord" and "ourselves as your slaves" are parallel and equivalent premises. This is the significance of his often-misunderstood declaration, "I have become all things to all people, that I might by all means save some" (1 Cor. 9:22). It is likewise what he has in mind when he introduces himself to the Roman believers:

I am a debtor [*opheilētēs*] both to Greeks and to barbarians, both to the wise and to the foolish—hence my eagerness to proclaim the gospel [*euangelisasthai*] to you also who are in Rome.

Romans 1:14–15

As if it were not enough to have yielded his own will to the "commission" entrusted to (or imposed on) him by Christ (so 1 Cor. 9:17), he is bound and obligated to the Gentiles by the content of the gospel itself. Christ's love constrains or (according to the RSV) "controls" him (2 Cor. 5:14), obliging him to serve their spiritual needs even as Christ did.

The integration of theological conviction and personal experience that lay at the heart of his recent affliction in Asia Minor continues to inform Paul's discipleship and the ministerial practice to which it gives rise. Paul sees a profound consonance between the cross that he proclaims, the humble manner of its proclamation, and the suffering that he experiences. Just as the paradigm of Jesus's crucifixion enables him to embrace suffering where the congregants reject it, and to see therein a gracious design where they find only degradation or divine malice, so the example of Jesus determines the nature of his relationship even with recalcitrant converts. Whereas for them abasement and exaltation, humiliation and glory, "slavery" and "Lordship" are antithetical and mutually exclusive, Paul seeks to demonstrate that for Jesus's followers, each is inherent in the other:

This explains why Paul can actually preach himself as *doulos hymōn* ["your slave"]. The gospel which he preaches is being worked out in his life. He is being transformed into the likeness of Jesus Christ, a likeness which, as we have seen, comes to expression pre-eminently in self-giving service. Paul's behavior among the Corinthians thus embodies the message he is proclaiming. His "service" is indivisible from his preaching.[46]

To live after the example of Jesus, in conformity to the cross, places the preacher or Christian leader in a position of almost intolerable vulnerability. The danger of what Paul proposes is that it risks subjecting the leader to the whims of a less spiritually mature congregation (although the Corinthians would not have seen things quite this way). Yet at the

46. Savage, *Power Through Weakness*, 153. It is in this sense that Gorman (*Cruciformity*, 30) speaks of Paul exemplifying "a *narrative* spirituality, an experience of re-presenting in living form the word of the cross" (emphasis original).

very least (and however imperfectly he or his congregants may practice them), Paul is perfectly consistent in his theological principles. Just as Jesus subjected himself to the will of others, even at the cost of his life, so Paul offers to do the same. What this meant for Paul vis-à-vis the believers at Corinth is only too clear from his correspondence, as he struggles to answer their questions, defend himself against their recriminations, and compete for the congregation's loyalty with other leaders whose style seems so much more straightforward, sensible, and rewarding. Nonetheless, declaring apostles to be "slaves" is part of Paul's larger program of redemptive vulnerability, whereby he knows himself to be in a humanly impossible situation, and for that reason to be also in the hands of a redeeming God. The risk is enormous, yet from all appearances it is one that Paul accepted throughout his ministry, even to the point (assuming the tradition to be accurate) of eventually being martyred for his faith. For one who sought to imitate Christ in all things, it proved a fitting end. Preachers might justifiably be reluctant to follow Paul too literally in this regard, but some at least will perceive an uncomfortable analogy to their own situations.

For Jesus's Sake

The key to the entire principle enunciated in 2 Corinthians 4:5, without which self-humiliation would remain in equal measures incomprehensible and unjustifiable, is the simple concluding phrase, *dia Iēsoun*: "We do not proclaim ourselves; we proclaim Jesus Christ as Lord and ourselves as your slaves *for Jesus' sake*." This construction appears only twice in the correspondence attributed to Paul: here and in 4:11 ("For while we live, we are always being given up to death *for Jesus' sake*").[47] Granted, the general principle of accounting for adversity by means of Christ's precedent appears elsewhere, as in 1 Corinthians 4:10, "We are fools for the sake of Christ [*dia Christon*]" (so also Phil. 3:7) and 2 Cor. 12:10, "I am content with weaknesses, insults, hardships, persecutions, and calamities for the sake of Christ [*hyper Christou*]." But by now we

---

47. Although the construction *dia* + the accusative (meaning "on account of") is not infrequent in combination with other nouns (e.g., 1 Cor. 7:5; 9:10, 23; 10:25, 27–28; 11:9–10; 2 Cor. 2:10; 3:7; 4:15, etc.), the phrase *dia . . . Iēsoun* appears elsewhere in the New Testament only at John 12:9.

recognize at once the significance of Jesus's name appearing alone: it is Paul's specific shorthand for the frail humanity of the human Savior—the fact that he is subject to suffering and death. Much as the believers' imitation of Jesus and devotional emulation of his cross run counter to historical precedent (the fact that the original disciples abandoned him), so in this instance Paul's summary of Christian homiletics contradicts the historical movement of Jesus's death and resurrection. As we noted earlier, it moves (both grammatically and conceptually) from self-abasement ("not ourselves") to the exaltation of the Risen One ("Jesus Christ as Lord"), then back to self-abasement ("ourselves as your slaves") before concluding with Jesus's human identity ("for Jesus' sake"). Not only do the apostolic message and example seem to participate in abasement alone, but in order to reinforce this emphasis the sentence ends by focusing on Jesus in his human state.

The description of Jesus's ministry set out in Philippians 2:6–11 again provides an apt comparison, for that account begins at the high point of "equality with God," descends into humanity, slavery, and death, then concludes on the upswing with heaven and earth alike declaring that "Jesus Christ is Lord." The Philippians' imitation of Jesus, however, will terminate abruptly at the halfway point, for Paul counsels only:

> Do nothing from selfish ambition or conceit, but *in humility* regard others as better than yourselves. Let each of you look not to your own interests, but to the interests of others. Let the same mind be in you that was in Christ Jesus.
>
> Philippians 2:3–5

That is, they are to imitate only the downward movement of Jesus's humility. Paul says nothing about the possible (e.g., eschatological) relevance of Jesus's exaltation, except that it should lead them to worship. Similarly in 2 Corinthians 4:5, the movement of apostolic imitation is a direct inversion of Jesus's own example, an abbreviated imitation of the Christ. In fact, Paul has from the outset taken care to deny any similarity between the manner of his ministry and the exaltation of Jesus. As we saw in chapter one, Paul suggests an analogy between Christ and Christians, between the Anointed One and the apostolic ministers whom God has in turn anointed (2 Cor. 1:22). He then continues:

175

But I call on God as witness against me: it was to spare you that I did not come again to Corinth. I do not mean to imply that we lord it over [kyrieuomen] your faith; rather, we are workers with you for your joy, because you stand firm in the faith.

2 Corinthians 1:23–24

His logic is straightforward, if implicit. Having already drawn the connection between Christ as "anointed" and the anointing of apostles, Paul does not want his readers to take the further (quite reasonable) step of linking Jesus as *Kyrios*, "Lord," with apostolic domination, "lording it over" (*kyrieuein*) the congregations in their charge. Imitation of Jesus goes only so far, all the more so as proud displays of power are something the Corinthians incorrectly expect of their religious leaders. Or, more precisely, disciples may initiate or acquiesce to abasement in imitation of Jesus, but exaltation and "resurrection" are the prerogatives of God alone.[48]

There is, admittedly, one exception to this rule. In 2 Corinthians 13:1, Paul warns that he will soon visit for the third time, and is prepared if needed to deal firmly with "those who sinned previously and all the others" (2 Cor. 13:2). It would appear that some have voiced doubts about his authority for, he says, "you desire proof that Christ is speaking in me" (13:3a). Paul's response is to assert the similarity between Christ's commanding presence and his own:

He is not *weak* in dealing with you, but is *powerful* in [*or*: among] you.
For he was crucified in *weakness*, but lives by the *power* of God. For we are *weak* in him, but in dealing with you we will live with him by the *power* of God.

2 Corinthians 13:3b–4

The apostles' apparent frailty and puniness—their lack of elegance or eloquence—of which the congregants have been so scornful should not, Paul insists, be mistaken for laxity or lack of spiritual authority. On balance, it would seem that Paul appeals to the power of Christ's resurrection

48. Cf. Mark 10:42–44, where Jesus refutes the example of Gentile rulers who "lord it over [*katakyrieuousin*]" their subjects, insisting instead that "whoever wishes to be first . . . must be slave [*doulos*] of all." Here the context is significant: when the sons of Zebedee demand a share in glory, Jesus asks them whether they are able to share his baptism of suffering.

only when left no other choice, and even then continues to assert that "we are weak in him."

That the idea of emulating Jesus primarily in abasement was not limited to Paul, but likely widespread in the early church, may be seen from 1 Peter, generally held to have been written in the last quarter of the first century:

> Like good stewards of the manifold grace of God, serve one another with whatever gift each of you has received. Whoever speaks must do so as one speaking the very words of God. . . . Beloved, do not be surprised at the fiery ordeal that is taking place among you to test you, as though something strange were happening to you. But rejoice insofar as you are sharing Christ's sufferings, so that you may also be glad and shout for joy when his glory is revealed. If you are reviled for the name of Christ, you are blessed, because the spirit of glory, which is the Spirit of God, is resting on you.
>
> 1 Peter 4:10–14[49]

Although the author addresses his remarks to the church as a whole, he has preachers and teachers specifically in mind ("Whoever speaks . . .") as he shifts his attention to the topic of their common ordeal. For the present, he says, they "are sharing Christ's sufferings"; although "the spirit of glory, which is the Spirit of God" already rests on them, the full revelation of glory—both their own and Christ's—remains a future hope. This passage, which links the ideas of suffering, imitation of Christ, glory, and the Holy Spirit, may itself ultimately depend on Pauline thought as set out in chapters three and four of 2 Corinthians. But whatever the source of these ideas, similarity here, too, between Jesus and his followers is construed primarily in terms of shared tribulation.

Few preachers in North America or Western Europe can legitimately complain of being similarly persecuted or harassed. Yet the words of 1 Peter and the teaching of Paul may nonetheless apply to our situation. Such is our expectation of being able to live "a quiet and peaceable life in all godliness and dignity" (1 Tim. 2:2) that any form of trial or difficulty

---

49. See further J. N. D. Kelly, *A Commentary on the Epistles of Peter and of Jude* (BNTC; London: Adam and Charles Black, 1982), 180–87 (citing 2 Cor. 2:17 and 4:13 for the same use of the verb *lalein*, "to speak," with reference to preaching and teaching, 180).

comes as a shock, and we need to hear with new ears the admonition "do not be surprised at the fiery ordeal that has come on you . . . but rejoice inasmuch as you participate in the sufferings of Christ" (1 Pet. 4:12 TNIV). The point of similarity is not the manner of the affliction, but the manner of its interpretation, and our ability to discern redemptive significance in whatever trials or difficulties ministry may bring.

Perhaps this is mere quibbling, an example of reading more into Paul's *dia Iēsoun* and 2 Corinthians 4:5 as a whole than the text warrants. After all, the sentence immediately following returns to the theme of glorification, with clear eschatological overtones: "For it is the God who said, 'Let light shine out of darkness,' who has shone in our hearts to give the light of the knowledge of the glory of God in the face of Jesus Christ" (2 Cor. 4:6). Yet no sooner has he said this than Paul immediately resumes the theme of apostolic frailty, acknowledging that "we have this treasure in clay jars, so that it may be made clear that this extraordinary power belongs to God and does not come from us" (4:7). This tendency toward emphasizing the humanly weak and negative aspects of Christian experience raises an important question. If, as we have argued, Paul believes that he has experienced a "resurrection" of sorts, indeed that imitation of or participation in Christ's death and resurrection are marks of apostolic ministry, how can he give such weight to abasement in his description of Christian preaching, and leave the bulk of "resurrection" to the future? Paul now turns to address this point.

Earthenware Vessels

Paul's confession that "we have this treasure in earthen vessels" (2 Cor. 4:7a RSV) amounts to a wry acknowledgment of the scorn with which the congregation apparently views him. He may not look like much, he admits, and his oratory may be nothing to write home about (2 Cor. 10:10), but that does not negate the power or value of his message. From the world of Paul's day we find examples of large collections of coins being carried about or stored in clay pots (for example, a hoard of 561 silver coins in three jars was unearthed at Qumran), and the Talmud tells of an emperor's daughter who, being impressed by the learning but repulsed by the ugliness of Rabbi Yehoshua ben Hananiah (fl. ca. AD 90–130), declared, "Glorious wisdom in a repulsive vessel" (*b. Ta'an.* 7a).[50] Although the metaphor may have been proverbial, it aptly captures the contrast between the glorious nature of the apostolic task and the generally unspectacular lives of most of God's servants—even those who do not suffer on the scale of Paul and the earliest apostles.

At the same time, it provides a fitting visual image of the balance between the complementary dynamics of death and resurrection that Paul finds to be at work in his life. As so often, he is able to turn the logic of his detractors on its head. They argue that his many afflictions and unimpressive personal appearance furnish proof that he and his message are far less than they claim to be. Paul agrees, at least where his own image is concerned. But in his mind such weakness, far from invalidating the Christian message, simply indicates "that the transcendent power belongs to God and not to us" (2 Cor. 4:7b RSV). That he is, so to speak "bloodied but unbowed" proves that far from having abandoned him, the God of Jesus sustains him through all of his trials. The catalogue that follows delineates the fine balance between profound suffering and sustaining grace in greater detail. This theological balance is reflected in literary form, as Paul lays out four sets of paired afflictions and consolations. He and his fellow apostles are:

> afflicted in every way, but *not* crushed;
> perplexed, but *not* driven to despair;
> persecuted, but *not* forsaken;
> struck down, but *not* destroyed . . .
>
> 2 Corinthians 4:8–9

First, that they are "afflicted [*thlibomenoi*]" recalls similar phrasing in the opening of the letter:

> Blessed be the God and Father of our Lord Jesus Christ . . . who consoles us in all our affliction [*thlipsei*], so that we may be able to console those who are in any affliction [*thlipsei*] with the consolation with which we ourselves are consoled by God. . . . If we are being afflicted [*thlibometha*], it is for your consolation and salvation . . .
>
> 2 Corinthians 1:3–4, 6

50. Thrall (1:322–23) cites this and similar examples.

More to the point, the language of being "afflicted [*thlibomenoi*] . . . but not crushed; perplexed [*aporoumenoi*], but not driven to despair [*ex-aporoumenoi*]" directly reflects the phrasing of his reported "affliction [*thlipseōs*]" in Asia Minor, because of which he and Timothy earlier "despaired [*exaporēthēnai*] of life itself" (1:8). This outright contradiction seems to reflect a new sense of theological insight and integration. Where once he had indeed been caused to despair, God's unexpected rescue has afforded him new confidence, furnishing grounds for the hope and consolation he now offers his congregants.

It is worth pausing once more to observe that Paul's reasoning, so often cited as authoritative and therefore to be imposed without question on subsequent audiences, testifies to the experiential nature of theological insight. Paul has little doubt either of the authority Christ has given him or of his right to wield it (as he testifies, for instance, in 2 Cor. 10:8 and 13:10). Yet it is an authority granted "for building up and *not* for tearing down," and therefore must allow for the unavoidable reality that different listeners (ancient as well as modern) appropriate new insights at different rates and in different manners. Indeed, if this has been Paul's own experience, as we see him gain deeper understanding of a foundational principle he has already preached at length, how much more does it apply in a more psychologically attuned culture such as our own.

Divine instrumentality is no less to the fore in the remaining two strophes. That apostles are "persecuted, but not forsaken [*enkataleipomenoi*]" echoes the language of the Septuagint in which God frequently promises not to abandon his people (Matera, 109). The early church took much comfort from such assurances. Employing the same verb, Peter in his Pentecost sermon quotes Psalm 16:10 (LXX 15:10) as a prophecy of Jesus's resurrection (Acts 2:27), while Hebrews 13:5 makes divine loyalty and provision the linchpin of a contented Christian lifestyle, citing Deuteronomy 31:6. More starkly, Paul's claim that apostolic preachers are "struck down, but not *destroyed*" uses the same participle [*apollumenoi*] that elsewhere refers to nonbelievers being subject to divine judgment, and therefore as "perishing" (1 Cor. 1:18; 2 Cor. 2:15; 4:3; 2 Thess. 2:10). By implication, therefore, it is not the apostles but those who strike them down who will ultimately find themselves "destroyed."

First Corinthians 4:9–13, which shares many similarities with the present passage, offers a telling comparison to this series of afflictions

180

and consolations. In that instance, Paul's deliberations on the mystery of apostolic weakness had led him to conclude, "When reviled, we bless; when persecuted, we endure; when slandered, we speak kindly" (1 Cor. 4:12–13). Perhaps he would have stood by these statements following his experience in Asia Minor, but it is telling that the second element of each earlier pair ("we bless . . . we endure . . . we speak kindly") focuses on personal agency on the part of those who suffer, whereas in 2 Corinthians 4:8–9 Paul's posttraumatic responses are consistently in the passive voice: "not crushed . . . not driven to despair . . . not forsaken . . . not destroyed." The catalogue in 2 Corinthians 6:8b–10 admits of only slightly greater personal agency:

> We are treated as impostors, and yet are true;
> as unknown, and yet are well known;
> as dying, and see—we are alive;
> as punished, and yet not killed;
> as sorrowful, yet always rejoicing;
> as poor, yet making many rich;
> as having nothing, and yet possessing everything.

In short, as Paul continues to reformulate the delicate balance between affliction and consolation, the lists from 2 Corinthians (1:3–4, 6; 6:8b–10) weigh more toward acknowledging the fragility of the "earthen vessels" and their theological (if not practical) passivity than does the earlier list from 1 Corinthians 4:9–13, in keeping with his posttraumatic insistence that "the transcendent power belongs *to God* and not to us" (2 Cor. 4:7b RSV).

On any reading, Paul's litanies of affliction seem a long way from the lofty and energetic ideal of "victorious Christian living" currently preached from many Protestant pulpits, especially in North America. Paul's claim, by contrast, is astonishingly modest: he says merely that having had the stuffing repeatedly knocked out of him, he is not yet dead (when by rights he should be). He began this letter by affirming that those who suffer share with equal abundance in both the afflictions and the consolation afforded Christ (2 Cor. 1:5). But as Paul enumerates his personal experiences of deliverance, it appears that God has in each instance intervened only enough to save his servant from outright destruction. The God of Paul, it seems, is not quite the God of John

Bunyan, for the apostle finds the grace accorded him to be "sufficient" (2 Cor. 12:9) but hardly "abounding."[51]

More to the point with respect to the conditions of apostolic ministry, Paul avers that such affliction is not merely incidental, an unfortunate accident of circumstance and history. Rather, he says, it is a necessary component of ministry, an essential requirement for the demonstration of divine power. Apostles, he says, are

> always carrying in the body the death of Jesus, *so that* the life of Jesus may also be made visible in our bodies. For while we live, we are always being given up [*paradidometha*] to death for Jesus' sake [*or:* on account of Jesus], *so that* the life of Jesus may be made visible in our mortal flesh.
>
> 2 Corinthians 4:10–11

In both sentences the conjunction (*hina* followed by the subjunctive) is unmistakably causal, indicating that God's constant or repeated deliverance of him to something like Jesus's death (with the passive voice of "being given up to death" implying divine agency) is necessary *in order* for Jesus's resurrection life to be revealed in and through him.[52]

Here Paul pursues the idea of identification with Christ to its bitter theological end. According to the apostle, Jesus was "*handed over*" to suffering and death (Rom. 4:25) by God, "who did not withhold his own Son, but *gave him up* for all of us" (Rom. 8:32), allowing him to be "*betrayed*" (1 Cor. 11:23) by one of his own; indeed, Jesus "*gave himself up*" (Gal. 2:20; Eph. 5:25) for the sake of others.[53] In each case, the key verb (*paradidosthai*) is the same as that with which Paul describes himself being "given up" or "delivered over" to suffering of his own—not as an end in itself, but for the sake of those to whom he ministers. Paul's cruciform theology and cruciform spirituality thus give rise to a specifically cruciform vision of ministry:

51. The English Puritan John Bunyan (1628–88) titled his 1666 spiritual autobiography, *Grace Abounding to the Chief of Sinners*.

52. Hafemann notes in this passage the "tension between the present and the future in Paul's eschatology." Specifically, "because the kingdom is not yet present in its fullness it becomes necessary for [Paul] to continue to carry in his body the 'death of Jesus.' Nevertheless, because the new age has already decisively broken into the present aeon in the resurrection of Christ, it is also possible for Paul's *present* suffering to be at the *same time* a *present* revelation of God's resurrection power" (*Suffering and the Spirit*, 72 [emphasis original]).

53. Cf. Gorman, *Cruciformity*, 313.

Cruciform ministry, Paul claims, makes visible (4:10–11) the life of Jesus—the power of God by the Spirit to bring life (cf. 3:6). These are not two things operating, life *and* death, but rather death *in* life, power *in* weakness (cf. 12:9–10).[54]

Paradoxically, therefore, the "power" or spiritual vitality that makes ministry both possible (from the perspective of those ministering) and effective (from the perspective of its recipients) emerges only out of yielding and being delivered over to the imitation of Jesus's *in*ability, weakness, and death.

There are at least two difficulties here, two issues likely to cause offense. The first is that Paul has no difficulty in seeing God's purpose in suffering. He does not, it is true, argue that God is the immediate cause of his affliction, but implies that God hands him over to the tribulations so generously provided by certain opponents within the congregation and elsewhere. As commentators observe (e.g., Thrall, 1.108, 332), Paul does not consciously seek the suffering that he undergoes, just as we are more likely to pray, "Deliver us *from* evil" (Matt. 6:13) than "Deliver us *into* it." But it is his confidence in God's ability to deliver that allows him to attribute divine causality to suffering as well: "He who rescued us from so deadly a peril will continue to rescue us; on him we have set our hope that he will rescue us again" (2 Cor. 1:10). That the prospect of God leading us into tribulation might prove difficult to preach is self-evident, not least because preachers themselves will find it sobering and severe. Yet if we are indeed to preach after the manner of Paul, then such a message can be proclaimed only from a post-resurrection—which is to say, a post-consolation—point of view, exactly as Paul attempts to do. That is, he interprets his trials retrospectively, having been led all the way through them and beyond (even if additional difficulties likely await him). The consolation he offers others is based on a deep-rooted trust in the God who raised Jesus from death and has rescued him as well. This implies that it is not, in the end, enough for later preachers to insist on the meaningfulness of Christian suffering (their own or that of others) simply on the basis of what *Paul* teaches. Rather, the experiential nature of Paul's theological method suggests that preachers are wise to balance

54. Gorman, *Apostle of the Crucified Lord: A Theological Introduction to Paul and His Letters*, (Grand Rapids: Eerdmans, 2004), 302–3.

the testimony of Paul with what they can state with confidence from their own experience of God's saving power. Or as Ahab once rebuffed an enemy king, "One who puts on his armor should not boast like one who takes it off" (1 Kings 20:11 NIV).

The second difficulty is less theological than personal: as elsewhere in his letters, Paul is willing to be seen as a functioning illustration of spiritual dynamics from which others may properly learn. In both Greco-Roman and Jewish worlds, instruction was as much by example as by words.[55] We, on the other hand, are considerably more reticent, reluctant not only to seem proud or overly confident in bidding others follow our example, but also wary of having our flaws exposed to critical congregational scrutiny. As pointed out earlier, 2 Corinthians provides evidence of the dangers to which such transparency can lead. Again, however, it is precisely his weakness that Paul is willing to expose, so long as it serves to highlight the contrast between his own obvious liabilities and the power of God. Because he believes this to be so, Paul understands himself to be nothing less than an instrument of revelation, a vivid demonstration of God's power manifest in Jesus. This is what he means by intending as the result of his suffering "that the life of Jesus may be made visible [or: revealed] in our mortal flesh" (2 Cor. 4:11). While he does not thereby replace Jesus as the source of God's revelation, he nonetheless serves as a living illustration whereby the meaning of what God has accomplished in Jesus may be presented to the congregation.

At this juncture the scope of Paul's "we" becomes critical, for he applies this model to himself and other apostles in a manner that is not fully shared by his audience. In his earlier letter Paul contrasted the Corinthians' pride in spiritual riches with his own and other apostles' more meager blessings:

> Already you have all you want! Already you have become rich! Quite apart from us you have become kings! Indeed, I wish that you had become kings, so that we might be kings with you! For I think that God has exhibited us apostles as last of all, as though sentenced to death, because we have become a spectacle to the world, to angels and to mortals. We are fools for the sake of Christ, but you are wise in Christ. We are weak, but you are strong. You are held in honor, but we in disrepute. To the present hour we are hungry and thirsty, we are poorly clothed and beaten and homeless . . .
>
> 1 Corinthians 4:8–11

55. See Fee, *First Epistle*, 186n24, on 1 Cor. 4:16, citing W. Michaelis, "*mimeomai*, etc.," *TDNT* 4:659–74.

Such contrasts are ironic to the point of sarcasm.[56] In his first letter, Paul is by no means convinced that the asymmetry between the self-satisfaction of the Corinthian believers and his own sorry state is as it should be. But by the time he writes 2 Corinthians, the sarcasm is clearly absent: "death is at work in us, but life in you" (2 Cor. 4:12). Paul's "we" and "us" apply to the preachers rather than the hearers: how are we to account for this disparity, and does it govern those who seek to preach like Paul?

Perhaps the simplest way of reading this verse is in its most literal sense. Normal life expectancy in the Roman world was between twenty and thirty years.[57] More precisely, "two thirds died by age 31, 80 percent by age 49 . . . [and only] 7.87 percent would be 50 years or older."[58] Assuming that Paul was born around the turn of the era[59] and that 2 Corinthians was written in the early to mid-50s AD would place Paul in a similar age range (that is, in his mid-fifties). He is conscious of his mortality ("death is at work in us") not only because of persecution, but also because he is almost certainly older than most of his congregants, and is nearing the uppermost range of usual life expectancy.[60] Although his age might normally

56. So C. K. Barrett, *The First Epistle to the Corinthians* (BNTC; London: Black, 1971), 110–11.

57. So Jo-Ann Shelton, *As the Romans Did: A Sourcebook in Roman Social History*, 2nd ed. (New York: Oxford University Press, 1998), 90–91; together with the highly technical analysis of life expectancy offered by Bruce Frier, "Roman Life Expectancy: Ulpian's Evidence," *Harvard Studies in Classical Philology* 86 (1982): 213–51; cf. Frier, "Roman Life Expectancy: The Pannonian Evidence," *Phoenix* 37 (1983): 328–44. This amply explains Paul's view that Abraham at 100 is "already as good as dead" (Rom. 4:19). See also the wide-ranging and entertaining analysis of M. I. Finley, "The Elderly in Classical Antiquity," *Greece and Rome* 28 (1981): 156–71.

58. Frier, "Ulpian's Evidence," 247–48.

59. Bornkamm, *Paul*, tr. D. M. G. Stalker (New York: Harper and Row, 1971), 3.

60. In Philemon 9 Paul calls himself an "elderly man [*presbutēs*]," which, according to Philo (*On the Creation of the World*, 105), denotes a man in the penultimate span of his life, between the ages of 50 and 56, or according to Hippocrates (*Aphorisms* 3.30–31) refers to the final stage of life (so Eduard Lohse, *Colossians and Philemon: A Commentary on the Epistles to the Colossians and to Philemon* [Hermeneia; Philadelphia: Fortress, 1982], 199n20); cf. J. B. Lightfoot, *St. Paul's Epistles to the Colossians and to Philemon. A Revised Text with Introductions, Notes and Dissertations* (Peabody, MA: Hendrickson, 1987), 338–39 ("On any showing he must have been verging on sixty at this time and may have been some years older"). Acts 7:58 refers to him as a *neanias* (most translations: "young man") at the time of Stephen's death, indicating an age "[from] about the 24th to the 40th year" (BDAG *s.v.*; cf. LSJ *s.v.*), which, if the

have occasioned more respect than disrespect from his contemporaries, and even though the cult of youth and the "midlife crisis" are modern psychosocial constructs, Paul's advancing years (at least by the standards of his day) invite identification on the part of preachers similarly conscious of their own aging. In this regard the looming prospect of death draws them, like Paul, closer to Jesus and the cross.

Perhaps, then, he is aging and others in the congregation are younger (although we have no direct proof of this). But even if this is so, Paul's main point is theological and, as he has been trying to explain since the beginning of his letter, concerns the nature of apostolic ministry:

> If *we* are being afflicted, it is for *your* consolation and salvation; if *we* are being consoled, it is for *your* consolation, which you experience when you patiently endure the same sufferings that we are also suffering.
>
> 2 Corinthians 1:6

With this, the apostolic imitation of Jesus, in which all preachers share, is complete. Paul grants that his audience may join him in the community of Jesus's suffering. But the role of apostolic leadership is to forge the way in this regard also. If, he says, "death is at work in us, but life in you," the implication is that participation in the death and resurrection of Jesus is not apportioned equally within the body of Christ. If "in the church God has appointed first of all apostles" (1 Cor. 12:28 NIV), then apostles are also first in receiving a greater share of suffering, in order that their teaching (so Paul argues) may bear greater witness to God's power of consolation. Just as Jesus's suffering is neither pointless nor impotent, but intended for the benefit of others, so it is with those who suffer like Paul, in imitation of Christ. So there is no question of preachers or pastors imagining themselves to be more important, powerful, or blessed than their congregants. On the contrary, Paul's view is that leaders may exceed their congregations neither in dignity, nor charisma, nor material blessings, but only in tribulation, and only in the degree to which they are thereby constrained to rely utterly on the resurrecting power of God. It is this experience that gives them voice, informs their theology, and grants their preaching the authenticity of a lived spiritual reality. In such

---

martyrdom of Stephen occurred prior to AD 37–40 (so Furnish, 522), is consistent with the reading proposed above.

circumstances, the preacher's authority is entirely independent of office, institution, or scholastic achievement. The charism of such proclamation does not even reside in the event or activity of proclamation itself, but in the saving divine action to which it testifies.

In support of this premise we may refer once again to the diary of Lilias Trotter, and to her citation of 2 Corinthians 4:12 in particular:

> So with ourselves; instead of a life of conscious power, ours will probably be, if he is going to do any deep work in us or through us, a path of humiliation and emptiness where no flesh may glory in his presence. Instead of the sense of power, there comes only more and more the sense of insufficiency; for in the spiritual [realm], as in the natural, if you want to seek for water, look in the very lowest place you can find . . . nothing to glory in at all except that one, wonderful glory of bearing the life-giving water. "Death worketh in us but life in you," is the message of the watercourses.[61]

The Spirit of Faith

What prevents Paul from giving up? How is it that he has not succumbed to posttraumatic stress, the sheer weight of anxiety, or simple exhaustion? With regard to "disputes without" (2 Cor. 7:5), we have already discussed at length Paul's confidence in divine rescue on the model of the resurrection. But what of "fears within" and the toll they must have taken? Or to pose the question in Paul's terms, on what grounds can he claim that "even though our outer nature is wasting away, our inner nature is being renewed day by day" (2 Cor. 4:16)? Paul's explanation comes several verses prior, in 2 Corinthians 4:13. Having recounted how "death is at work in us," he alertly anticipates his audience's next question: how can he claim not to "lose heart" (4:1, 16)? As with his earlier answer, which appealed to the encouragement of God's mercy, so here he cites the empowering presence of the Holy Spirit:[62]

61. St. John, *Until the Day Breaks: The Life and Work of Lilias Trotter, Pioneer Missionary to Muslim North Africa*, (Bromley, Kent: OM Publishing, 1990), 129.

62. Although Thrall (1:338–39) proposes that *to auto pneuma*, "the same spirit," refers only to a human attitude or outlook (so the identical phrase in 2 Cor. 12:18, although not cited by Thrall), Paul frequently uses this locution with reference to the Holy Spirit (Rom. 8:16; 1 Cor. 12:4, 8, 9, 11), a reading favored also by Paul's indirect allusion in this verse to scriptural inspiration.

Just as we have the same spirit of faith that is in accordance with scripture—
"I believed, and so I spoke"—we also believe, and so we speak.

2 Corinthians 4:13

In all likelihood Paul has in mind the larger context of Psalm 116, even
though, in contrast to the Hebrew original, the Greek translation from
which he quotes (i.e., LXX Ps. 115:1; cf. MT Ps. 116:10) divides the work
into two separate compositions. Psalm 116 describes the mortal peril of
a righteous believer—"The snares of death encompassed me; the pangs
of Sheol laid hold on me" (Ps. 116:3)—and God's gracious deliverance
of him:

> For you have delivered my soul from death,
> my eyes from tears, my feet from stumbling.
> I walk before the LORD in the land of the living.

Psalm 116:8–9

Paul would have been familiar with this psalm as one of a series (Pss.
113–118) known as the "Egyptian Hallel" and cited at major festivals,
especially Passover, where they formed an integral part of the public liturgy
during the slaying of the sacrificial lambs (*m. Pesah.* 5:7). Paul identifies
both with the suffering of the psalmist and with his rescue, which allows
him to claim that the two of them "share a common faith in the God
who raises the dead" (Matera, 112). According to the Septuagint, the
psalmist writes, "I believed, therefore I spoke, having been exceedingly
humbled." In other words, such is his faith that great affliction ultimately
leads to proclamation rather than silence. Paul attributes such fortitude
and conviction to the Holy Spirit, the same "spirit of faith" who sustains
him also amid his own trials.

It is certainly the case that pastors and preachers sometimes "burn out"
due to the pressures and demands of ministry, even as it is true that some
would attribute such an outcome to lack of faith or an insufficient experience of the Holy Spirit. But such a conclusion cannot be drawn from the
present passage, if only because Paul has earlier counted himself among
the faithless and the failing, and would hardly accept such criticism of his
own ministry. He can account for failure easily enough, since its causes
are constantly before him and within. But it is the surprise of having survived that leads him to seek an explanation in the working of God's Holy

Spirit. This is simply an extension of attributing to divine intervention his survival of external adversity. Internally, the same is true, as God's Spirit sustains his hope that ultimately "the one who raised the Lord Jesus will raise us also with Jesus, and will bring us with you into His presence" (2 Cor. 4:14). Similarly in Philippians 4:7, Paul speaks with gentle humor of forbearance amid suffering made possible by "the peace of God, which surpasses all understanding [or: thought]." This is doxology, to be sure, but it is also a wry admission that being at peace in the face of affliction, and the ability to maintain such an outlook, is humanly inexplicable. It escapes understanding as much as it surpasses it.

In the fourth chapter of 2 Corinthians, Paul's reasons for preaching seem almost prosaic. Because he has been delivered from his enemies, and has not given in (this time, at any rate) to anxiety or despair, he concludes that the Spirit of God is at work in him, sustaining his ministry. Or at least this is one of several experiential elements that contribute to a multidimensional faith. Reading the Psalms devotionally, he finds affirmation for this aspect of his discipleship, since looking to God for deliverance from affliction is the essential pattern of faith for people of the first Jewish covenant as much as for those who look to Jesus. His preaching, then, like faith itself, claims the same origins and foundation as scripture, which is the inspiration of the Holy Spirit. That the verdict of the apostolic church has been to accept Paul's writings as canonical—something that cannot be said for last Sunday's sermon—should not prevent other preachers from making a similar claim. Despite its later inclusion in the Christian canon, Paul is by no means asserting scriptural authority for his own work. He is simply affirming that God works through the Spirit to deliver and sustain, to inspire faith and empower faithful proclamation. That much surely continues to be true for subsequent preachers, the spiritual efficacy of whose ministries likewise depends on the power of the resurrection.

It is one thing to see oneself as a servant—or slave—of God, and another thing entirely to be enslaved to the unrelenting demands and frequently unrealistic expectations of a local congregation. For Paul, however, the one not only explains the other, but also makes it possible. Just as Paul is in the first instance the slave of *Jesus*-as-Lord, so only the primary Lordship of Jesus makes it possible to serve the Corinthians—even to be enslaved to them. So it is possible to follow Paul's example with regard to one's own congregation only to the degree that we have first followed him with regard to his Lord. The fate of slaves, we recall, was frequently crucifixion—and not a few preachers might imagine enslavement to their congregation having a similar outcome! The critical paradox, however, is that while slavery to the Lord Jesus requires that we join him at the cross, it also promises that we will be raised and reign with him in glory. And Paul's experience in Asia Minor has clearly shown that such vindication begins even now—not only for him, but for those who share in trials like his.

Paul may be an old man, his ministry is highly controversial, and sometimes not even his own converts can figure him out. Were he alive today, no one in his or her right mind would allow him on television, much less make him a poster boy for the victorious Christian life. But for all his oddity, he can do the one thing his competitors seem incapable of, which is to set forth the real Jesus with power and clarity, and to lead those who will heed him into the presence of the one true Lord. In many respects, he is the very antithesis of how we tend to view ministry, and the ministry of preaching in particular. Yet the challenge he presents is straightforward: the more we seek to avoid Jesus's cross, with the humiliation and lack of self-reliance it implies, the less we will know the grace, empowerment, and divine affirmation that are the gifts of his resurrection. Paul's next move is to explain how these seemingly contradictory aspects of the Christian life are both essential to the preacher's task.

5

Glory and Hope
(4:16–5:15)

As Christians, we find ourselves caught between two worlds: between the apparently contrasting realities of flesh and spirit, sacred and secular, heaven and earth, time and eternity, now and not yet. In the history of Christian spirituality, the pendulum has swung back and forth between these extremes; as we struggle to live faithfully in a fallen world, we never quite seem to get the balance right. Yet this is what Paul seeks to do in this letter to Corinth. His explanation draws on a wide range of models and metaphors: architecture, body image, citizenship, clothing, creation, even his own profession of tent making. He then goes on to describe his personal motivation for preaching in terms of love and fear of God, and of appearing crazy while hanging on to hope. In the end, however, Paul is less concerned with metaphysics or psychology than with moral and theological responsibility. For he knows that at the very end, Christ will be the one to judge him and his ministry. Both for him and for us, therefore, the resolution and integration of these confusing opposites lies in the recognition—so obvious yet so difficult to grasp—that they are brought together in the person of Jesus, whose life our lives reflect.

So we do not lose heart. Even though our outer nature is wasting away, our inner nature is being renewed day by day. For this slight momentary affliction is preparing us for an eternal weight of glory beyond all measure, because we look not at what can be seen but at what cannot be seen; for what can be seen is temporary, but what cannot be seen is eternal.

2 Corinthians 4:16–18

As far as we know (and we have only Luke's account to go by), Paul's experience of Christians and Christianity begins with persecution and the murder of Stephen. For it is with this tragic episode that the author of Acts introduces the future apostle: those who formally witness the first martyrdom following Jesus's own death lay their garments "at the feet of a young man named Saul. . . . And Saul approved of their killing him" (Acts 7:58; 8:1). Saul, the narrator continues, is responsible for imprisoning believers (Acts 8:3) and for threatening, if not actually carrying out, further murders (9:1; cf. 22:4; 26:10–11). Paul admits as much: "You have heard of my previous way of life in Judaism," he tells the Judaizers of Galatia, "How intensely [*kath hyperbolēn*] I persecuted the church of God and tried to destroy it" (Gal. 1:13 NIV). It is this shameful history, he confesses, that makes him unworthy of the name "apostle": "I am the least of the apostles, unfit to be called an apostle, because I persecuted the church of God" (1 Cor. 15:9).

On the basis of this experience, Paul would have entered into Christian discipleship and ministry in the full knowledge that martyrdom was a real possibility at any juncture. The intense persecution he encountered only matched the intense persecution he had once meted out himself (as the recurrent *kath hyperbolēn* implies). Tradition holds that he was executed in Rome, beheaded on the Ostian Way at the command of the Emperor Nero.[1] And although we have no contemporary record of his death, Paul writes from prison that he is ready to meet the martyrdom that awaits him (Phil. 2:17).

Advancing age and physical affliction, together with the constant threat of violent death, all interpreted through the lens of Jesus's actual encounter with it, have a profound effect on Paul's vision of the spiritual life in general and of ministry in particular. His own tenuous grasp on earthly life accords well with the inherently apocalyptic and eschatological tendencies of early Christian tradition, which anticipates the Lord's imminent return (1 Thess. 1:10; 4:16–5:5, etc.). Nonetheless, he insists once more,

---

1. See the brief discussion in Bornkamm, *Paul*, tr. D. M. G. Stalker (New York: Harper and Row, 1971), 105.

"we do not lose heart" in the face of such adversity (2 Cor. 4:16). In fact, Paul's language suggests that the threat of death is not his main concern: 2 Corinthians 4:16 explicitly echoes the earlier phrasing of 4:1 with its reference to ministry ("since it is by God's mercy that we are *engaged in this ministry*, we do not lose heart"). According to Furnish, this "makes it certain that Paul is not referring to boldness in facing death, but to boldness in preaching the gospel despite all manner of afflictions and despite the way some have falsely interpreted [them]" (Furnish, 288).

The ongoing reality of religious persecution thus provides the backdrop as Paul resumes his apostolic apologia. Maintaining his focus on ministry amid affliction and weakness (rather than treating the latter as problems of their own), Paul sets out a series of contrasts that juxtapose in turn the human interior with its exterior, the mundane (and visible) with the transcendent (and invisible), and the temporal (or temporary) with that which is eternal. Although the three pairs of opposing realms are closely interlinked, we will discuss each set separately, since each offers distinctive insights for homiletic practice.[2]

Because of our concern for preaching, the perspective from which we interpret Paul's argument here is especially important. Western culture, as we have repeatedly observed, favors personal appearance and material acquisition as primary determinants of human identity. The Western church, on the other hand, has a long legacy of material or cosmological dualism, according to which an emphasis on "spirituality" implies the denigration of material existence, the human body in particular.[3] On such a view, a truly "spiritual" life comes at the expense of the "flesh," with all of its carnal appetites. These contrasting positions are stated here in extreme form, and exceptions can be found on both sides. But what both have in common is the tendency to distinguish strongly between "material" and "spiritual," to separate the physical from the metaphysical realm. Paul, by contrast, manages a careful balance of the two, again indicating the way forward as to the manner and content of our own Christian proclamation.

2. It is well to note at the outset, however, that 2 Cor. 5:1–10 has been more intensely studied and debated than any other passage in this letter, yet without any clear consensus so far arising as to its proper interpretation.

3. For a brief and helpful introduction to various kinds of dualism, especially as they apply to the interpretation of Paul, see N. T. Wright, *Jesus and the Victory of God*, vol. 1, *Christian Origins and the Question of God* (Minneapolis: Fortress, 1996), 252–56.

Interior and Exterior; Internal and External

Paul's first set of "opposites" poses a problem for those Corinthians who expect transformation of the human interior (whether construed as "heart," "mind," "soul," or "spirit") to be accompanied by measurable external change. Unlike certain congregants and their super-apostles, who believe that social prominence and personal grandeur are marks of spiritual superiority (cf. 5:12), Paul insists that (at least in terms of physical circumstances) the relationship between inner renewal and outward change is inverse rather than commensurate. "Even though our outer nature is wasting away," he contends, "our inner nature is being renewed day by day" (2 Cor. 4:16). Paul proceeds from the uncomfortable fact of his own mortality and weakness, arguing that his unimpressive personal deportment does not indicate proportionate spiritual poverty within. Since persecution is not a condition over which he has any control, he is not advocating masochism or even asceticism, but simply declaring the benefits of spiritual consolation amid difficult circumstances. He does not maintain either that spiritual regeneration necessitates poverty and weakness, or (at least in the present passage) that battering one's body is good for the soul (but cf. 1 Cor. 9:27). Rather, he simply wants to argue that being continually "given up to death" (2 Cor. 4:11) should not be taken to mean that he is also dying on the inside. To the extent that they may be countered by spiritual renewal, material loss and physical affliction suffered for the sake of Christ, he says, are signals not of the end of human existence, but of an "eternal weight of glory" (4:17) yet to come.

Although his main emphasis is on continuing to explain his own ministry, Paul's plural may here extend to include the addressees, if only because he goes on to reiterate that a glorious eschatological future is the promised heritage of all believers. Keeping this in mind, three questions arise: first, what does Paul intend by the contrast between the "outer nature" and the "inner nature"; second, to what does "wasting away" refer; and third, what does it mean to be "renewed day by day"? The first of these finds a ready answer in Romans 7:22–23 and 2 Corinthians 7:5. In Romans 7, speaking not only for himself but of the human condition in general, Paul explains:

> I delight in the law of God in my inmost self, but I see in my members another law at war with the law of my mind, making me captive to the law of sin that dwells in my members.
>
> Romans 7:22–23

On the one hand there is his "inmost self" and "mind," which serve as "a slave to [*douleuein*] the law of God" (Rom. 7:25); against these are ranged the "members" of his "body of death," the "flesh" that is "a slave to the law of sin" (Rom. 7:24–25). Here Paul is primarily concerned with the issue of obedience to God, yet even beyond this specific concern he thinks of the "inner" self or "mind" as the aspect of human identity that is initially subject to transformation and renewal (so Rom. 12:2; Col. 3:10), and which is the particular object of the ministrations of the Holy Spirit (Eph. 3:16).[4] Conversely, the "outer" person is all that the "inner" is not: perishable, liable to affliction and decay, the domain of conflict and physical strife (2 Cor. 7:5). It is, as we have seen so often, part of the human identity that Jesus shared, with which suffering believers can identify in turn. Indeed, the fact that the sufferings of the *embodied* life provide the point of contact and identification with Jesus prevents us from dismissing the "flesh" as somehow unimportant (as Paul will emphasize again in his treatment of "nakedness" and embodiment [5:1–5], as well as by his insistence that Christ will judge what we have done "in the body" [5:10]).

Nonetheless, what is "wasting away" is the "clay jar" that hides the treasure of new life within itself (2 Cor. 4:7), the "mortal flesh" in (and not despite) which the life of Jesus becomes visible (4:11). Yet Paul's outlook is one of confidence and hope: "our inner nature is being renewed day by day" (2 Cor. 4:16). As in 1:4 and 6 ("being consoled"), 2:15 ("being saved"), 3:18 ("being transformed"), and 4:11 ("being given up"), so the language of 4:16 ("being renewed") conveys the sense that such inner renewal is accomplished by God rather than its recipient, and is a process rather than a single event (as also in Eph. 4:23–24 and Col. 3:10). Similarly, just as earlier Paul spoke of transformation by degrees "from one degree of glory to another" (3:18) so here the renewal of the believer proceeds "day by day" (4:16). Again, Paul is careful not to claim too much, for, as he will go on to argue in a moment, complete change takes place only at the Lord's return, and not before (cf. Phil. 3:20–21).

It might occur to a modern observer that Paul's lack of consonance (the disparity between physical circumstances and psychic well-being) is a consequence of the repeated psychological trauma and physical suffering that he chronicles, a defense mechanism and coping strategy that he

4. "The inner person is the unseen reality of the embodied person that has the possibility of being renewed" (Matera, 115).

recommends to sufferers like himself. And it might be no more than this were it not for the direct agency of the Holy Spirit to sustain him. Paul's challenge, as much to later readers as to his initial audience, is for our sense of spiritual well-being to be based on something other than physical circumstances alone. His example suggests that the key to maintaining such an outlook is attentiveness to the work of God within oneself (so also Phil. 2:13), to which Paul now directs our attention. It is, no doubt, a difficult ethic to implement at the best of times, requiring concentration, inner quiet, and a keen sense of spiritual perception. An abundance of psychological and physical "white noise" in daily life conspires to prevent us from having to face this place of renewal, let alone enter into it. To be governed by this orientation to the holy and to commend it to others requires preachers, paradoxically, to acknowledge the reality of personal suffering within themselves and their congregants, whatever form that suffering might take. For only the painful acknowledgment that one is, indeed, "wasting away" will likely be sufficient to sustain the search for alternative sources of life, or to elicit the discipline required for such careful listening. The confident and polished rhetoric of the "super-apostles" and their ilk (however illusory) will otherwise prove far too appealing.

Even so, we immediately recognize the truth of what Paul has to say. In a sermon she titled "Why Me?" Kathy Black reflects on her own physical disability, the result of exposure to toxic waste, to question the all-too-common assumption that Christian discipleship will bring us health, wealth, and happiness. On the contrary, she says,

> Accidents happen . . .
> Illness, disease, and disability happen . . .
> But when something does happen . . . God is there . . .
>   offering us opportunity for healing and transformation
>   at every moment of our lives.[5]

Striking a fine theological balance similar to Paul's acknowledgment that both death and life are at work in him, that he is both "wasting away" and simultaneously "being renewed," so Black insists that while God is not the cause of our suffering, nor does Jesus take away all suffering, yet,

5. Kathy Black, "Why Me?" in Ronald J. Allen, ed., *Patterns of Preaching: A Sermon Sampler* (St. Louis: Chalice, 1998), 196-97. The layout of the quotation follows the original text, which "is printed in the form of an oral manuscript" (191).

God accepts us and is supporting us . . .
nurturing us . . .
  bringing healing into our lives at every moment . . .[6]

Having assured his hearers that he and they are indeed "being renewed" despite appearances to the contrary, Paul must immediately counsel patience. To the extent that apostles "always [*pantote*]" carry with them the death of Jesus, and are "constantly [*aei*]" being given up to it (2 Cor. 4:10–11), "being renewed" is no more instantaneous or final than "death" itself. Both are ongoing and incremental processes. The believer's imitation or appropriation of both Good Friday and Easter Sunday is, for the time being, fragmentary and incomplete. In this respect, the experience of the disciple is quite unlike that of the Master, whose death was "once for all [*ephapax*]" (Rom. 6:10). Although certain models of conversion and/or sacramental initiation may encourage us to think of discipleship in similarly accelerated terms, "the daily renewal of Christian existence . . . is not guaranteed by an act of faith, or by baptism, in the past, but continues only in virtue of continual contact with the Lord" (Barrett, 147). Whether, then, by virtue of suffering and affliction, or as an expression of their longing for a fuller encounter with the life of God, preacher and congregation alike are impelled to draw near and remain close to Jesus as Messiah, Savior, and Lord. The frustration of incomplete spiritual vision and understanding (1 Cor. 13:12) is thus equally the consolation of incomplete death, for only when one has suffered the ultimate effects of mortality will one also experience resurrection in its totality. Until that point, all aspects of one's experience of God are "in part."

To recapitulate: Paul is here defending his ministry, in particular his apostolic proclamation, by explaining the theological vision and devotional orientation that underlie it. While using himself as an example, he is implicitly commending the same outlook to his audience. To preach on this model is to urge one's hearers, as does Paul, "Be imitators of me, as I am of Christ" (1 Cor. 11:1). That is, one preaches on the basis of one's experience of Christ, not in the sense of imposing a spiritual regimen from above, but rather offering (in self-defense if necessary) an explanation of what has proven spiritually sustaining in personal experience, and therefore may be of benefit to others. Paul's preaching points to the

6. Ibid., 198.

possibility of Christ being at work in his hearers, and, by implication, seeks to identify evidence of that reality within them, amid whatever difficulties they currently face. His homiletic method, if we may call it that, consists primarily of conveying a vision of Christ's gracious activity among them. Although it is heavy with theology and has many implications for morality, his message hinges on spirituality.

It is daunting to think that one's main qualification as a pastor or preacher should be the depth of one's spiritual need (which is not, fortunately, quite the same as emotional or psychological need). Yet this is what Paul confesses to be his own qualification. True, he is also certain of having been divinely commissioned, but the claim of commissioning is in itself no proof of personal qualification. Even if it had been, subsequent events have convinced him that the source of his ministerial authority and effectiveness does not lie within him. This being the case, the model he proposes is one of vulnerability and transparency, of confessing that one is (in a number of senses) "wasting away," in continual need of spiritual sustenance, and at the same time constantly "being renewed" by the power of God. Although there is the danger in such an approach of narcissism and excessive introspection (all the more so given the narcissism and excessive introspection of Western culture), Paul seems to escape this trap, managing as every preacher must to maintain a focus on Christ.

Mundane and Transcendent; Visible and Invisible

We noted earlier the discipline of reading circumstances "against the evidence," of giving priority to the "unseen" over that which is "seen." This characteristically Christian and cruciform way of viewing one's physical circumstances takes the resurrection of Jesus as its starting point. Paul is as aware as any more recent skeptic that resurrection is no ordinary event. Even in Corinth—in the church itself!—certain vociferous critics "say there is no resurrection of the dead" (1 Cor. 15:12). Yet his conviction that Christ has indeed been raised is based not on adherence to some general philosophical possibility, but on eyewitness testimony, his own included (1 Cor. 15:3–8, 20). On this basis, and because it represents an acknowledgment of God's life-giving power, he is willing to give credence to something that is outside the bounds of normal human experience. Of course, it helps that he already accepts the existence of a supernatural realm inhabited by God, Satan, and their respective emissaries. He may, indeed, be more open to supernatural irruptions than a modern or even postmodern Westerner, but that would not have lessened the shock of being personally confronted by the resurrected Jesus. This encounter above all has encouraged Paul to prioritize the "unseen" over the "seen," and the reality of the transcendent realm to which Christ now belongs over the physical sphere of normal human activity. This is what it means to "walk by faith, not by sight" (2 Cor. 5:7).

There is, of course, a certain contradiction here: Paul has in fact seen what is normally "unseen," both in the person of the risen Christ and—assuming that he is referring to his own experience—in the course of a mystical vision of "Paradise" and "the third heaven" (2 Cor. 12:2–4). Those to whom he preaches, by contrast, may not have encountered such wonders firsthand. To the extent that this is so they must, as it were, take his word for the resurrection and all that it implies, living out a tension between "seen" and "unseen" that is widely acknowledged in the early church (e.g., John 20:29; 1 Pet. 1:8). Preachers who depend on Paul are in the same situation, especially so since the closing of the Christian canon: all of us must—in some sense—take Paul's word for it. This does not deny that Christ is "in" oneself and one's hearers, and they "in" Christ, or that God's resurrection power is at work in preacher and hearers alike. But there is no mistaking the fact that Paul's experiences of the risen Christ (like those of Jesus's earliest followers and the five hundred eyewitnesses to whom Paul appeals [1 Cor. 15:5–7]) are more direct and intense than is likely to be the case, say, among the members of a small congregation today in rural Saskatchewan or Nebraska. Preachers and congregations thus stand together before the testimony of Paul and other apostolic witnesses: both are confronted with the dual challenge, first, of trusting in a spiritual reality that is at variance with the way the rest of life functions and, second, of having to rely on the testimony of others for whatever aspects of that reality are not otherwise immediately evident or available to them. Thus it is not only the congregation who must trust the preacher, but preacher and congregation alike must decide which literal and metaphorical "voices" from apostolic tradition and contemporary testimony to trust, to question, or to reject. All the more so if we do not share the depth of Paul's experiences, both preacher and congregation can find in him an apt model for proclaiming and living with the tension between "seen" and "unseen."

On April 3, 1968, Martin Luther King, Jr., spoke from the pulpit of Bishop Charles Mason Temple in Memphis, Tennessee, to a gathering of sanitation workers whose labor strike he was there to support. The conclusion of his sermon offers especially poignant (and prescient) testimony to the power and dual focus of Christian vision:

> Well, I don't know what will happen now. We've got some difficult days ahead. But it doesn't matter with me now. Because I've been to the mountaintop. And I don't mind. Like anybody, I would like to live a long life. Longevity has its place. But I'm not concerned about that now. I just want to do God's will. And He's allowed me to go up to the mountain. And I've looked over. And I've seen the promised land. I may not get there with you. But I want you to know tonight, that we, as a people, will get to the promised land. And I'm happy, tonight. I'm not worried about anything. I'm not fearing any man. Mine eyes have seen the glory of the coming of the Lord.[7]

He has seen God's promised land, he declares, yet may not reach it together with his listeners. He longs for redemption in this life: like Moses, he has glimpsed it from afar. His language is intentionally ambiguous, for the "promised land" of which he speaks implies both a new heaven and a new earth. It was the last sermon King ever preached, for he was assassinated the next day. More fully than he could have known at the moment of speaking, King comes to embody in his words, his life, and his looming death the tension between affliction and glory, seen and unseen, temporal and eternal, that we find expressed here in 2 Corinthians.

Paul captures this dichotomy, and the role of the preacher within it, in the metaphor of dual citizenship, of having two homes:

> So we are always confident; even though we know that while we are *at home in the body* we are away from the Lord—for we walk by faith, not by sight. Yes, we do have confidence, and we would rather be away from the body and *at home with the Lord*. So whether we are at home or away, we make it our aim to please him.
>
> 2 Corinthians 5:6–9

7. Martin Luther King, Jr., "I See the Promised Land," in James Melvin Washington, ed., *A Testament of Hope: The Essential Writings of Martin Luther King, Jr.* (San Francisco: Harper & Row, 1986), 286.

His opening phrase, "So we are always confident," picks up the running motif of confidence, boldness, and not "losing heart" from earlier in the letter (3:4, 12; 4:1, 16, etc.), indicating that he is again speaking of apostolic ministry. Although he had earlier made an indignant protest—to the same hearers—"Have I not seen Jesus our Lord?" (1 Cor. 9:1), here he acknowledges that "we are away from the Lord—for we walk by faith, *not* by sight." In this he is no different from any other believer, of his own or a later day, who must also trust the "minority opinion" of personal consolation and survival (i.e., "*not* crushed . . . *not* driven to despair . . . *not* forsaken . . . *not* destroyed") against pressures that not infrequently seem overwhelming. To preach on the model of Paul is to acknowledge with one's hearers that the evidence of Christ's power is, by contrast, *not* overwhelming. That is to say, insofar as the God of Jesus Christ does not compel belief, neither does preaching employ coercion, but is an expression of trust that invites others to similar trust. Indeed, communication of the Christian message can be no more commanding or coercive than was Jesus himself in choosing self-sacrifice over the use of force as the means to inspire faith (cf. Matt. 26:53, 55).

Such social and epistemological humility is implicit in the ambiguity of Paul's "we," for (notwithstanding his interest in apostolic proclamation) the statement "while we are at home in the body we are away from the Lord" (2 Cor. 5:6) applies alike to congregants and preachers, as much to Paul's readers as to Paul himself. If the evidence of Christ's death and resurrection is less than overpowering, and preachers are to rely on grace rather than coercion, the latter provides another example of how Paul and other apostolic preachers illustrate the conditions of discipleship that apply to all Christ's followers. However much he and they may yearn to be elsewhere, so long as they are "in the body," they are "at home" in that state: not, that is, alienated from self and the physical circumstances that God has allotted them. This is a remarkable assertion given both the extent of Paul's suffering and the ambiguity of having to "walk by faith, not by sight." Accordingly, that he immediately adds "we would rather be away from the body and at home with the Lord" (2 Cor. 5:8b) is hardly surprising.

This last statement adds a final and transcendent dimension to Paul's axiom that "we do not proclaim ourselves" (2 Cor. 4:5). If, in addition to the personal, congregational, and political dimensions of this theme, preachers declare that they "would rather be away from the body and at home with the Lord," their "not ourselves" extends to the entire range of physical human existence, and confesses a desire for full communion with the risen Christ. As Paul writes to Philippi:

> For to me to live is Christ, and to die is gain. . . . Yet which I shall choose I cannot tell. I am hard pressed between the two. My desire is to depart and be with Christ, for that is far better.
>
> Philippians 1:21–23 RSV

In that instance, Paul avers that it is his obligation to care for his congregation that keeps him "in the flesh" (Phil. 1:24–26). To the Corinthians, his emphasis is slightly different, for here he makes no distinction between himself and other believers. His inference is that all of Christ's followers long for their mortality to be "swallowed up by life" (2 Cor. 5:4).

As was the case with his earlier discussion of Christ's and Christian "glory," so in the fifth chapter of 2 Corinthians Paul sets before his converts a vision of physical transformation. To this end he employs (and combines) two metaphors: that of an impermanent tent versus a permanent building, and that of nakedness versus being clothed, or re-clothed. The first of these pairs is richly suggestive in light of similar language elsewhere in early Christian tradition, although it is difficult to be sure either that the full range of these associations had developed by the time Paul wrote, or that the congregation would necessarily have appreciated them. What follows must therefore be considered a maximal reading of the text. Paul, we recall, was himself a tent maker, and practiced this trade along with Priscilla and Aquila upon his arrival in Corinth (Acts 18:3; cf. 1 Cor. 4:12a). Perhaps reflecting his program of self-abasement, Paul metaphorically relativizes his own livelihood, implying that God has something better in store than anything Paul has the skill to fashion.

Specifically, Paul's contrast is between bodily existence as a "tent [skēnos]" or temporary dwelling place and "a house not made with hands," a heavenly abode (oikodomē, whether as a metaphor for community or perhaps the resurrection body itself) created for believers by God (2 Cor. 5:1). The distinction between that which is "made with hands [cheiropoiētos]" (that is, of human origin) and "not made with hands [acheiropoiētos]" (furnished by God alone) appears in a number of places throughout the New Testament: at Jesus's trial, in apparent reference to the temple (Mark 14:58); in Stephen's relativizing of the same temple (Acts 7:48–50); in

202

Paul's polemic against idolatry (Acts 17:24); and above all in the letter to the Hebrews, which explains that Christ as high priest has entered not into an earthly tabernacle or tent (*skēnēs*, a different spelling) but into a heavenly sanctuary "not made with hands" (so Heb. 9:11–12, 24; cf. 8:2, 5; also Rev. 15:5). Elsewhere in the Corinthian correspondence (although without the crucial adjectives *cheiropoiētos* and *acheiropoiētos*), Paul reminds the believers that both individually (1 Cor. 6:19) and collectively (1 Cor. 3:16–17; 2 Cor. 6:16) they already constitute a temple in which God dwells. All these passages focus on the dwelling place of God, whereas 2 Corinthians 5:1–4 has in mind God's provision of a dwelling for believers. Nonetheless, the two sets of metaphors are complementary, joined by common vocabulary and their common focus on the fact that God alone provides the sanctuary and meeting place in which divine-human communion will be complete.

What may a preacher make of these complex metaphors? Our contemporary concern for the opposite extremes of materialism and over-spiritualization suggests two possibilities. First, preaching that follows Paul's intended contrast between "seen" and "unseen," between the impermanent "tent" of physical existence and the permanent home prepared by God, firmly resists the reduction of human existence to what is merely physical and marketable. It opposes the absolutizing and commodification of daily life that are so characteristic of materialist culture; it insists, with Paul, that "our citizenship is in heaven" (Phil. 3:20); and it diagnoses our dissatisfaction with economic consumption as a form of spiritual nostalgia, literally, "pain for homecoming." Unafraid to name the true cause of human discontent, preaching calls forth our spiritual longing to return to God. Conversely, to preach that "we would rather be away from the body and at home with the Lord" is to acknowledge that no amount of human effort and ingenuity (of which both homiletics and tentmaking are good examples) can dictate the terms or establish the conditions for intimacy with God. It is not that homiletics and tentmaking are unnecessary or irrelevant, but that both are radically relativized by the ministry of Christ. They are the work of human hands, and as such they are important in their own right. But no such work can substitute for that which comes by the hand—and voice—of God. The distinction is subtle, but critical, since Paul is arguing for the priority of grace. Human actions are important, and we are answerable for them (2 Cor. 5:10); for believers, however, even the most pious of human actions are less determinative than the actions of the human Jesus, to which our own acts merely respond. To preach after the manner of Paul avoids materialism, on the one hand, and excessive otherworldliness, on the other, by insisting that the truest denial of the flesh and the only certain satisfaction of our hunger for God have already been accomplished by the crucifixion and resurrection of Christ, into which we may now enter and rest.

Paul's second contrast, between being "naked" and "clothed" or "reclothed," conveys much the same sentiment. He speaks of longing to be "clothed" anew: not "unclothed" and thereby reduced to nakedness, but "overclothed" with new life (cf. Thrall, 1:381–82). Paul's logic appears less tangled once we recognize that for a Hellenistic audience, the "nakedness" of which he speaks would have seemed desirable. This is because the Greeks also thought of human existence in dualistic terms, esteeming flesh and physicality to be essentially base and ephemeral. Only when these were stripped off might the eternal soul be laid bare, freed to ascend once more to its celestial habitation (cf. Barrett, 153–54). For Paul, by contrast, creation and all that it contains is essentially good, since it too is the handiwork of God. The apostle's longing to be "away from the body" does not at all imply that physical existence is inherently evil. Nor is it as a result of being trapped in flesh that, he says, "we groan and are burdened [*baroumenoi*]" (2 Cor. 5:4 NIV). The "burden" in question is the kind of crushing affliction that he has been trying to account for throughout this letter (so 2 Cor. 1:8 of Asia Minor: *ebarēthēmen*). Rather, he says, a physical existence that is already good will ultimately be overlaid by something better.[8] Indeed, Paul's language implies an ironic comparison: although the burden of current affliction causes him to sigh or groan (2 Cor. 5:2, 4), he and other believers look forward to "an eternal weight [*baros*] of glory beyond all measure" (2 Cor. 4:17).

Particularly in our discussion of 2 Corinthians 3:18 (being transformed into the "image" of Christ), we have already touched on the implications for our sense of personal and corporate identity of the multibillion-dollar fashion, cosmetics, and entertainment industries. Perhaps for a majority

---

8. Some interpreters (see Furnish, 268, 296) see here a more specific reference to the fate of the individual: that Paul does not wish to be found naked (i.e., to die before the return of Christ), but to move directly from natural life to the transformed state of resurrection, "so that what is mortal may be swallowed up by life" (2 Cor. 5:4).

in our society, our physical bodies are a constant source of discontent and anxiety. Nor is this a purely modern concern:

> As is abundantly clear from their art and literature, the ancients attached great importance to ideals of bodily perfection and to outward appearance in general. Both the Greeks and the Romans demonstrated, from their earliest history, an extraordinary awareness of the potential of the body (and various modifications that could be made to it) as a means of marking social, political, religious, and even moral distinctions, aside from the opportunities dress and body decoration represent for self-expression or the pursuit of beauty.[9]

To be sure, Paul is not primarily concerned with the dictates of fashion (although his audience may well be).[10] Nonetheless, his theological anthropology addresses deeper issues of corporeality and human identity that underlie the preoccupation with "body image" among ancients and moderns alike. As such, his teaching is relevant to both extremes of contemporary sensibility (or lack thereof). On the one hand, Paul clearly affirms that physical bodies are among the many things that God has declared "good" in creation. Any Christian asceticism must reckon with this fact. Yet, conversely, believers are freed from the socially dictated obsession with a perfect body (and our despair that the ideal is unattainable)

9. Jeri B. DeBrohun, "Power Dressing in Ancient Greece and Rome," *History Today* 51.2 (2001): 18. Further: "Perfumes and scented ointments were wildly popular in antiquity. . . . While ancient garments did not undergo the swift and often capricious changes in fashion that regularly occur in modern clothing, innovations in material, colour, and decoration were common. . . . Women's hairstyles also changed rapidly in antiquity, especially in Rome. . . . The ancients idealized the beauty of the human body, and in this respect perhaps more than any other their concerns and efforts equal—or even surpass—those of modern men and women . . . it is difficult to imagine a more fashion-conscious society than that of ancient Greece or Rome" (ibid., 23–25). In his encyclopedic *Natural History*, Paul's contemporary Pliny the Elder (AD 23–79) noted that a perfume scented with iris and associated with Corinth (although also produced elsewhere, as at Pompei) had enjoyed long popularity in his day (*Nat. Hist.* 13.2.5).

10. "Given their penchant for self-display it is hardly surprising that the Corinthians placed a premium on personal appearance and impressive speech . . . the literature portrays Corinth as a city of beautiful people" (Savage, *Power Through Weakness: Paul's Understanding of the Christian Ministry in 2 Corinthians* [SNTSMS 86; Cambridge: Cambridge University Press, 1996], 46). In our discussion of 2 Cor. 3:18, we have already noted the political dimensions of personal fashion in Roman society.

by Paul's assurance that our "groaning"and longing will at last be satisfied only when frail flesh is "swallowed up by life" (2 Cor. 5:4).

To say this is not simply a matter of trying to find a contemporary application for each of Paul's theological points. Rather, Paul exemplifies a basic orientation to life—life as defined by the gift of Christ—that characterizes good preaching. For all his personal angularity and occasional inconsistencies, Paul embodies what he tries to proclaim. He models the movement toward integration of believing and being in which all preachers are engaged. Without doubt he believes more than he is able to embody or achieve, but in this too we resemble him, and he us: preachers always declare the vision of human identity as set forth in Christ so that they and their hearers will see the way ahead and together seek the grace to move toward it.

Temporal and Eternal; Transient and Timeless

This third axis of Pauline theology, which is the lived tension between present experience and future hope, has attracted more scholarly attention by far than the personal dynamic of internal versus external identity, or the metaphysical polarity of physical and spiritual existence. This is partly because of the prominence of eschatological themes within Second Temple Judaism, but more particularly because the maturation of the early church is often thought to have been marked by a waning of apocalyptic fervor, as believers came to realize that the Lord would not return as imminently as they had first hoped. The latter concern, however, does not seem to be an issue in 2 Corinthians 5, which envisages believers appearing before Christ rather than Christ appearing to believers.

Strictly speaking, Paul's treatment of temporal issues consists of two separate sets of concerns. His first contrast is between "things that are . . . transient" and "things that are . . . eternal" (2 Cor. 4:18 RSV), while the second involves simple futurity, contrasting the present with all that is yet to come (5:10). The first of these provides a bridge or point of transition from Paul's consideration of physical existence: what he has previously described as fragile "clay jars" (4:7) or an outer nature that is "wasting away" (4:16) he acknowledges here to be merely "temporary" (NRSV, NIV) or "transient" (RSV: *proskaira*, 4:18). Indeed, he now declares, the affliction that believers suffer is itself "momentary" (*parautika*), even "slight" (NRSV) or "easy to bear" (*elaphron*, 4:17, as in Matt. 11:30, "My yoke is easy and my burden is *light*").

We must keep in mind that, however much the conditions he describes apply to believers in general, and however much he has since the opening verses been concerned to delineate the shape of Christian consolation in its broadest sense, these assertions apply in the first instance to those who suffer the most—in this case, to the apostles as a group and to Paul in particular. As such, they are nothing short of astonishing. Elsewhere in contemporary Judaism the notion of present suffering and a future, glorious reward is commonplace. In the roughly contemporary *Fourth Maccabees*,[11] for instance, the mother of seven martyred sons is said to have weighed the "temporary safety [*proskairon sōtērion*]" of her children against "the religion that preserves them for eternal life according to God's promise" (4 Macc. 15:3, 8). Likewise *2 Baruch*, an apocalyptic work reflecting on the first century AD destruction of the Jerusalem temple, says of the righteous, "this world is to them a struggle and an effort with much trouble. And that accordingly which will come, a crown with great glory" (*2 Bar.* 15:8; cf. 48:50). Yet as Furnish (290) rightly points out, Paul here finds consolation neither in the Hellenistic virtue of "reason" or "rationality" that sustained the seven martyrs and their mother, nor in the prospect of a glorious recompense that evidently comforted those who mourned the loss of the sanctuary. His point, in the words of Rom. 8:18, is simply that "the sufferings of this present time are not worth comparing with the glory about to be revealed to us." Of course, he does compare them, only to discover that the very tribulation that had earlier caused him to despair "of life itself," and by which he has been so amply afflicted, perplexed, persecuted, and struck down (2 Cor. 4:8), now appears easy, manageable, even trivial by contrast. That "what cannot be seen is *eternal* [*aiōnia*]" (2 Cor. 4:18) does not in this case refer to the future (since the unseen realm is already present) but rather—as his contrast to transitoriness implies—to permanence or eternal duration. This, then, is a further aspect of divine consolation. Just as God may rescue and console believers amid the particular circumstances of their present affliction,

---

11. Although the question of its date and origin have been the subject of much debate, this work is usually held to have originated some time in the first century CE: see H. Anderson, "4 Maccabees: A New Translation and Introduction," *OTP* 2:533–34.

so suffering as a characteristic of the human condition will not last. By contrast, Paul insists, the "eternal weight of glory beyond all measure" (2 Cor. 4:17) will endure forever, and is available already by means of the believers' communion with Christ.

The very real danger in these words is that they threaten to trivialize human suffering. Whether speaking for himself or others, Paul "makes light" of trauma, raising the possibility that his overwhelming theological convictions have occasioned a measure of psychological denial. Of course, attempting such an analysis would be ethnocentric and anachronistic in the extreme—Paul did not see the world in post-Freudian terms. Yet the critique becomes immediately valid once we attempt to preach from this text. Thus we must keep in mind what Paul has in view: as much as his theological analysis may apply to believers in general, he is speaking in the first instance of what sustains *him* as a preacher. This is a text, and a set of theological principles, for preachers to apply to themselves before they may apply them to anyone else. As such, we must make sense of Paul's argument as a report of his own experience and the convictions to which that experience has given rise: he reports that however deeply he may have suffered, the vision of enduring glory he has glimpsed simply beggars all that preceded it.

First, then, we must say what this text is not. It is not a declaration that human suffering in general is trivial or unimportant, for that is not what Paul says. Neither, for the same reason, can such a text be used to impose a value on the affliction experienced by one's congregants, as if their suffering were somehow negligible. If we are to follow Paul's theological method and not simply seize on his results, we will recognize that his radical reassessment of personal affliction constitutes an invitation for those who aspire to preach like him not just to reevaluate their own adversity, but—as a prior step—to so seek "the Father of mercies and the God of all consolation" (2 Cor. 1:3) as to find in him the divine solace that makes such reappraisal possible. After all, Paul's words are a testimony and invitation to divine grace, not a new legalism that imposes itself on all hearers. Once again, Paul's homiletic method entails an invitation to theological vision and spiritual experience, to a cruciform spirituality that arrives (at least in his case) via the depths of theological ambiguity, physical suffering, and emotional despair at an openness to divine consolation.

Two minor observations tend to confirm this reading. First, having characterized apostolic affliction as "slight" and "momentary" (2 Cor.

208

4:17), Paul nonetheless goes on to say that "here indeed we groan" (5:2) and "sigh with anxiety" (5:4, RSV, both translating the verb *stenazein*, "to groan, sigh, complain"). In other words, he continues to affirm the reality of human suffering (his own included), even while being sustained by a vision of something greater. Far from devaluing or denying affliction, he acknowledges both that it continues, and that it wears down those who suffer it. Second, he says in 4:17 not that "affliction is *preparing us* for an eternal weight of glory beyond all measure" (so NRSV), but that "affliction is preparing *for us* an eternal weight of glory" (RSV; similarly NIV). The subject of the verb, in other words, is not "us" but "affliction" (so Furnish, 290–91). Although Romans 5:3–4 (employing the same verb, *katergazetai*, "to prepare, accomplish, result in") affirms that "suffering *produces* endurance; and endurance, character, etc.," here Paul adopts a less utilitarian perspective. Speaking out of the midst of affliction, he draws back from advocating its potential for spiritual growth. Not even the blessing of his "near-resurrection" experience will make him suggest that suffering is somehow "beneficial." Whatever "preparation" or benefit may ensue is not the fruit of suffering itself; it is the direct handiwork of God, as he goes on to clarify in 2 Corinthians 5:5, again making use of the same verb: "He who has *prepared us* for this very thing [i.e., life] is God." Some readings of Paul depict him as a solitary spiritual hero, bravely facing each new danger and boldly challenging subsequent generations to do the same. The interpretation suggested here is more circumspect: Paul knows his own weakness, and the cautious tone of even his clearest affirmations acknowledges the extent of his dependence on God's grace:

> since it is by God's mercy that we are engaged in this ministry, we do not lose heart. . . . we do not proclaim ourselves . . . we have this treasure in clay jars . . . So we do not lose heart. Even though our outer nature is wasting away . . . we are always confident; even though . . . we are away from the Lord . . .
>
> 2 Corinthians 4:1, 5, 7, 16; 5:6

By the same token, Paul's assessment of the future "eschatological horizon"—the final consummation of the present age and the universal manifestation of Christ's reign—is less triumphalist than is implied, for instance, by Romans 8:18 (quoted earlier). The future is not one, he says, of unqualified glory, but entails moral accountability and judgment as

209

well: "For *all of us* must appear before the judgment seat of Christ, so that each may receive recompense for what has been done in the body, whether good or evil" (2 Cor. 5:10). The personal and ministerial affirmation implied by his recent rescue might have inspired greater confidence in God's approval of him. Yet his outlook here is consistent with what he wrote in a previous letter to the congregation:

> I am not aware of anything against myself, but I am not thereby acquitted. It is the Lord who judges me. Therefore do not pronounce judgment before the time, before the Lord comes, who will bring to light the things now hidden in darkness and will disclose the purposes of the heart. Then each one will receive commendation from God.
>
> 1 Corinthians 4:4–5

First Corinthians envisages judgment at the point of Christ's return, whereas 2 Corinthians has believers answering the summons of a seated Lord; while the earlier letter speaks only of "commendation," the later correspondence anticipates believers receiving either reward or punishment, according to their earthly deeds. This is a sobering prospect, and one that cuts both ways. The congregation once more presumes to judge his ministry, and Paul concurs that he will indeed be judged. But, he reminds them, so will they: "*all of us* must appear before the judgment seat of Christ."

This orientation to the future is a direct response to the enduring problem of theodicy, which is the question of divine justice in an unjust world. Paul's ancestors in faith could more confidently declare, referring to the temporal realm, that "the wicked are snared in the work of their own hands" (Ps. 9:16), and of the righteous, "wealth and riches are in their houses. . . . Their hearts are steady, they will not be afraid" (Ps. 112:3, 8). But the tradition of lament, equally present in Israel's literature and worship, had proven more accurate with regard to the ambiguity of present experience, and Israel's hope of righteous vindication subsequently came to be expressed in the doctrines of resurrection and post-temporal judgment. Paul would certainly have argued on the basis both of Christ's experience and his own that the innocent indeed suffer and that God's justice is difficult to discern within the bounds of the present age. Being equally substantial, present suffering and future hope are each bound to the other in a delicate balance.

Paul's reticence in this regard is instructive for ministries of a later day. For instance, we shrink from preaching "Pie in the sky when you die,"[12] instinctively believing that present piety will bring present reward. Likewise it is difficult—above all for pastors and preachers—to escape the temptation of believing one's sacrifices and piety to be deserving of special (if discrete) divine favor. On the other side of the ledger are the voices proclaiming AIDS, for example, to be a punishment from God, or that other human misfortunes represent divine justice at work. The prospect of immediate divine punishment and present heavenly reward proceed from similar convictions: not simply that God's handiwork can be discerned in daily events, but that such interventions are essentially moral in character. But Paul, suffering as he does, and mindful above all of the human injustice of Jesus's death, is less confident of the moral shape of present experience. He might say that temporal moralizing amounts to seeking evidence of final judgment "before the time," "before the Lord comes" and before his advent brings to light the hidden purposes of the human heart.[13] In the meantime, as Paul sees it, ethical judgment and righteous conduct are primarily human responsibilities, above all of believers and preachers rather than of God. Hence, he maintains, "whether we are at home or away, we make it our aim *to please him*" (2 Cor. 5:9).

The situation of the preacher brings into clear focus how difficult it is to conduct one's daily affairs if true justice is elusive at present and accurate compensation (whether for good or ill) is deferred until the day of judgment. One cannot be certain of the ultimate value of one's actions because they are not yet subject to the full light of divine evaluation. Preaching itself, to the extent that it too is compromised by the mixed motives and imperfect spiritual vision of the preacher, cannot be fully evaluated, and can only be offered in full acknowledgment that (Reformation claims to the contrary notwithstanding) a sermon is never "the word of God" in

12. This memorable phrase is attributed to Swedish-American union organizer Joe Hill (1879–1915), "The Preacher and the Slave," in Geoffrey Grigson, ed., *The Faber Book of Popular Verse* (London: Faber and Faber, 1971), 328.

13. Note, by comparison, how in such widely differing texts as Luke 14:14; Rom. 2:5–10 and 12:19; 2 Thess. 1:6–10; Heb. 10:26–31; and Rev. 22:12, judgment is consistently reserved for the eschaton. The one exception Paul allows (2 Thess. 1:4–5) is that the ability of believers to endure persecution provides evidence of divine vindication, foreshadowing fuller vindication on the day of judgment.

the sense that this is said of scripture.[14] Preaching may echo or be based on scriptural authority, even as it may appeal to the authority of Christ, but it can never equal or replace scripture. Paul makes clear distinctions between pronouncements offered on his own authority and those that appeal to the authority of Christ (1 Cor. 7:10–12). However much it may appeal to the "eternal," preaching belongs to the realm of the "transient" and temporal, and cannot claim more than this for itself.

In the balance between present suffering and future hope, the fact of apostolic tribulation thus de-absolutizes apostolic preaching. If affliction is evidence of temporal injustice, then even faithful proclamation must also be less than the full expression of God's will. God may be present in both, and God's will may be accomplished in both (perhaps in different ways or to different degrees), but both fall short, as it were, of the full glory of the Lord. This recognition is what impels Paul to declare that it is God alone who gives the growth (1 Cor. 3:6–7): not himself, other apostles, or their joint theological heirs, among whom we may count ourselves. In other words, while both participate in the frail and transitory nature of present existence, both are subject to the dynamic of redemption and resurrection, and both look forward to inalterable future glory.

The Fear of the Lord

Paul's explanation of his apostolic ministry has contrasted the respective realms of interior and exterior, visible and invisible, present and future, transient and timeless. While each of these antitheses contributes to his exposition of apostolic proclamation, Paul summarizes the conditions of his preaching in more directly personal terms: "Therefore," he says, "knowing the fear [*phobon*] of the Lord, we try to persuade [*peithomen*] others" (2 Cor. 5:11). Forms of the word *phobos*, "fear," occur frequently enough in New Testament literature (19 times in the gospels and Acts, 15 in the larger Pauline corpus, and 13 in the general epistles), often referring to "holy awe" (e.g., Phil. 2:11). It is also the word that Paul uses to describe his own uncertainty and self-doubt upon

14. According to the Second Helvetic Confession of 1566 (written by Heinrich Bullinger), "The preaching of the word of God *is* the Word of God [Praedicatio verbi Dei est verbum Dei]."

first preaching to the Corinthians (1 Cor. 2:3), as well as the effect that bodily affliction had on him as he prepared to return from Macedonia (2 Cor. 7:5). But only rarely does Paul refer to God as the object of such reverence or "fear." In Romans 3:18, Psalm 36:1 (LXX 35:2) concludes an extended series of quotations to the effect that the absence of the "fear of God" is the ultimate proof of universal human rebellion. Rom. 8:15, on the other hand, just as clearly indicates that believers are freed from such fear, as their relationship before God moves from one of "slavery" to "adoption" as "children of God" and "joint-heirs with Christ." Nonetheless—assuming 2 Corinthians 6:14–7:1 to be authentic—Paul also cites "fear of God" as the believers' motivation for holiness of body and spirit (2 Cor. 7:1).

Even rarer are instances in which Paul names Christ as the object of holy fear: in fact, 2 Corinthians 5:11 is the only such occasion in the undisputed letters (cf. Eph. 5:21). Yet it is unmistakable that this is the one to whom Paul refers in the present instance, a conclusion dictated by the progression from "we are away from *the Lord* . . . at home with *the Lord*" (2 Cor. 5:6, 8) to "we . . . must all appear before the judgment seat *of Christ*" (5:9–10), and back again in 5:11 to "knowing the fear of *the Lord*." The context, in other words, implies more than holy awe or reverence in general. Rather, Paul has in view the prospect of personal judgment by the risen Christ. Preachers and congregants alike will "receive recompense for what has been done in the body, whether good or evil" (5:10).

In what specific sense, then, does "the fear of the Lord" govern his proclamation—or ours? The most obvious meaning would be that Paul expects to be judged on the basis of whether or not he has completed the apostolic commission entrusted to him. As he previously explained to the same congregation, "an obligation is laid on me, and woe to me if I do not proclaim the gospel!" (1 Cor. 9:16). This interpretation of being motivated to preach by "fear of the Lord" envisages ministry in its entirety as an occasion for obedience or disobedience (as in the case of Paul's admonition to Archippus: "See that you complete the task that you have received in the Lord," Col. 4:17). But while obedience in principle is an obvious requirement, it is likely that Paul also has something more specific in mind. His similar protest in Gal. 1:10 provides an indication of this added dimension:

Whom am I trying to convince [*peithō*] now, human beings or God? Am I trying to please human beings? If I were still doing that I should not be a servant [or "slave," *doulos*] of Christ.[15]

Here the *New Jerusalem Bible*, alone among modern translations, makes obvious in English the similarity between Galatians 1:10 and 2 Corinthians 5:11, albeit at the expense of comprehensibility: both texts hinge on the meaning of *peithein*, variously "to persuade, convince, please, or conciliate."[16] Recourse to an alternative (and likely more accurate) translation such as the NRSV seems advisable: "Am I now *seeking* human *approval*, or God's approval?" (Gal. 1:10). In Galatians, seeking to "please" God rather than one's congregants or detractors expresses a relationship of pious obedience between *kyrios* and *doulos*, between Jesus as "Lord" and Paul as his "slave." Here Paul speaks not of obedience in principle, as in the fulfillment of an apostolic mandate, but rather of obedience that must choose between competing claims of allegiance, and submit to the true "Lord."

The relevance of this detail for 2 Corinthians 5:11 is suggested by the fact that having to choose between human approbation and divine is likewise a constant theme throughout the Corinthian correspondence. Paul wishes to contrast his own manner of preaching—his endeavor to please Christ—with the preaching of the "super-apostles" who (as he sees it) concern themselves merely with appearances in an effort to please their immediate audience. Indeed, Paul sounds this very note in the verse immediately following:

> We are not commending ourselves to you again, but giving you an opportunity to boast about us, so that you may be able to answer those who boast in outward appearance and not in the heart.

> 2 Corinthians 5:12

Accordingly, the meaning of his "knowing the fear of the Lord, we try to persuade others" extends beyond general notions of obedience to a divine call, and invokes the more specific issue of the manner in which such ministry is conducted. His intended sense is that "we persuade others,

15. *The New Jerusalem Bible* (Garden City, NY: Doubleday, 1985).
16. On this verse, see BAGD *s.v.*, and on the meaning of Gal. 1:10, Richard N. Longenecker, *Galatians* (WBC 41; Dallas: Word, 1990), 18.

not in order to please them, but in order to serve and please the *Lord* who is also eschatological judge." There is even, perhaps, a degree of irony in Paul's use of the verb *peithein*: the phrase could be read, "knowing the fear of the Lord, we seek to *placate* people." But that is the opposite of his true intent, a sense that applies only to the false apostles who are trying by this very means to usurp Paul's place.

On such a reading, 2 Corinthians 5:11 invokes once more the earlier themes of confidence, adequacy or sufficiency, and self-commendation as opposed to the commendation bestowed by Christ. The apostolic mandate for which Paul will be answerable demands that he neither be ashamed of the gospel, nor that he in any way curtail its counterintuitive message of death and resurrection for fear of offending his hearers. He will be judged, he believes, against the standard of an uncompromising adherence to apostolic "boldness" that refuses to retreat from the "folly" and "weakness" of the cross, evade the "slavery" of apostolic obedience, or resort to self-promotion and rhetorical trickery. Although believers are in one sense set free from "fear" and "the spirit of slavery" (Rom. 8:15), Paul maintains that "fear of the Lord" nonetheless still governs preachers and their message.

If we have read this passage correctly, Paul again declares it essential for there to be complete consonance between the message of the Christian gospel and the manner of its proclamation. Because the cross entails abject humility and utter reliance on God, and the resurrection implies a saving divine intervention beyond the power of human agents to initiate or imitate, so apostolic proclamation conducts itself in the same manner. We gain a more detailed sense of how this might work from Paul's earlier discussion of how others are now building on the foundation he laid:

> For we are God's servants [*sunergoi*; NIV: fellow workers], working together; you are God's field, God's building. According to the grace of God given to me, like a skilled master builder I laid a foundation, and someone else is building on it. Each builder must choose with care how to build on it. For no one can lay any foundation other than the one that has been laid; that foundation is Jesus Christ.
>
> 1 Corinthians 3:9–11

His metaphor is curiously contradictory. On the one hand he is conscious of having worked as "a skilled master builder," yet the church is "*God's* building"—not simply in the sense of belonging to God, but more particularly in that Paul's own ability to "build" is a specific gift of grace (*charis*), and therefore not something for which he can claim credit. He may, like Apollos and others, be a "fellow worker" through whom God works, yet even the foundation he has laid by preaching in Corinth is one that, paradoxically, has been laid already by the work of God in Christ. Reliance on God to accomplish the bulk of apostolic ministry is thus as critical to the metaphor of architecture and building as for the previous metaphor from agriculture: "So neither the one who plants nor the one who waters is anything, but only God who gives the growth" (1 Cor. 3:7).

Reliance on the work of God helps to explain the way in which Paul further develops this metaphor:

> Now if anyone builds on the foundation with gold, silver, precious stones, wood, hay, straw—the work of each builder will become visible, for the Day will disclose it, because it will be revealed with fire, and the fire will test what sort of work each has done.

> 1 Corinthians 3:12–13

The point of contrast, as Fee observes,[17] is between building materials that are permanent and impermanent, respectively: those that are consumed by fire—"wood, hay, straw"—and those that are forged by or relatively impervious to fire—"gold, silver, precious stones." Thus to build on the foundation of Christ that Paul has by grace set down requires materials that, metaphorically, share in the enduring character of the gospel message itself. Paul does not specify what sort of building superstructure (that is, what issues of congregational development) he has in mind.[18] Nonetheless, his imagery recalls the contrast between things "temporary" and "eternal" from 2 Corinthians 4:18. In sum, whether by crediting the bulk of ministerial effectiveness to God (1 Cor. 3:5–9) or by highlighting metaphorical building materials that share in the glory and permanence of the divine

17. Fee, *The First Epistle to the Corinthians* (NICNT; Grand Rapids: Eerdmans, 1987), 140–41.

18. "This could refer to organizational development, elaboration of scriptural and doctrinal understanding, leadership of worship and witness, and/or congregational social service" (William F. Orr and James Arthur Walther, *I Corinthians: A New Translation with Introduction and Commentary* [AB 32; Garden City, NY: Doubleday, 1976], 173).

(1 Cor. 3:12–13), Paul underscores the need for ministerial conduct to share in the character of the gospel itself. Just as, in 1 Corinthians, he declares that the work of congregational leaders will be judged on this basis, so in 2 Corinthians he says that "the fear of the Lord" motivates him to conduct the whole of his ministry in a manner commensurate with the work of Christ.

This is hardly a comforting thought, particularly in light of the more hopeful and much preferable perspective offered by the first letter of John:

> Love has been perfected among us in this: that we may have boldness on the day of judgment, because as he is, so are we in this world. There is no fear [*phobos*] in love, but perfect love casts out fear; for fear has to do with punishment, and whoever fears has not reached perfection in love.
>
> 1 John 4:17–18

Whether Paul and the Johannine writer can be reconciled on this issue need not concern us here. Yet however we resolve the issue, preachers cannot afford to affirm one at the expense of the other. Whether or not Paul has "reached perfection in love," he insists that apostolic preachers must expect to be judged on the basis of the message they proclaim. Much as it may seem confusing, or even contrary to social expectation, the life and ministry of the preacher is to be an expression and embodiment of the cross and resurrection.

Divine Madness and the Love of Christ

The Corinthians, it seems, think Paul "crazy." The accusation is not infrequent; according to Luke, this was Festus's opinion of him (Acts 26:24–25, *mainomai*), and Paul himself suggests that the Corinthians may be subject to a similar charge if outsiders behold them speaking in tongues (1 Cor. 14:23, *mainesthe*).[19] Festus and the Corinthians apparently concur on this issue, as Paul concedes: "If we are out of our mind

---

19. Thomas Gillespie (*The First Theologians: A Study in Early Christian Prophecy* [Grand Rapids: Eerdmans, 1994], 157) points out that the verb *mainesthai* is a technical term for divine inspiration or ecstatic possession, and not simple "madness." But this need not obviate the sense of irrationality (so Luke Timothy Johnson, quoted in ibid., n127).

[*exestēmen*], it is for the sake of God; if we are in our right mind, it is for you" (2 Cor 5:13, NIV).[20] It is by no means impossible that Paul knows the tradition that Jesus's own family accused him of insane behavior (Mark 3:21, *exestē*; John 10:20, *mainetai*). If so, this is one more respect in which he resembles Christ, although it is the sole instance in which Paul uses such language of himself.

Particularly in cultures with a strong sense of behavioral norms and boundaries, "craziness" is largely a social construct; it may be defined differently and carry different consequences in differing social contexts. Just as certain opponents accused Jesus of being a Samaritan and having a demon (John 8:48), the charge against Paul is intended as slander, as a shaming device that conveys a sense of radical social discontinuity; that is, he offends the norms of acceptable social conduct. What seems remarkable is that (once again) rather than denying the accusation, Paul concedes it. As he has argued all along, the nature of the gospel is such that it causes its adherents to conduct themselves in a way that many find incomprehensible and socially offensive. His only defense is that he acts in this way on account of God, while anything they do not find offensive they may take as being done out of concern for the congregation's well-being.

As a more recent parallel, we may cite the conduct of Hudson Taylor, who earned the scathing contempt of his English compatriots by adopting Chinese dress, Chinese customs, even a Chinese tonsure as part of his attempt to spread the Christian gospel.[21] By the standards of the British Empire, Taylor had lowered himself and brought shame on his own people:

> To [those] who believed that the white man's dignity rested in strict adherence to British dress and British habits, his action was deeply shocking. He had gone native. He had lost face. He had broken the magic ring of white solidarity. The word *traitor* was not too harsh to describe him.[22]

20. Similarly, it is by no means accidental that this is the only congregation to whom Paul characterizes himself as "foolish [*aphrona*]" (2 Cor. 11:16), or among "fools [*aphronōn*]" (2 Cor. 11:19), or "foolish [*aphrōn*]" (2 Cor. 12:6, 11); cf. "foolishness [*aphrosunēs*]" (2 Cor. 11:1) or "as a fool [*aphrosunē*]" (2 Cor. 11:17, 21).

21. See, e.g., A. J. Broomhall, *Hudson Taylor and China's Open Century*. Book Two: *Over the Treaty Wall* (Littleton, CO: Overseas Missionary Fellowship, 1985), 279–80, 285–86, 293–94.

22. George Woodcock, *The British in the Far East* (London: Weidenfeld and Nicolson, 1969), 99, quoted in Broomhall, *Hudson Taylor*, 293 (emphasis original).

Ironically, by conforming in certain respects to the social customs and expectations of his "foreign" audience he had transgressed those of his own, nominally Christian nation. We recall from our earlier discussion that Paul too wishes to be "all things to all people," yet there is also much that he rejects. As in the case of Hudson Taylor, the desire to be conformed to the pattern of Christ, to act in a manner that is consistent with the proclamation of the cross and resurrection, risks earning the incomprehension and condemnation of those whose sense of cultural propriety (that is, moral, social, or ethnic superiority) is thereby offended. How this works itself out in various situations will differ according to the setting. In one, union members may be offended by the preacher's charity toward management; in another, those holding strong views concerning the Lord's Table may find it difficult to countenance admission of newcomers from another denomination; or members of a socially disadvantaged group may find themselves less welcome in the congregation than the pastor wishes them to be. Alternatively, it may be the preacher who balks at closer imitation of Christ, as the conduct of certain congregants contravenes accepted social norms. Both may have difficulty discerning the proper contours of Christlikeness, distinguishing what is consonant with the message of the cross from what is contrary to it.

The rule that Paul invokes to bring clarity to the social chaos of his own and every preacher's situation is stunning in its simplicity:

> For Christ's love compels us, because we are convinced that one died for all, and therefore all died. And he died for all, that those who live should no longer live for themselves but for him who died for them and was raised again.
>
> 2 Corinthians 5:14–15 NIV

The Corinthians are no strangers to the topic of Christian love, since it was to them that Paul addressed perhaps the most famous passage on the subject in religious literature of the classical period (1 Cor. 13:1–13). There, as elsewhere in his letters, Paul emphasized the paramount virtue of love as a hallmark of Christian identity and the most perfect and enduring of all charisms bestowed by God's Spirit. Yet, from a theological point of view, that passage is inexplicable apart from this one in 2 Corinthians.

Its meaning hinges on our interpretation of "Christ's love" and of how such love exercises compulsion or constraint. References to "the love of

Christ [*ho agapē tou Christou*]" (so Rom. 8:35; Eph. 3:19; cf. Gal. 2:20; Eph. 5:2, 25) are less frequent in Paul than references to *God's* love for humanity (Rom. 5:5, 8; 8:39; 2 Cor. 13:13; Eph. 2:4; 1 Thess. 1:4; 2 Thess. 2:16; 3:5; cf. 2 Cor. 13:11).[23] Nonetheless, the two are inseparable and their meaning unmistakable, as the apostle explains in his letter to the Romans: "God proves his love for us in that while we still were sinners Christ died for us" (Rom. 5:8); "I am convinced that [nothing] in all creation, will be able to separate us from the love of God in Christ Jesus our Lord" (Rom. 8:38–39). Thus while the believers' love of God and one another are indispensable for the life of faith (so 1 Cor. 16:14, "Let all that you do be done in love"), both reflect and derive from the love that God has shown them in Christ. So in declaring that "the love of Christ urges us on" (2 Cor. 5:14 NRSV), Paul does not claim that his ministry is guided or constrained by his own love of Christ, but rather that he proclaims the message of the cross and resurrection by virtue of Christ's love for him, as demonstrated by these pivotal events.

Less obvious, however, is the meaning of *synechein*, a verb with a broad range of meanings that interpreters variously translate as "to urge" or "impel" (so Vulgate, NRSV, NAB), "to direct, control" (RSV; Barrett, 167–68; Matera, 133; Thrall, 1:408–409; cf. NEB, "leaves us no choice"), or else "overwhelm" (JB), "lay claim to" (Furnish, 309), or even "possess."[24] Of particular interest is the fact that in common usage, for which we have evidence from contemporary papyri, the verb conveys a sense of obligation, and became "the usual word for stating the executory force of a judicial decision."[25] Along the same lines, Furnish points out that the ensuing verb *krinantas* ("for we *are convinced*" [NRSV]) likewise has "a juridical connotation," and means to come to a firm decision or final conviction about an issue. Perhaps such language reflects Paul's conviction that, in Christ, God has already pronounced judgment on the world—and that it is a judgment of love. In any

23. "Love" is also the domain of the Holy Spirit: Rom. 5:5; 15:30; Gal. 5:22. For a comprehensive survey of the topic, see William Klassen, "Love (NT and Early Jewish)," *ABD* 4:381–96, esp. 392–93.

24. Jean Héring, *La Seconde épître de Saint Paul aux Corinthiens* (CNT 8; Neuchâtel: Delachaux & Niestlé, 1958), 50–51 ("l'amour pour Christ nous *possède*").

25. Ceslas Spicq, *Agape in the New Testament*, tr. M. A. McNamara and M. H. Richter (London: Herder, 1965), 2:193; quoted in Furnish, 309. According to Spicq, "by using the verb *synechō*, [Paul] suggests the almost irresistible force of the charity of the crucified Christ" (ibid., 193–94).

event, we may paraphrase Paul as saying that Christ's love, summarized in the universal Christian conviction that "one has died for all," sets clear boundaries for the preacher's task. The theological dictates of cross and resurrection establish the conditions of the preaching life and constrain the preacher into conformity with its strangely loving decree. Thus it is *God's* love (rather than Paul's), exemplified and enacted by Christ, that provides the standard against which the apostle's "madness" must be judged.

There is a strong element of determinism in this assertion. However we translate the verb *synechein*, it conveys a clear sense of constraint and direction entirely in keeping with the metaphor of religious "slavery" that lies just beneath the surface of the discussion as a whole. Whether or to what degree Paul has willingly yielded himself to divine obligation is not the point. Nor does he seem overly troubled by loss of personal freedom or self-determination. For, he insists, it is *love* that compels him so strongly. On the face of it, such divine determinism appears to contradict his earlier argument that "where the Spirit of the Lord is, there is freedom" (2 Cor. 3:17), although in that instance (to use Margaret Atwood's incisive distinction) Paul has in mind not "freedom *to*" but "freedom *from*"—freedom from impersonal cosmic necessity, condemnation, and death.[26]

No less paradoxical is the contrast between Paul's assertion, only three verses earlier, that he preaches "knowing the *fear* of the Lord" (2 Cor. 5:11) and his present insistence that "the *love* of Christ controls us" (RSV). Yet both statements are true, for both express the absolute character of Christ's determinative role vis-à-vis humanity—that this Christ is *Kyrios*, "Lord" (4:5). And both premises are implicit in the representative death of the Messiah which, while certainly an act of divine love, nonetheless invokes death upon all of humanity:

> we are convinced that one has died for all; *therefore all have died*. And he died for all, so that those who live might live *no longer for themselves*, but for him who died and was raised for them.
>
> 2 Corinthians 5:14b–15

That is, the death of Jesus is an act both of love and of judgment, an act that constrains as well as liberates, and an act that brings death and life

26. Cf. Margaret Atwood, *The Handmaid's Tale: A Novel* (Toronto: Bantam, 1986), 24.

equally as God's Word to the world. Having been, as it were, captured by the death of Christ, and thus having "died" with him, Christ's followers now live "in Christ," acknowledging that he has been raised from death as the universal "Lord" who commands their allegiance and bids them no longer live for themselves.[27]

Again we note how awkward and unwelcome such views appear, not only to their ancient audience but also to modern or postmodern readers for whom freedom of self-expression and personal fulfillment are self-evident, even inalienable rights. Cruciform discipleship comes as a shock. As Lauren Winner puts it, "Sometimes I feel God has taken a paring knife to me. I know the way an apple feels."[28] According to Paul, Christian believers are indeed freed from condemnation, yet constrained by God's love; liberated by Jesus as "Lord," they nonetheless become his "slaves"; like Paul, they are ruled not by cosmic "necessity" but by the deeper "obligation" of God's saving purpose.[29] In addition to these constraints, preachers must also reckon with the paradox of their apostolic calling: just as the "glorious liberty" (Rom. 8:21, RSV) that they proclaim comes only by way of enslavement, so their ministry is not one that they adopt or conduct of their own volition. It is, rather, an expression of the will—the constraining love—of a merciful God, its conditions dictated by the suffering and vindication of Jesus.

Paul's unusual logic is all the more appropriate if, as we have surmised, the Corinthians subscribe to a theology of exaltation by which they understand death (whether of Adam, of Christ, or of believers) to be a thing of the past. Certainly there are grounds for interpreting Paul's thrice-repeated assertion in 2 Corinthians 5:14–15 that Jesus died *hyper* ("on behalf of") others to mean that since he has died in their place, believers are freed from death. As Wedderburn observes, "examples of . . .

27. Cf. Gorman, *Cruciformity: Paul's Narrative Spirituality of the Cross* (Grand Rapids: Eerdmans, 2001), 128.

28. Lauren F. Winner, *Girl Meets God: On the Path to a Spiritual Life* (Chapel Hill: Algonquin, 2002), 260.

29. As Gorman (*Cruciformity*, 125) observes, such apparent contradictions express the cruciform nature of faith itself, for "faith actualizes all the intended outcomes of Christ's death. Faith *liberates* and *enslaves*; it *incorporates* and *inaugurates*. It liberates from the interlocking directorate of hostile powers that enslave human beings in order to make them servants of God; it incorporates people into Christ; and it inaugurates in them a new life of faithfulness made possible by the Spirit. All of this is an experience of cruciformity" (emphasis original).

the death of an individual for the sake of the many, a death that rescues the many, abound in the Graeco-Roman world."[30] Yet here the thought is that rather than rescuing humanity from a similar fate, Jesus's death unexpectedly invokes it upon them, confronts them with the very thing from which "religion" might normally be expected to save them: "one has died for all; *therefore all have died*"!

The daunting scope of Paul's theological analysis may obscure the fact that he is still in process of offering an apologia for his conduct, an explanation for "crazy" behavior. His apparent madness, he insists, cannot be evaluated on its own terms or in light of social custom alone. He may even be suggesting that christomorphic (that is, Christ-shaped) conduct is necessarily puzzling and unexpected, precisely because its explanation does not lie within the human realm alone. The rationale for Paul's tendency to self-effacement (however imperfectly implemented) and his willing submission to suffering and abuse is that Christ also has acted this way as a demonstration of God's love for humanity. To understand why Paul acts incomprehensibly, they must look not to him but to Christ.

The challenge that this represents for preaching cannot be underestimated. In keeping with the emphasis in contemporary theology on the humanity rather than the divinity of Christ, Western missiology in particular has tended to emphasize points of contact and continuity between "gospel" and "culture." More specifically, preaching to the converted and the unconverted alike seeks to make sense of scripture and theology in light of culture. But as William Willimon rightly points out, the task of preaching is to articulate God's purpose for humanity so as to make sense of culture and contemporary experience in light of scripture's unique categories (rather than the other way around):

> The Bible is not content to be translated into the categories of the contemporary world, but rather the Bible wants to absorb the contemporary world into its text. . . . The Bible is not content to leave modern people as they are. It wants to convert and change them. . . . So the question is not,

30. A. J. M. Wedderburn, "2 Cor. 5:14: A Key to Paul's Soteriology?" in Trevor J. Burke and J. Keith Elliott, eds., *Paul and the Corinthians: Studies on a Community in Conflict. Essays in Honour of Margaret Thrall* (NovTSup 109; Leiden: Brill, 2003), 274 (and passim, 267–83), with additional examples provided by Martin Hengel, *The Atonement: The Origins of the Doctrine in the New Testament*, tr. John Bowden (London: SCM, 1981), 6–31.

How can we interpret the Bible to suit the limitations in church, but, *How can we re-interpret the church to suit the demands of the Bible?*[31]

This too is paradoxical, since (like every preacher) Paul appeals to any number of cultural commonplaces in order to make his argument. At issue, however, is the question of hermeneutical priority rather than the use of culture and language in their own right. Preachers employ language, metaphors, and concepts that they hold in common with their audiences, but only in order to convey a salvific reality that exceeds the bounds of normal human experience. As we will soon see, Paul understands this interpretative task on the analogy of Jesus's incarnation. For the moment it is sufficient to observe that the message of the cross and resurrection, while necessarily employing human language, is not limited to the meaning of that language. Although conveyed in human language, the gospel derives its meaning in the first instance from the events themselves, from the claim that God has acted in those events, on which basis God continues to act in and through their proclamation.

Present Affliction and Pious Hope

Many aspects of Paul's thinking will seem incomprehensible to the Western church of the third millennium, for any number of reasons. First, we do not readily admit the practical relevance of the transcendent realm. That is to say, the concerns of "mysticism" and "economics," "spirituality" and "plumbing," "prayer" and "skin care" are thought to belong to entirely different domains. The customary separation between a public, scientifically verifiable world and a private realm of spirituality and religious conviction remains intact despite the more fluid boundaries of a postmodern worldview. It is not unusual to encounter highly educated and thoughtful Christian lawyers, public administrators, or university faculty who have never considered the possible relevance of faith and spirituality to their particular spheres of professional competence. Second, Western churchgoers on the whole seem to put little stock in the consolation of heavenly reward, no doubt because the material compensations of our present life are so ample. Third, we are (at best) uncertain what to make

31. Willimon, *Shaped by the Bible* (Nashville: Abingdon, 1990), 62–63 (emphasis original).

of the negative dimensions of final judgment. Given Jesus's emphasis on love and acceptance (so the argument goes) and our own preference for tolerance and inclusiveness, the possibility of damnation seems (to say the least) intolerant, and therefore intolerable. Being uncomfortable with the "negative" overtones of God's rule, we sometimes leave its "positive" aspects to one side as well. Fourth and most determinative is the fact that we do not experience persecution. Admittedly, the history of the European Reformation offers a litany of persecutions perpetrated and suffered by Catholics and Protestants alike. But recent examples are extremely rare— if only in the privileged West. By contrast, Paul's intense interest in the dual horizons of transcendence and eschatology is impelled in no small measure by a conviction of its practical immediacy. Given the cruciform character of his experience, it is no wonder he exclaims, "If for this life only we have hoped in Christ, we are of all people most to be pitied" (1 Cor. 15:19). Likewise for the majority of the church throughout the world today, Christian confession entails the likelihood of being deprived of food, shelter, family, freedom, education, or employment, even life. As has been extensively documented, for example, by Paul Marshall,[32] their persecution is as real as Paul's.

How, then, can Paul's cruciform spirituality make sense to those who (to borrow the unflinching analysis of 1 Cor. 4:8) "already . . . have all [they] want" and to that extent experience neither affliction nor personal need? The simple fact is that to the extent one is satisfied, "rich," and powerful, it is unlikely to do so. Yet at the same time, pastors in particular are acutely aware of the fragility of their own and their congregants' lives. Even the most confident and successful fall victim to accident or disease; material abundance may only heighten loneliness or spiritual want; leaders and congregations alike have to contend with difficult relationships, overwhelming temptations, and secret fears.

Perhaps the movement of Paul's thought between the first and second canonical letters to Corinth can prove instructive in this regard. As we have seen, Paul at first assails the congregation's sense of self-satisfaction, ironically contrasting his own circumstances with theirs in mock self-

32. See Paul Marshall with Lela Gilbert, *Their Blood Cries Out: The Worldwide Tragedy of Modern Christians Who Are Dying for Their Faith* (Dallas: Word, 1997); for evaluations of religious freedom and/or persecution in particular countries, see Paul Marshall, ed., *Religious Freedom in the World: A Global Report on Freedom and Persecution* (Nashville: Broadman & Holman, 2000).

deprecation (again, 1 Cor. 4:8). Although it is possible that their attitude and situation have changed radically by the time Paul writes his second epistle, it is at least as likely that the primary change has been in the apostle's own outlook. Perhaps (although this is no more than conjecture) the increased intensity of his own affliction has led Paul to acknowledge the extent to which some or all of his congregants have also experienced opposition and suffering. In any event, it seems reasonable to conclude that increased awareness of the fragile, transitory character of his own life and ministry has given rise to greater sensitivity concerning the pastoral needs of his congregation. In turn, to the extent that preachers can identify and identify with such needs, the better they may be able to communicate a Christian hope that transcends the limitations of physical and temporal existence.

Ironically, this may be an instance in which the widespread "graying" of the mainline North American church will prove to be an asset, for older congregants will be more conscious of their mortality, more likely to acknowledge the ambiguity of human accomplishment and, potentially, more attracted to a transcendent hope and the prospect of eschatological glory. Of course, for this to be so requires preachers and denominational leaders to abandon the criteria of "bigger is better" and "more money represents greater worth" that we have adopted from the surrounding culture. The eschatological horizon of a cruciform spirituality implies, rather, that personal and ministerial validation cannot be measured simply in material terms, indeed that neither suffering nor well-being is inherently vindicatory. Conversely, sensitivity to the physical and chronological limits of human life leaves room for consideration of an otherworldly and extra-temporal validation that is the domain of God alone.

Thus to preach after the manner of Paul requires, first, that we be so convinced of Christ's love and so uncertain of human—even religious— endeavor that we yield to the priority of interior over exterior, unseen over seen, and eternal over transient that Christ's death and especially his resurrection exemplify. It requires that we enter into the dynamic of divinely imposed death and resurrection to such an extent that we begin to yield up our prerogatives of self-determination, social dignity, and cultural identity, and thereby become conformed to the reality of Christ, with the new life that this entails. This is the challenge not merely of preaching about Paul, or even of preaching like Paul, but of being caught up in the process of spiritual transformation that makes Paul—and every follower of Jesus—a *Christianos*, or "little Christ."

6

Ambassadors for Christ
(5:16–6:13)

One of the problems Paul faces in Corinth is that he disagrees in important respects with his congregation's "horizon of interpretation." Even when contemplating spiritual matters, their thinking is too limited by the expectations and perspectives of their culture and day. It is as if they are standing on the earth, looking into the sky for Jesus's return. Paul insists that this is "carnal" thinking. Characteristically, he takes the opposite view. Followers of Jesus—apostles and preachers foremost among them—are not simply rooted on earth, reaching up; they are also anchored in heaven, looking down. They are "ambassadors for [and from] Christ," to whom God has now delegated the ongoing work of proclaiming reconciliation. Paul adopts this stance toward his congregants and Corinth in general, even as the congregants both represent and proclaim God's "new creation" to others in their city. In so doing, he employs a hermeneutic of grace, not viewing Christ in human terms, but viewing all humanity in terms of Christ. Like every preacher, Paul wants his hearers to see themselves as Christ sees them: as recipients and representatives of God's grace, humbly imitating, in some measure repeating, thus faithfully continuing the ministry of Christ.

From now on, therefore, we regard no one from a human point of view; even though we once knew Christ from a human point of view, we know him no longer in that way. So if anyone is in Christ, there is a new creation: everything old has passed away; see, everything has become new! All this is from God, who reconciled us to himself through Christ, and has given us the ministry of reconciliation; that is, in Christ God was reconciling the world to himself, not counting their trespasses against them, and entrusting the message of reconciliation to us. So we are ambassadors for Christ, since God is making his appeal through us; we entreat you on behalf of Christ, be reconciled to God.

2 Corinthians 5:16–20

The Human Point of View

Preachers necessarily employ human language, human rhetoric, and analogies or illustrations from human life in order to communicate the Christian gospel, thereby seeking to present a reality that in its fullness exceeds the bounds of such categories. As Paul argues concerning the interpretation of revelatory speech, "There are doubtless many different languages in the world, and none is without meaning; but if I do not know the meaning of the language, I shall be a foreigner to the speaker and the speaker a foreigner to me" (1 Cor. 14:10–11 RSV). Accurate interpretation is thus the central challenge of communicating divine revelation. But the question of how human language can convey divine content is already both posed and resolved in terms of early Christian debate concerning the "two natures" of Christ. Just as theologians of the patristic era concluded that Jesus's divine and human natures coinhere without contradiction, so we may take the incarnation to represent God's commitment to communicate transcendent reality in human form and human language—not only the words of Christ and scripture, but of preachers as well.

The surprise, as we have seen, is that God chooses to communicate by means of an event so despicable and in language so vulgar as to represent the very antithesis of anything "divine," that is, via "the word of the cross" (*ho logos . . . tou staurou*, 1 Cor. 1:18). Paul wrestles repeatedly with the fact that Jesus's incarnational weakness is easily misconstrued. Nonetheless, he insists that even crucifixion—the basest possible expression of human suffering and cruelty—accurately conveys the divine nature,

228

even if conceiving of God in the form of a condemned slave (Phil. 2:7–8) seems shockingly counterintuitive. This same conundrum, as we have also discovered, lies at the heart of the Corinthians' difficulties with Paul and his message. Hence he must assure them, "From now on . . . we regard no one from a human point of view [*kata sarka*, literally, 'according to flesh']; even though we once knew Christ from a human point of view [*kata sarka*], we know him no longer in that way" (2 Cor. 5:16). For to perceive Christ *kata sarka* is to reckon only with his human frailty, to judge him by purely human criteria, and thus to overlook or ignore the implied opposite, which is his embodiment of divine power. It is this "more than merely human" perspective that Paul now urges upon his hearers.

In similar terms, Paul protests that he does not conduct his own ministry *kata sarka* (2 Cor. 1:17; 10:3), although others accuse him of doing so (2 Cor. 10:2). In fact, he retorts, behaving "according to the flesh" is more characteristic of his opponents (2 Cor. 11:18). In his letter to the Galatians, he uses the parallel expression, *kata anthrōpon* ("according to humanity" or "human standards") to make much the same point regarding the source and content of the gospel that he preaches:

> For I want you to know, brothers and sisters, that the gospel that was proclaimed by me is not of human origin [*kata anthrōpon*]; for I did not receive it from a human source [*para anthrōpou*], nor was I taught it, but I received it through a revelation of Jesus Christ. . . . But when God, who had set me apart before I was born and called me through his grace, was pleased to reveal his Son to me, so that I might proclaim him among the Gentiles, I did not confer with any human being [*literally*: "flesh and blood"].
>
> Galatians 1:11–12, 15–16[1]

Just as the gospel he preaches is divine rather than human, so his commissioning for the task of proclamation does not rely on "flesh and blood"—human affirmation, authority, or empowerment. Both here and in 2 Corinthians 5:16, Paul chooses to view himself, the message of the cross, Christ, and all believers in the same light: as subject to profound misunderstanding should one account for them as merely human constructs, yet by means of those same ambiguous human forms communicating an even more profound divine reality.

---

1. For a summary of the intense scholarly debate that this passage has engendered, see Longenecker, *Galatians* (WBC 41; Dallas: Word, 1990), 23–25.

In all likelihood, the apostle's assertion that "we once regarded Christ from a human point of view" (RSV) is as much personal and biographical as rhetorical.[2] Doubtless Saul the Pharisee once regarded Jesus's crucifixion as the epitome of shame, and proof positive of God's rejection. The same may well be true of some to whom he now writes. Therefore his "*we* regard him thus no longer" amounts to a confession of former error, and of the change in perspective at which he has now arrived. Yet the ultimate focus of this passage is not on Christ, but on those to and about whom Paul now writes:

> So from now on we regard *no one* from a worldly point of view. Though we once regarded Christ in this way, we do so no longer. Therefore, if *anyone* is in Christ, he is a new creation: the old has gone, the new has come!
>
> 2 Corinthians 5:16–17 NIV

He is arguing, in other words, from Christ to Christians, in the assurance that what God has accomplished in the case of Christ will be replicated in the lives of his followers. This is an all-important principle for pastoral ministry in general and preaching in particular. Nor does this perspective apply only to those already within the church, since it refers to "all" (5:15) for whom Jesus died. "*Therefore*," Paul continues, "we regard *no one* from a human point of view." So if perceiving Jesus *kata sarka* means seeing no more than an ignominious execution, regarding one's fellow human beings in the same way means being unable to see beyond their human folly, frailty, and error. At best it is to see them as no more than self-made, the sum of their human parts. Paul proposes, by contrast, an

---

2. So J. Louis Martyn, "Epistemology at the Turn of the Ages: 2 Corinthians 5:16," in W. R. Farmer, C. F. D. Moule, and R. R. Niebuhr, eds., *Christian History and Interpretation: Studies Presented to John Knox* (Cambridge: Cambridge University Press, 1967), 274n4. Martyn (followed by Resner, *Preacher and Cross: Person and Meaning in Theology and Rhetoric* (Grand Rapids: Eerdmans, 1999), 110–18) takes his cue from Paul's "no longer" (5:15–16) and "from now on" (5:16) to argue for a distinctly Christian "epistemology at the turn of the ages" that hinges on the death and resurrection of Jesus. He understands the implied converse of knowing *kata sarka* to be knowledge and understanding *kata stauron*, "according to the cross," which means that "the cross is *the* epistemological crisis for the simple reason that while it is in one sense followed by the resurrection, it is not replaced by the resurrection" (286); "the essential failure of the Corinthians consists in their inflexible determination to live either *before* the cross . . . or *after* the cross . . . rather than *in* the cross" (285).

interpersonal hermeneutic *kata Christon*, which is choosing to see others "according to Christ," according to the principle of divine action manifest in the resurrection of the broken Messiah.

To preach, then, not *kata sarka*, according to flesh, but *kata Christon Iēsoun*, "in accordance with Christ Jesus" (so Rom. 15:5; cf. Eph. 4:7),[3] is to preach in light of the resurrection of "the Lord Jesus Christ, who . . . will transform our lowly bodies so that they will be like his glorious body" (Phil. 3:21 NIV). This is a radically liberating and transformative perspective for preachers to adopt. Pastoral care, as often as not, acquaints preachers with the extent of their congregants' emotional, material, and spiritual needs. Pastoral burnout, as often as not, results from trying in good conscience to bear these burdens while neglecting to care for one's own. Even where burnout is not the result, pastors and preachers alike can feel overwhelmed by the needs of those to whom they minister. But to see oneself and one's congregation "according to Christ" is to know and be able to declare before them, "God is at work in you, both to will and to work for his good pleasure" (Phil. 2:13 RSV). It is to see them not just in their weakness and failure, but according to God's transformative power. Again, this is possible not because the preacher is an optimist and believes in the human capacity to adapt and triumph. At least for Paul and the apostolic proclamation that he models, the possibility of a cruciform and Christomorphic life is enabled only by the unexpected and humanly inexplicable resurrection of Jesus.

Still, the structure of Paul's argument adds an important nuance to this perspective and the prospect of transformation that it implies. More clearly in Greek than in English, 2 Cor. 5:15, 16, and 17 represent three separate assertions, of which the latter two are each introduced by the conjunction *hōste*, "wherefore" or "therefore":

> He died for all, so that those who live might live no longer for themselves . . .
> *Therefore*, we regard no one from a human point of view . . .
> *Therefore* if anyone is in Christ, there is a new creation . . .

3. This seems preferable to Martyn's choice of *kata stauron*, which does not appear in the New Testament. Giving full weight to each element of the formula from Rom. 15:5 allows us to speak of Jesus's human weakness transformed and risen: to preach *kata Christon Iēsoun* means to acknowledge the full human *and* divine dimensions of his identity.

Verse 15 reiterates the general principle of salvation: Christ has died and been raised from death for the sake of all. Verse 16 articulates the general hermeneutical principle that results: the perspective of the apostolic preacher is to regard all humanity as subject to the death and judgment, resurrection and life expressed in Christ. This, as we have seen, is what motivates preaching: the knowledge that preacher, audience, and humanity as a whole are caught up in the compassionate saving initiative of God. All are subject to grace. Were it not for the following verse, Paul might be expressing a universalist salvation. But the fact that he adds a further qualification indicates his awareness of the distinction between those for whom salvation is potential and those for whom it is in process of actualization. "Therefore," he adds, "if anyone is *in Christ*..." The second "therefore" parallels the first but introduces a distinct qualification: those who are "in Christ"—those who participate by faith in the identity of their Lord and Messiah—become already subject to the "new creation" that Jesus's resurrection has inaugurated.

Accordingly, we may say that preaching is motivated in principle by the universal implications of Jesus's death and resurrection. But in terms of the practical consequences that it foresees, apostolic preaching stands between the potential and actual dimensions of human salvation, between the divine offer of life that enables preachers to envisage their hearers as subject to resurrection, and the reception of that offer on the part of those who are indeed "in Christ" (or its rejection on the part of those who choose not to be). Preaching does not seek by its own power to move the hearers between one position and the next; it simply articulates and bears witness to God's invitation for hearers to enter into the death and life of Christ. To preach in this way is neither fully universalist nor narrowly particularist: it acknowledges both the full scope of Christ's salvation and the possibility of its rejection. Indeed we may say that apostolic preaching derives its urgency equally from the overwhelming magnitude of God's offer and from the irreplaceable freedom of the human response.

New Creation

The power of Paul's declaration regarding the impact of Christ is conveyed at least in part by its remarkable brevity, impossible to render into English but evident even in transliteration: *ei tis en Christō, kainē ktisis.*

Paul explains in a mere six words (no verbs among them) what it requires nearly twice as many to present in translation: "if anyone *is* in Christ, *there is a* new creation" (2 Cor. 5:17). The economy of his expression suggests that Paul has already instructed his hearers on this subject, so that its import may be more immediately evident to them than to subsequent readers. As he tells the Galatian believers, "Neither circumcision counts for anything, nor uncircumcision, but a new creation" (Gal. 6:15 RSV). However, the prospect of preaching the full form of Paul's statement confronts us with the realization that it is not—in a certain sense—entirely true:

> Therefore, if anyone is in Christ, [there] is a new creation: the old has passed away; behold, the new has come.
>
> 2 Corinthians 5:17 RSV

If Christ is the "firstfruits" or (more colloquially) the "first installment" of the new creation (1 Cor. 15:20, 23), so also by virtue of its association with him is the church as a whole (cf. 2 Thess. 2:13). To this extent, the church serves as a sign of the renewal of all things, all the more so in a world for which the presence and relevance of Christ may be otherwise altogether obscured.

But therein lies the problem. Paul's experience of this very congregation is that the "old" has by no means fully passed away, nor by any means has the "new" yet adequately replaced it. Indeed, the entire letter testifies to the force and extent of their resistance to cruciform and Christomorphic ways of thinking. As Paul sees it, they are too easily persuaded by "super-apostles" and other imposters, too easily swayed by less contrary or demanding portrayals of the spiritual life. Elsewhere Paul characterizes life between Jesus's resurrection and the eschaton as one of sighing or "groaning" in anticipation (Rom. 8:22–23; 2 Cor. 5:2–4). Saints and the cosmos alike groan precisely because they are not nearly "new" enough. Likewise in a later day it is possible to preach about untrammeled Christian victory—"new creation"—only by jettisoning any possibility of identification with the checkered circumstances of one's listeners. Conversely, given the inescapable fact of human weakness, it is possible to speak of "everything old [having] passed away," or of "everything [having] become new" only by virtue of a selectively steadfast gaze upon Christ. Insofar as such affirmations are true of the resurrected Christ, they are true also of those who are "in Christ." But to view believers apart from Christ is to be struck by the painful dissimilarity between the risen Lord and his quarreling, fractious, and self-absorbed followers (preachers not least among them!). Once again, this is the importance of Paul insisting that we regard no one any longer *kata sarka*, but rather *kata Christon Iēsoun*. He proposes nothing short of a hermeneutic of grace. Whereas the Corinthians apparently wish to view Christ and *Christianoi* in human (that is, culturally and socially defined) terms, Paul exhorts them to view humanity in terms of Christ. The one is a kind of theological and hermeneutical minimalism, a reduction of the divine to human parameters; the other offers a properly *theo*logical and *christo*logical perspective on human existence. Indeed by refusing to be reduced to an anthropological solipsism, Paul's hermeneutic of grace offers the prospect of divinely authored transformation, while not denying the painful and ever-present reality of human limitations. Apostolic preaching on the model Paul proposes is the expression of this perspective, the declaration of a hermeneutic of grace.

By the same token, the prospect of a "new creation" suggests the all-encompassing scope of salvation, and therefore too the all-encompassing scope of Christian preaching. Western Christians, nurtured in an individualist culture, are predisposed to read Paul's "new creation" with reference to personal salvation, and the transformation of the individual. Paul's language no doubt encourages interpretations such as that of Eugene Peterson: "Now we look inside, and what we see is that anyone united with the Messiah gets a fresh start, is created new."[4] But to see no more than this would be to overlook the larger implications of this principle for Christian ministry, Christian mission, and the Christian worldview as a whole. Certainly Paul suggests that the transformed individual reflects God's christological "renovation" of the created order, but as such, that individual is but a small part of a vast transformation. According to Paul, the whole of creation groans in anticipation, because "creation itself will be set free from its bondage to decay and obtain the glorious liberty of the children of God" (Rom. 8:21 RSV). This being the case, the church's proclamation and teaching can hardly be reduced to the subject of personal salvation alone, but necessarily embraces a wide range of concerns, among them environmental degradation, international economic policies, the weaponization of space, ethical treatment of animals, appropriate use of natural resources, and much else

4. 2 Cor. 5:17 from Peterson, *The Message: The New Testament in Contemporary English* (Colorado Springs: NavPress, 1993).

besides. In short, the Christian worldview, Christian responsibility, and therefore also Christian preaching, encompass everything that Christ's death and resurrection have previously embraced, without exception. To proclaim the gospel in any less comprehensive terms would fall short of what Paul in Acts 20:27 calls "the whole purpose of God."

This is especially important to note insofar as socially current ethical concerns are sometimes inconsistent and often subject to change. At present, for example, personal sexual preferences are not to be criticized, but economic exploitation is; oppression of indigenous populations in other countries is roundly condemned, but the social conditions of aboriginal people in North America escape notice; Westerners impose their systems of government and finance on subject populations overseas, but strenuously object when non-Western nations attempt the same thing. To preach the "new creation" of Christ, by contrast, is to declare that all of life and the entire cosmos have been made subject to his cross and resurrection, whether prevailing cultural norms and one's fellow citizens concur or not.

God's Envoys

As we have seen throughout, Paul is in constant conversation with analogies and illustrations from the world of his day, whether the concept of divine "favor," Roman military ceremony, the divinization of the Roman emperor, the social significance of crucifixion, the bronze trade in Corinth, cosmic "necessity," master-slave relationships, or the language of the law court—to name only a few of innumerable examples. The climax of his apologia is governed by yet another of these: the concept of the apostolic preacher as a divine envoy or "ambassador."

There is a long-standing and lively debate among scholars as to the best scriptural model for preaching.[5] Karl Barth, for example, championed the image of the preacher as "herald" of the gospel:

> [The preacher's] authority rests on the authority of him who sends the herald. Being a *kērux*, a herald, means coming from the epiphany of Christ and going toward the day of the Lord. It is in the double movement, namely,

5. The following discussion is indebted to the analysis offered by Thomas G. Long, *The Witness of Preaching* 2nd ed. (Louisville: Westminster John Knox, 2005), 18–51.

that God *has* revealed himself and *will* reveal himself, that preaching conforms to revelation in the New Testament sense.[6]

This title is used of Paul only in 1 Timothy 2:7 and 2 Timothy 1:11 (and a variant reading in Col. 1:23) although, as we saw earlier, the corresponding verb *kērussein* ("to proclaim") and the substantive *kērugma* ("proclamation, preaching") are not infrequent in his correspondence. The opposite emphasis is exemplified by Harry Emerson Fosdick (1878–1969), who thought of preaching as an exercise in pastoral care:

> People come to church on Sunday with every kind of personal difficulty and problem flesh is heir to. A sermon was meant to meet such needs; it should be personal counseling on a group scale. . . . That was the place to start—with the real problems of the people.[7]

This position too can claim Scriptural authority, both in the image of the leader as "shepherd" or pastor (so Acts 20:28) and more specifically in the admonition to take proper care of the "flock" in one's charge (1 Pet. 5:1–4). A third model, rooted largely in narrative theology, envisages the preacher as narrator or storyteller. Narrative theology proposes

> that the Bible presents us with a "world" of its own. Thus by implication the task of theology is to describe the character and identity of this world. And the task of preaching is to tell the Bible's stories about that world.[8]

On such a view, the biblical text is allowed to speak for itself, appealing to the audience's own experience so as to draw preacher and hearer alike

6. Barth, *Homiletics*, tr. Geoffrey W. Bromiley and Donald E. Daniels (Louisville: Westminster John Knox, 1991), 50, and, more extensively, Gerhard Friedrich, "*kērux,* etc.," *TDNT* 3:683–96; cf. Beaudean, *Paul's Theology of Preaching* (NABPR Dissertation Series 6; Macon: Mercer University Press, 1988), 103–4, 118.

7. Harry Emerson Fosdick, *The Living of These Days: An Autobiography* (New York: Harper, 1956), 94.

8. Ellingsen, *The Integrity of Biblical Narrative: Story in Theology and Proclamation,* (Minneapolis: Augsburg Fortress, 1990), 19. Perhaps the most influential example of a "storytelling" approach to preaching—although emphasizing rhetorical methodology rather than narrative theology *per se*—is Eugene Lowry, *The Homiletical Plot: The Sermon as Narrative Art Form* (Atlanta: John Knox, 1980), and see Eugene Lowry, "Narrative Preaching," in William H. Willimon and Richard Lischer, eds., *Concise Encyclopedia of Preaching* (Louisville: Westminster John Knox, 1995), 342–44.

into its characteristic account of reality. Tom Long advocates a fourth possibility, arguing persuasively for the quasi-juridical model of the preacher as "witness," in keeping with the explanation Luke attributes to Paul:

> I do not count my life of any value to myself, if only I may finish my course and the ministry that I received from the Lord Jesus, to testify [*diamarturasthai*] to the good news of God's grace.
>
> Acts 20:24[9]

Nor is this merely Luke's view, for Paul himself characterizes his preaching to the Corinthian church as "testimony [*marturion*] to Christ" (1 Cor. 1:6 RSV).[10] At least as Luke tells it, Paul's address to the elders of Ephesus describes his ministry in a variety of ways: as one of "serving [*douleuōn*] the Lord" (Acts 20:19), "proclaiming" and "teaching" (*anangeilai, didaxai*; 20:20, 27), "testifying" (20:21, 23, 24), "warning [*noutheton*]" believers (20:31), and "preaching [*kērussōn*] the kingdom" (20:25). Paul summarizes the elders' own leadership as "shepherding [*poimainein*] the flock of Christ" (20:28). The range of vocabulary in this one passage should be sufficient to dissuade us from adopting a single image or description to the exclusion of all others. Each image simply highlights particular aspects of the larger task.

In 2 Corinthians 5:20 Paul explores yet another analogy: that of apostles as "ambassadors." The exact nuance of the Greek text is difficult to convey, for whereas most translations employ a noun—"we are *ambassadors* for Christ"—the original has a verb, which may be translated over-literally, "so we *serve as representatives* [*presbeuomen*] on behalf of Christ." In other words, although the verb in question indeed means "to be an ambassador," Paul appears not to be establishing the terms of a formal position or ministerial office so much as describing a concrete activity.

The role of a legate or ambassador in the Greco-Roman world was well-established, and involved two essential principles. The first of these was "that proper reception of the envoy necessarily entails proper reception of

9. Quoted in Long, *Witness of Preaching*, 45. The idea of the apostles as witnesses is frequent in Acts (e.g., 1:8, "you will be my witnesses in Jerusalem, in all Judea and Samaria, and to the ends of the earth"), as are the verbs *marturein* ("to bear witness, speak well of") and *diamarturesthai* ("to testify").

10. On this passage see Barrett, *The First Epistle to the Corinthians* (BNTC; London: Black, 1971), 37–38.

the one who sent him," such that "the envoy should be received according to the status of the one by whom he was sent"; the second, that envoys were accorded "significant power and authority to speak for those who sent them in accordance with their instructions."[11] Indeed, it was frequently the case that the envoy not only served on behalf of the original sender, but also represented the original recipients in conveying their response back to the initiator of the exchange. Such an envoy was, in an important sense, an intermediary and mediator between the two parties.

In keeping with this "social and diplomatic commonplace," the influence of which can be traced throughout the New Testament, Paul sends a letter by the hand of Titus in order to convey his wishes and bring about a reconciliation between the Corinthians and himself. He carefully stresses Titus's qualifications as "my partner and co-worker in *your* service" (2 Cor. 8:23) and, in a manner that has close parallels in contemporary personal and diplomatic correspondence, relates the history of his emissary's successful missions both to and from Corinth (2 Cor. 7:5–16).[12] Such clear use of diplomatic conventions provides an important background for understanding Paul's claim that apostles also serve as emissaries or ambassadors for Christ.

On the one hand, the claim is by no means unique either to Paul or to this letter (cf. Matt. 10:40; Mark 9:37; Luke 10:16; John 13:20; *1 Clem.* 42:1–2, etc.). Yet it is central to Paul's understanding of himself as one commissioned and sent by God (Rom. 10:15; 1 Cor. 1:17; Gal. 1:15). Mitchell translates Galatians 4:14 accordingly: "you welcomed me as a *messenger* [*angelon*] of God, as Christ Jesus."[13] The Corinthians, by contrast, seem to question his apostolic credentials. They seek proof, he says, "that Christ is speaking in me" (2 Cor. 13:3). Yet Paul understands himself to represent Christ bodily to his congregations: he bears in his body "the marks of Jesus" (Gal. 6:17), even "the death of Jesus" (2 Cor. 4:10), and together with other messengers of the gospel represents "the smell of Christ" in the

11. Margaret M. Mitchell, "New Testament Envoys in the Context of Greco-Roman Diplomatic and Epistolary Conventions: The Example of Timothy and Titus," *JBL* 111 (1992): 645, 647, 649: Mitchell cites numerous examples from contemporary Greek and Latin literature.

12. Mitchell, "New Testament Envoys," 651–61.

13. Mitchell, "New Testament Envoys," 646n17. Paul's term here, *angelos*, is usual in diplomatic literature for a non-Greek envoy (Frank Adcock and Derek J. Mosley, *Diplomacy in Ancient Greece* [London: Thames and Hudson, 1975], 152).

world, whether the stench of death or the sweet fragrance of new life.[14] This, then, is Paul's intent in the present passage:

> We are ambassadors for Christ [*hyper Christou*], since God is making his appeal through us; we entreat you on behalf of Christ [*hyper Christou*], be reconciled to God.

2 Corinthians 5:20

As Furnish (339) comments, "the repetition [of *hyper Christou*] emphasizes the official and authoritative capacity in which Paul writes"—although we should add that his choice of the plural voice extends this authority to all apostles.[15] Moreover, the particular phrase *hyper Christou* means more than "on behalf of" or "in place of" an apparently absent Christ. It "must be interpreted on the basis of the verb *presbeuein*: 'with the full authority of Christ who has sent me'" (Furnish, 339).

The context of social and diplomatic convention further explains why Paul represents such a conundrum for his Corinthian charges. For a start, "diplomats were men of importance and influence," invariably wealthy and well-connected, deemed suitable for representing the public interests of their native state as well as being acceptable to the recipients.[16] No mention is made of "slaves" serving such a function. The very idea would have seemed ludicrous. More to the point:

> It was a familiar Greek saying that "an ambassador is neither beaten nor insulted," which appears to have been corroborated in actual practice:

14. Cf. Mitchell, "New Testament Envoys," 651.

15. This also explains his preference for the image of "ambassador" over "herald" (as well as the greater suitability of the former for the task of preaching): "Heralds usually served singly and were sent to take simple messages or requests and to make formal pronouncements, whereas ambassadors were sent in larger numbers to advocate, persuade, and plead. . . ." (Derek J. Mosley, *Envoys and Diplomacy in Ancient Greece* [Historia Einzelschriften 22; Wiesbaden: Steiner, 1973], 81). On the other hand, "heralds in Greek diplomacy were regarded as inviolate in states to which they were sent, whereas ambassadors were not automatically so regarded. It was a deeply embedded facet of Greek thought that heralds were agents who functioned under some form of divine patronage." In any event, the two titles and functions were often confused (ibid., 87, 89). On the religious function of heralds, see also Friedrich, "*kērux*," etc., *TDNT* 688–92.

16. Mosley, *Envoys and Diplomacy*, 94 (and, more fully, 43–47).

"ambassadors fared comparatively well and were usually treated with considerable respect."[17]

The Corinthians clearly understand and abide by this principle, for they welcome Paul's own representative "with fear and trembling," falling over themselves in eagerness to affirm their affection for the apostle (2 Cor. 7:7, 11, 15). How, then, are they to explain the fact that Paul, the emissary of God in Christ, is by his own account repeatedly beaten and insulted? More to the point, what are they to make of the fact that God's emissary was crucified? Insults to ambassadors usually precipitated war, or (in the case of the herald, who undertook the risky task of announcing hostilities or negotiating an end to them) formalized a state of war already in place.[18] Whereas for those familiar with Jewish sacrificial tradition, the death of the Messiah could be viewed as a peace offering effecting reconciliation between heaven and earth, a Hellenistic audience would probably see greater significance in the unexpected absence of divine retribution as a consequence of that death. Heralds and (to a lesser extent) ambassadors were by definition divinely sanctioned, all the more so in the case of a messenger actually sent by God. It would have been nothing short of astonishing to contemplate God's response to the murder of his emissary—and firstborn Son—as one of making peace with the malefactors (so 2 Cor. 5:19b: "not counting their trespasses against them"). Yet Paul bids his audience not to view the matter *kata sarka*, according to mere human understanding. They must view him and Christ alike as emissaries whose shameful treatment at human hands bespeaks a God of enduring peace, patient forbearance, and unswerving commitment to reconciliation.

We may infer, therefore, that Paul's intent in 2 Corinthians 5:20 is not to announce his own position as an envoy or emissary of Christ—for that would have been self-evident from the outset—so much as it is to redefine and explain that role in light of Christ's own ministry as the ambassador of God. As God sent Christ, so Christ sends his own representatives and

17. Mitchell, "New Testament Envoys," 645–46n14, citing Mosley, *Envoys and Diplomacy*, 89.

18. So Adcock and Mosley, *Diplomacy in Ancient Greece*, 153–54; Mitchell, "New Testament Envoys," 645–46, citing Dietmar Kiernast, *Presbeia: Griechisches Gesandtschaftswesen* (*PWSup* 13; Munich: Alfred Druckenmueller, 1974), 561–62, and, most fully, the dramatic examples furnished by Mosley, *Envoys and Diplomacy*, 82–87.

"apostles." As Christ suffered calumny and rejection, so does Paul. The unexpected result in both cases, however, is reconciliation: an end to hostilities rather than a beginning.

Nor is the apostolic preacher beyond the scope of God's forbearance and grace, says Paul, for only insofar as such a one is antecedently the object of God's reconciliation may he or she bear its message to others:

> All this is from God, who reconciled *us* to himself through Christ, and has given *us* the ministry of reconciliation; that is, in Christ God was reconciling the world to himself, not counting their trespasses against them, and entrusting the message of reconciliation to *us*.
>
> 2 Corinthians 5:18–19

The ministry of Christian proclamation cannot therefore be undertaken abstractly, or apart from personal experience. For that would be to place oneself above the message or to impose it "from above," as if it applied to one's audience but not to oneself. In this case, to preach "not ourselves" means that the same conditions apply equally to all, for in Christ God has reconciled the entire *kosmos*, "world," to himself.

In yet a further reversal of social expectation, preaching as Paul explains it is a radically democratizing activity. It is already axiomatic for Paul that all human beings share the same need (so Rom. 3:23, "*all* have sinned and fall short of the glory of God"), all have access to God ("there is no distinction between Jew and Greek; the same Lord is Lord of all," Rom. 10:12), and all are reconciled by the work of Christ (so Gal. 3:28, "all of you are one in Christ Jesus"). But to be both the recipient of grace and its delegated representative requires preachers to identify closely with their audiences—not in terms of similarity of social situation, ethnic background, or other worldly criteria, but in terms of acknowledging their own need of the same mercy and divine compassion that God offers to all humanity. Indeed, to follow the model for preaching that Paul proposes is to highlight this need by means of reference to one's own experience. In this sense, preaching cannot but be a compassionate activity, for it emulates God's compassion in extending to one's hearers the same grace that one has already received. The preacher has compassion on the hearers because he or she knows from personal experience what it is to long for life, to feel spiritually impoverished, or to be mired in shame. "For the love of Christ urges us on" (2 Cor. 5:14) is thus not a principle of external constraint, as if preachers were forced by Christ to love others. Rather it represents an internalized dynamic of urgently inviting others to share one's own experience of Christ, and one's own cruciform spirituality.

As we have repeatedly seen, the preacher is thus an "anti-example" of sorts, a model of human weakness and spiritual indigence that illustrates the relevance of divine grace. Notwithstanding claims of special divine commissioning on the part of some, this—rather than the commissioning itself—is what constitutes one's basic qualification for the role of apostolic "ambassador." It is the equivalence of citizenship in the heavenly "commonwealth" (Phil. 3:20 RSV) and the sign of a disciple's submission to the reign of Christ. Again, notwithstanding the commissioning of some, this implies that all followers of Christ are qualified to serve as witnesses and ambassadors—preachers—of the gospel message. The role accorded those officially designated as the church's ministers and teachers is theirs as a sign not of extraordinary but of "ordinary" grace. If preachers differ at all from those to whom they speak it is, as we noted previously, not in kind but in degree, perhaps particularly in the acuteness with which they are conscious of their own spiritual poverty and their reliance on God's sustaining power. Certainly this is what Paul seeks to explain in divulging the extent of his personal affliction and adversity.

God's Appeal

A good portion of the "folly" of the cross is the fact that God entrusts "the message of reconciliation" to those who crucified his Son, thereby, says Paul, "making his appeal through us" (2 Cor. 5:19–20). For John the Evangelist, the conditions of Jesus's incarnation apply equally to his followers, who, he explains, are "born, not of blood or of the will of the flesh or of the will of man, but of God" (John 1:13). Paul has a similar view of apostolic proclamation: just as God initially delegated to Jesus the ministry of reconciliation, so the furtherance of that reconciliation is now entrusted to Jesus's newly repentant followers. This is the high point of repeated parallels in this letter between Christ and Christians, who emulate their Lord in calling God "Father" (2 Cor. 1:2, 3); sharing "the sufferings of Christ" (1:5); being afflicted and consoled for the sake of others (1:6); experiencing God's power of resurrection (1:9); being "anointed" for ministry (1:21); bearing the "aroma" of Christ (2:15–16);

being "sent from God and standing in [God's] presence" (2:17); being "transformed into the . . . image" of Christ (3:18); assuming the position of slaves (4:5; cf. Phil. 2:7); in short, "always carrying in the body the death of Jesus, so that the life of Jesus may also be made visible in [their] bodies" (4:10). Perhaps we say that all these aspects of the Christian life are subsumed within the larger category of the disciple's ambassadorial role, for they are all means by which disciples demonstrate the true source of their new life and the authority by which they speak.

Paul seems fully aware of the risk that such imitation entails. In Corinth and elsewhere (e.g., Phil. 1:15–17), he knows of unworthy representatives of the Christian message. On this point the paradox of ministerial identity is most acute, for nothing is as it seems. What commends the would-be apostolic preacher according to the standards of popular culture—influence, eloquence, material assets, and self-commendation—is, for Paul, proof of disqualification for the task. Conversely, what disqualifies Paul by the standards of popular culture is, by the measure of Christ's cross, what indicates the authenticity of his ministry:

> We put no obstacle in any one's way, so that no fault may be found with our ministry, but as servants of God we commend ourselves in every way: through great endurance, in afflictions, hardships, calamities, beatings, imprisonments, riots, labors, sleepless nights, hunger . . . in honor and dishonor, in ill repute and good repute. We are treated as impostors, and yet are true; as unknown, and yet well known; as dying, and behold we live; as punished, and yet not killed; as sorrowful, yet always rejoicing; as poor, yet making many rich; as having nothing, and yet possessing everything.
>
> 2 Corinthians 6:3–5, 8–10 RSV, *alt.*

The "folly" of the Christian message thus governs its proclamation—and its proclaimers—as much as its content.

On such a view, the role of an apostolic ambassador is more than merely nominal, as if one might announce the message of the cross without being personally constrained by its terms and conditions. No, ambassadorship is substantive. A Christian emissary such as Paul embodies the paradox of divine grace prevailing over human weakness, testifying to that paradox in the message of Jesus's cross and resurrection. Indeed, we may be more precise: recalling Barth's comments on preaching (cited in chapter two), the impossibility of representing God in this matter is such that any preacher with the least self-awareness or merest sense of the enormity of the task is at once thrown back on the sufficiency of God. Apostolic proclamation is thus by nature transformative: even those who do not incur the violent wrath of religious rivals will recognize their own inadequacy once they begin to preach. They are, on Paul's example, turned into material representatives of the gospel—conformed to the message they proclaim—by the conditions of proclamation itself. Or to press the matter to its logical conclusion, *not* to be constrained into a cruciform spirituality would, on Paul's view, indicate that one had, in fact, been preaching something other than the message of Christ all along. The first test of the authenticity of the message, then, is its effect on the messenger.

Yet the demands that the message of the cross itself places on its hearers are no less enormous, above all that of deciphering a "word of the cross" that is, in important respects, if not incomprehensible then at least radically counterintuitive and intellectually challenging. In this sense the preacher and the preached cross are jointly parabolic—enigmatic and indirect, yet simultaneously revealing a deeper truth both about themselves and about those who behold them. They function, in other words, much as do the parables of Jesus: as challenges to understanding by which hearers discover their own orientation with regard to the reign of God. This, as we saw earlier, is a second indication of the authenticity of preacher and proclamation: the effect they have on their audience. Perhaps we may understand this by analogy to the principle Paul enunciates in 1 Corinthians 11:19: "Indeed, there have to be factions among you, for only so will it become clear who among you are genuine." Just as social interaction among congregants discloses the degree to which each member has or has not been transformed by grace, so the true character of the hearers is revealed by their response to the message of the cross. Indeed we may say that the message, its messengers, and the nature of the response they engender are mutually illuminating. This is simply to reiterate Paul's own assertion from earlier in the letter: "You yourselves are our letter . . . to be known and read by all" (2 Cor. 3:2). The point of repeating it here, however, is to note that just as the apostolic "ambassador" is a substantive representative of the cross, reflecting its message in his or her own lived experience and cruciform spirituality, so the aim of such a ministry is for its recipients to share the same transformative encounter with cross and resurrection.

244

As to the authority of the divine ambassador, Paul makes three partly overlapping statements. In the first instance, he says, God makes his appeal "through us" (2 Cor. 5:20b): he and his fellow preachers are directly "servants of God" (6:4). At the same time, however, apostles are ambassadors "for Christ" (5:20a), making their entreaty "on behalf of Christ" (5:20c; both *hyper Christou*). That is, third, "we work together with him" (*sunergountes*, 6:1)—the phrase "with him" being an interpolation added for the sake of clarity. Although the verb has no direct object, Paul's intended sense must again be that apostolic preachers work together with God, who is mentioned both immediately prior ("the righteousness of God," 5:21) and immediately following ("the grace of God," 6:1c; cf. Thrall, 451).

These statements affirm once more the divine initiative that underlies both the ministry of Christ and Christian proclamation, yet without either the salvific centrality of Christ or the responsibility of the preacher being curtailed or eliminated from the equation. Indeed, Paul asserts nothing less than that human agency (beyond Jesus's own) continues to be essential for the outworking of God's purpose of salvation. Still, the nuances are important. Again, Paul significantly limits the contribution of human initiative with his insistence that the substance of divine-human reconciliation has been accomplished by God "in Christ"; only the "message [*logos*] of reconciliation" (5:19) is entrusted to human agents. The latter may be God's "co-workers," but they are by no means "co-redeemers," much less (as is sometimes claimed) "co-creators." Apostolic ministry is thus made possible by its function as imitation, repetition, and continuation of the ministry of Christ. In the words of Schütz, "Christ is thus extended through his ambassadors . . . [so that] the gospel is the extension of the Christ-event."[19] More specifically, Paul implicitly sets the representative role of an emissary within the context of Christ's ministry "on behalf of" humanity. As we saw earlier, Paul understands the foundational Christian conviction to be that Christ died and was raised "on behalf of [*hyper*] all" (2 Cor. 5:14, 15; cf. 5:21; Rom. 5:8; 14:15; 1 Cor. 15:3; 1 Thess. 5:9–10, etc.). In direct imitation of Christ, he understands himself to suffer affliction "on behalf of [*hyper*]" the "consolation and

19. *Anatomy of Apostolic Authority*, 181; quoted in Beaudean, *Paul's Theology of Preaching* (NABPR Dissertation Series 6; Macon: Mercer University Press, 1988), 145.

salvation" of his congregations (2 Cor. 1:6; cf. Eph. 3:1; Phil. 1:29). At the same time, he and other apostles proclaim the message of reconciliation "on behalf of Christ [*hyper Christou*]" (2 Cor. 5:20).[20] In each case the key preposition could equally be translated "for the sake of" or "to the benefit of," but whichever shade of meaning one selects, this is language of benefaction (cf. L&N 90.36). The critical issue for ministry is not, therefore, the precise degree of representation Paul implies (does the apostle partly "replace" Christ, or merely "mediate" between Christ and the congregation?), but rather its focus away from the preacher and toward the one who is preached.

The ministerial ethic Paul has appropriated is, once more, an extension of the principle of imitation. In this respect also, the servants copy their Lord. Thus, he says, "[Christ] died for [*hyper*] all, so that those who live might live no longer for themselves, but for [*hyper*] him who died and was raised for them" (2 Cor. 5:15). As he explains in Romans 14:7–8: "We do not live to ourselves, and we do not die to ourselves. If we live, we live to the Lord, and if we die, we die to the Lord." And in the case of apostolic ministry, living "for the sake of" Christ means acting also "to the benefit" of those for whom Christ died. This too is part of his message to the Romans:

> We who are strong ought to put up with the failings of the weak, and not to please ourselves. Each of us must please our neighbor for the good purpose of building up the neighbor. For Christ did not please himself; but, as it is written, "The insults of those who insult you have fallen on me."
>
> Romans 15:1–3

Thus Paul's characteristic motifs—"not ourselves," "on behalf of Christ," and "for the sake of" neighbor or congregation—are correlative aspects of apostolic identity and ministry, distinct yet commensurate corollaries of Jesus's death and resurrection "on behalf of" or "for the sake of all" (2 Cor. 5:14–15). Accordingly, preaching as Paul defines it is far more than a simple activity or event. It is one aspect of a holistic orientation to the identity of Jesus as Messiah and Lord, formed by and bearing witness to the defining events of his crucifixion and resurrection.

20. Likewise, he adds, his experience of "weaknesses, insults, hardships, persecutions, and calamities" is "for the sake of Christ [*hyper Christou*]" (2 Cor. 12:10).

God's Message of Reconciliation

Paul has already summarized the theological content of preaching: "For we do not proclaim ourselves; we proclaim Jesus Christ as Lord and ourselves as your slaves for Jesus' sake" (2 Cor. 4:5). Yet that is a theological explanation, more a homiletical principle than an actual sermon. The message itself is more immediate, personal, and urgent: "We entreat you on behalf of Christ, *be reconciled to God.*" (2 Cor. 5:20c). It is not immediately clear how this applies to the Corinthians, who must surely consider themselves already reconciled to and at peace with God. Perhaps this is simply typical of Paul's preaching, given as a general example rather than specifically directed to the audience at hand. Or, more probably, Paul is convinced that his converts are farther from God than they imagine. In any case, it is notable that Paul directs his appeal to humanity's point of greatest need. We have already alluded to the sense of impersonal destiny and constraint, or *anankē*, that typified the Hellenistic outlook on life. Paul responds by announcing God's urgent disposition toward reconciliation, using innovative language that is without grammatical or conceptual precedent in the Hellenistic world.[21] Nor are the passive voice and imperative mood—"be reconciled"—accidental. On the one hand, "the imperative is significant, since it shows that man [*sic*] is not merely a passive participant in a purely automatic process" (Thrall, 437). To "be reconciled" implies moral responsibility, a willingness to accede to and participate in reconciliation. On the other hand, it is *God* who initiates this reconciliation, of which human beings are the recipients and beneficiaries. Paul's choice of language nicely balances the asymmetry of the relationship with the reality of human responsibility. Finally, while his use of an aorist imperative may perhaps imply a "once-for-all moment of conversion which the readers had already experienced" (so

21. "Paul uses *katalassō* in ways unattested in earlier Greek . . . [namely] in the active voice with the offended and hence angered party in a relationship (i.e., God) as (grammatical) subject taking the initiative in effecting reconciliation between himself and the offending party": so Stanley E. Porter, *Katallassō in Ancient Greek Literature, with Reference to the Pauline Writings* (EFN 5; Cordoba, Spain: el Almendro, 1994), 16; on 2 Cor. 5:18–21, see esp. 125–44. See further H. Merkel, *s.v.* "*Katallassō*, etc.," *Exegetical Dictionary of the New Testament*, ed. Horst Balz and Gerhard Schneider; tr. G. Schneider (Grand Rapids: Eerdmans, 1990–93), 2:261–63.

Thrall, 1:438),[22] Paul typically uses this verb form to "express the coming about of conduct which contrasts with prior conduct," especially so "where the *new* life of the Christian, corresponding to the divine call which creates a new beginning, is meant."[23] While conversion is indeed a moment of reconciliation (and *vice versa*), the condition of "being reconciled" remains characteristic of discipleship as a whole, and thus retains its high priority on the preacher's agenda.

This is not the place to comment extensively on the meaning of 2 Corinthians 5:21a, "For our sake he made him to be sin who knew no sin." We may simply observe that (unlike certain of his modern successors) Paul does not shrink from naming the "problem" between God and humanity as that of sin, and that the sense of the passage is probably best clarified by comparison with 5:19a. There Paul asserts that God does not count human transgressions against the perpetrators; here he declares the converse, which is that by making him "to be sin who knew no sin" God has counted the offenses instead against Christ.[24] In any event, Paul's argument offers a suitable model for proclaiming the human situation in light of Christ. His treatment once more emphasizes the divine initiative in reconciliation, balances human responsibility with Christ's response, and incorporates both retrospective and prospective aspects of salvation. Even so, Paul does not dwell on the problem of human sin (however much it confounds him in Corinth and elsewhere), but looks forward to the completion of divine-human reconciliation, even while that outcome is still in process: "that in [Christ] *we* might *become* the righteousness of God" (5:21b; the "we" is emphatic).

Three comments are in order regarding Paul's restatement of the goal of the life of faith, each of which is integral to the theological foundations of Christian preaching. First, and most broadly, whatever sense we attribute to the assertion that Christ was "made sin," it is clear that a principle of identification and exchange is operative: Christ becomes what is least characteristic of God and most characteristic of humanity ("sin") so that humanity can become what is most characteristic of God and, arguably, least characteristic of themselves ("righteousness"). Second, this statement

22. *Pace* Porter, *Katallassō in Ancient Greek Literature,* 140–41. Greek imperatives distinguish between action that is complete (discrete and at a specific moment, indicated by the aorist tense) or in progress (repeated or continuous, indicated by the present tense).

23. BDF §337(1) [emphasis original], with further examples.

24. Porter, *Katallassō in Ancient Greek Literature,* 142.

entails a significant revisioning of the divine character—whether for Jews, Corinthians, or Canadians. The instinctive human understanding of divine holiness or "righteousness" seems to be that this is a quality embodied by God and demanded by God of human beings. Paul's position is the exact opposite: that God is *dikaion kai dikaiounta* (Rom. 3:26): "just and justifying," holy and bestowing holiness on the unholy. Or, as he explains here, God's intent is "that we might *become* the righteousness of God": holiness and righteousness are not so much owed by humans to God as flowing from God to humans. This is essential to the Christian worldview, the hermeneutic of grace: to view the world *kata Christon Iēsoun* is to recognize the unexpected intersection of humanity and holiness; not simply to see human beings from the perspective of Christ or as Christ himself would, but to see ourselves in process of becoming Christlike (cf. 1 John 4:17b). Third, both in Romans and here, the agency of Christ is as indisputable as it is indispensable. All three points emerge from the intensity of Paul's own identification with the cross and resurrection of Jesus. Paul expresses a simultaneously grim and rosy outlook on the human situation: he is neither so optimistic as to overlook the evidence of the crucifixion, nor so pessimistic as to ignore the reality of resurrection. Holding the two in balance, and providing the key to each, is the person of Jesus. Whether with respect to our understanding of the human condition, the divine character, or the agency of Christ, preaching participates in God's purpose to transform humanity, through the person of his Son, from sin and death to righteousness and life.

Just as the grammar and logic of 2 Corinthians 5:15–17 move from general to specific, from the universal scope of Christ's work to its manifestation in the lives of his followers, so Paul follows up the general example of apostolic preaching in 5:20–21 with a message more directly suited to his Corinthian audience:

> Working together with him, then, we entreat you not to accept the grace of God in vain. For he says, "At the acceptable time I have listened to you, and helped you on the day of salvation." Behold, now is the acceptable time; behold, now is the day of salvation.
>
> 2 Corinthians 6:1–2 RSV[25]

25. The quotation is from Isa. 49:8: "Thus says the Lord: 'In a time of favor I have answered you, in a day of salvation I have helped you; I have kept you and given you as a covenant to the people. . . .' "

Paul began his first letter to the congregation on a similar note: "*Grace to you and peace from God our Father and the Lord Jesus Christ. I give thanks to my God always for you because of the grace of God that has been given you in Christ Jesus*" (1 Cor. 1:3–4). We recall from our introductory section how radical it would have seemed to a Hellenistic audience that God had poured out abundant "favor," *charis*, on humanity, making them the beneficiaries of Jesus's self-offering. Paul does not insist—as the Corinthians might have expected—that it is now their responsibility to reciprocate, returning "favor" to God for divine favors received. Much more remarkably, he implies that while they likely claim to have received an abundance of divine *charis*—favor, grace—it may yet prove void, having little or no effect on them.[26] "Most probably," according to Thrall, Paul "fears lest they should fail to understand and practise the full moral consequences of their new state of being" (Thrall, 1.451). No doubt he also has in mind their obvious need for reconciliation with the one who first announced this "grace" to them—himself (so Matera, 149–50)!

But something larger than either of these issues is at stake, as suggested by Paul's concern in 2 Corinthians 11:4 about the danger of receiving "another Jesus . . . a different spirit . . . or a different gospel" (cf. Barrett, 183). Paul now launches into an extensive recitation of personal hardships, by which, he says "as servants of God we commend ourselves in every way" (2 Cor. 6:4 RSV). He is being consciously ironic, for he and his audience know full well that these are the very things that *fail* to commend him, in fact debasing him in their eyes. Taking seriously the apostolic apologia that has occupied him from the beginning of this letter and setting this catalogue of affliction within its context leads to the conclusion that—in pointed contrast to Paul—the Corinthians make "void" the grace of God by thinking themselves no longer in need of it. By following the "superapostles" with their love of power and self-commendation, they have failed to grasp the central dynamic of the cross that Paul himself embodies (cf. Gal. 3:1). They seem to have forgotten that their present spiritual "abundance" has come at the expense of Christ's poverty (so 2 Cor. 8:9). And in rejecting the scandal of Paul's humiliation, they turn away from the only means by which *charis* can be received—through identification

26. Applying the same critique to himself, Paul is elsewhere concerned to show that God's grace has not been "in vain [*eis kenon*]" in his own ministry (1 Cor. 15:20; Gal. 2:2; Phil. 2:16).

with the yet more humiliating scandal of Jesus's crucifixion. Indeed, Paul implies, they obviate *charis* itself. This has been their error all along, as is indicated by his previous, ironic protest:

> Already you have all you want! Already you have become rich! Quite apart from us you have become kings! Indeed, I wish that you had become kings, so that we might be kings with you! For I think that God has exhibited us apostles as last of all, as though sentenced to death, because we have become a spectacle to the world, to angels and to mortals. We are fools for the sake of Christ, but you are wise in Christ. We are weak, but you are strong. You are held in honor, but we in disrepute.
>
> 1 Corinthians 4:8–10

The Corinthians have grasped the wrong end of the cross, so to speak, embracing its glory while eschewing its shame. In practical terms, they are so taken with their newfound favor with God that—aided by congregational leaders of their own choosing—they have an entirely inflated sense of themselves (so 1 Cor. 4:6; cf. 1 Cor. 8:1).

The implication of this argument is that the only barrier to grace is the conviction—characteristic of this congregation, if no other—that one is no longer truly in need of it. As they see it, Paul's life lacks evidence of Christian perfection; his conduct and deportment are a stumbling block to the gospel. This is, equally, Paul's view of them. The apostle's diagnosis is not that they lack grace, but that they are impervious to it. He puts no obstacles in anyone's way (2 Cor. 6:3); the only resistance or obstruction derives from the hearers themselves: "Our heart is wide open to you. There is no restriction in our affections, but only in yours" (2 Cor. 6:11b–12).

These are more than occasional observations on the situation at hand. Rather, they again articulate key principles that govern Paul's ministry and apply equally in our own day. First, we may perceive here another grave warning against Christian triumphalism and spiritual smugness. Second, we cannot exaggerate or reiterate too often the radical implications of the Christian message for our understanding of God. Whether with respect to humanity as a whole or as concerns this congregation in particular, Paul is insistent that divine favor—*charis*—is fully available to his audience, and that such favor also determines his own attitude toward them. All that remains is for the congregants to respond—not just once, but continually. Apostolic preaching therefore proceeds on the theological assumption of divine favor. "*Now* is the day of salvation!" (2 Cor. 6:2), Paul says, because this is the inalterable divine intent. Granted, every preacher is liable to doubt whether God will "show up" for a given sermon, and may utter a fervent plea for mercy on the way up the pulpit steps. And every preacher encounters "dry spells," when God seems aloof or absent and the task of preaching, futile. But these are purely personal, emotional, and psychological uncertainties, not theological ones. Particularly when—like Paul!—preachers are constrained by personal adversity, preaching is only possible because it proceeds from and expresses God's antecedent, persistent self-declaration in "favor" of preacher and hearers alike.

This suggests, at last, the proper place of rhetoric, as an appropriate means by which one recipient of grace may persuade others that they too may receive the same. The rhetoric of proclamation by no means seeks to replace divine action in the context of proclamation, but stands alongside it, working "together with him." The dichotomy between "theology" and "rhetoric" is thus revealed to be false: insofar as God "makes his appeal *through* us," the two are brought into cooperation. Nor is it necessary to construe one's audience as the homiletical "enemy," ever resistant to God and therefore in need of forceful persuasion. Or, to the extent that this may indeed be the case, the condition is not limited to one's hearers. Every astute preacher will recognize his or her own intermittent resistance to grace, acknowledging the need to be reminded and persuaded while seeking to do the same for others. In this sense, preaching is no more or less than a reappropriation or reintegration of the basic Christian insight that in the person of Christ, God is revealed as being no longer estranged from humanity, as one who pursues every possible avenue of reconciliation. On the theological assumption that God's favorable disposition is unchanged and unchanging, and the ensuing conviction that "*now* is the day of salvation," preaching puts before its hearers a gracious opportunity and challenge to respond. The fact that in the first six chapters of 2 Corinthians Paul must expend more than two thousand words pleading and arguing with his (apparently) reluctant interlocutors provides a case in point. That he found such argumentation necessary makes it all the more likely that something similar will be required of his imitators and successors. This being so, we no less than the Corinthians are the beneficiaries of his tribulation, both because of his exemplary (if epistolary) preaching, and in terms of the cruciform spirituality that it articulates.

That Paul must still preach to this church testifies to the necessity of the cross, and to the ongoing need for grace that it answers; that Paul has a ready audience in Corinth testifies to the reality and effectiveness of that grace, both in general terms and with regard to preaching in particular. Were it not for the fractiousness of his converts, neither the gospel nor Paul's proclamation of it would be necessary; were it not for the efficacy of the gospel, and of the events to which it bears witness, proclamation itself would be futile. We can hardly imagine this being any less so for subsequent preachers. It remains the case therefore, that—by themselves— neither the theological content of Paul's message, nor the language with which he proclaims it, nor even the method that he embodies are alone sufficient to convey the full meaning of God's purpose in Christ. Rather, all three aspects of apostolic proclamation function together, jointly deriving their significance from a divine reality that shapes them from without. Because, as Paul repeatedly argues, the efficacy of preaching is ultimately dependent on the God who gives life to it and to the dead, cruciform spirituality—whereby preacher and message are conformed to crucifixion so as to become subject to resurrection—serves as the point at which God's appeal "to us" becomes God's appeal "through us," and apostolic preaching of Jesus's death and resurrection assumes its proper dimensions as divine activity conveyed in paradoxically human form.

7

Conclusions

By the time we follow his thinking only halfway though 2 Corinthians, Paul's account of Christian life and ministry begins to look as strange to us as it surely did to the letter's first recipients. By contrast, at least a few features of the ancient world have come into clearer focus. We have a better sense, for instance, of how ambassadors functioned in Hellenistic society, how long people typically lived, and how letters were written; of how words such as "grace," "freedom," "necessity," "peace," "Lord," and "Savior" likely sounded in Corinthian ears; and of how Paul's description and embodiment of the Christian message ran counter to virtually everything his converts would normally have expected from religious experience, and from religious leaders in particular. Rather than completely distancing us, however, clarifying the differences between ourselves and ancient Corinth helps to identify valid parallels and analogies between our respective situations. Not unlike postmodern Westerners, the Corinthians are concerned with body image, personal success, and social advancement; they are eager for divine "blessing," proud of their accomplishments, offended by their uncouth, unconventional preacher, and tempted to look for new leaders more inclined to assist them in their quest for glory. Like the letter's first recipients, we too are troubled by the theological strangeness of Christ, and the apparent madness of the manner in which Paul imitates him. He makes the task of preaching seem more difficult by far than we already knew it to be.

Even so, we are forced to recognize that Paul's version of the gospel—at least if we have read it correctly—seems more faithful to the message and example of Jesus of Nazareth than certain other models and interpretations with which we may be familiar from recent experience. As expected, Paul argues that Jesus's death and resurrection provide a new pattern for human existence, restoring an estranged creation and its creatures by, as it were, subjecting the whole of God's handiwork to death so as to re-create it anew. We are familiar from Paul's other correspondence with the forensic, moral, and eschatological dimensions of this preemptory initiative on God's part—its offer of forgiveness, its call to holy living, and its promise of future glory. Recent and traumatic events in Paul's own life, however, have provided new insight into the present, experiential dimensions of conformity to Christ. Recognizing that every aspect of his discipleship and apostolic ministry is governed by Jesus's death and new life, Paul proceeds to defend himself in the face of severe criticism, articulating a vision of preaching in particular that gives absolute priority to the principle of divine grace. He is concerned to show how the cross and resurrection establish the basic pattern of Christian discipleship, provide the conceptual content of the Christian message, and determine the manner of its proclamation. John Stott offers a concise summary of what Paul seeks to convey:

> ... the central theme of Paul's Corinthian correspondence is power through weakness. We have a weak message, Christ crucified, which is proclaimed by weak preachers who are full of fear and trembling, and is received by weak hearers who are socially despised by the world. God chose a weak instrument (Paul) to bring a weak message (the cross) to weak people (the Corinthian working classes), but through that triple weakness he demonstrated his almighty power.[1]

The crucial issue for Paul is the inclusion of both death *and* resurrection as essential to Christian experience. But herein lies the difficulty, as much for ourselves as for the Corinthians. In the course of his correspondence, Paul highlights a series of contrasts that describe particular aspects of Jesus's ministry and/or its consequences for the life of faith. Among them we may note the following (although the list is far from complete and its order is not essential):

1. John R. W. Stott, "Power Through Weakness (1 Cor. 1:17–2:5)," in Michael P. Knowles, ed., *The Folly of Preaching* (Grand Rapids: Eerdmans, 2007), 138.

Humanity	—	Divinity
Shame	—	Honor/Glory
Enslavement	—	Emancipation
Mundane/temporal	—	Transcendent/timeless
"Away from the Lord"	—	"In the presence of God"
"Not ourselves"	—	"Jesus Christ as Lord"
Crucifixion	—	Resurrection
Death	—	Life
Old creation	—	New creation

To lay out matters in this fashion, however, risks repeating the same error that apparently confounded the Corinthians, which is to suggest that the elements of each pair are antithetical or contradictory. On the contrary, the paradox of the Christian message is that God speaks by means of the unspeakable: both the unspeakably "human" (or, we might say, "inhuman") and the unspeakably divine. That is, crucifixion and resurrection *alike* reflect the divine purpose; abasement and glorification are *both* integral features of Christian discipleship; "glory"—whether for Jesus or his followers—emerges out of shame rather than in spite of it; "enslavement" to Christ as Lord represents liberation from impersonal destiny; and only by continuing to embrace the death and degradation implied by crucifixion does a disciple become subject to resurrection and the new creation.

The problem is not, in all likelihood, that the Corinthians reject the idea of conformity to Christ—more likely, they embrace it in principle. But they seem to recoil at the particular demands of *cruci*formity; at the thought that cross-like abasement in the presence of God and life-giving rescue or exaltation by God are equally integral and ongoing features of Christian discipleship. The paradox of the message Paul proclaims and embodies is that it calls for "near-death" and "near-resurrection" alike, but not one at the expense of the other. It is in this sense that the components of each set turn out to be complementary rather than contradictory—at least when viewed (as Paul insists they must be) in relation to Christ himself. These inseparable aspects of the gospel are perhaps best symbolized by the image of an empty cross, the enduring and irreplaceable sign of an inhuman death whose human victim neither hangs on it nor is subject to its power any longer.

But this explanation only compounds the difficulty that preachers face. On the one hand the Christian message finds coherence and harmony in combining otherwise incoherent and contradictory premises: hope amid suffering, glory by means of shame, life through death, new creation emerging from Jesus's mortal embrace of the old. Or to use a more concrete example from Paul's own preaching: the Christian gospel, announcing God's gift of salvation, is conveyed via illustrations from military ceremony, social convention, and local industry. Like the incarnation itself, this strategy seems to imply the affirmation of human culture. Yet Paul rejects the "Lordship," "Peace," and "Fatherhood" of Caesar, radically subverts social norms, and insists that the glory yet to be revealed is "beyond *all* comparison" (2 Cor. 4:17 RSV). How, then, is the Christian preacher to discern which human (or social, or cultural) principles are ultimately contrary to God's saving purpose, and which cohere with it? How does one speak from within a culture in a manner that nonetheless transcends even the terms in which the message itself is expressed?

Paul, we recall, explains this dilemma as a problem of perspective, of choosing to view matters either *kata sarka*—"according to the flesh, from a human point of view"—or *kata Christon Iēsoun*, "according to Christ Jesus" (2 Cor. 5:16; Rom. 15:5). The latter title refers to Jesus of Nazareth both in his human weakness and as the exalted Messiah, implying that the two aspects of his identity are inseparable. In similar terms, Paul explains that "we preach *Jesus* as *Christ* and *Lord*" (2 Cor. 4:5a; author's translation), that is (to anticipate the categories of later christological debate), one whose human identity does not nullify his messianic exaltation, any more than his divine sonship nullifies his humanity. As a pattern of experience for his followers, the example of "Christ Jesus" combines abasement and exaltation, death and life, old order and new, to express the full range of human identity both before and after God's saving purpose is complete, both with and without the life-giving intervention of God (since, in each instance, both poles reveal the truth of the human situation in relation to God).

The Corinthians have evidently embraced the glory of their exalted Lord, and look for leaders who act accordingly; leaving behind all that is merely human (epitomized by the scandal of the cross), they have yielded to all that seems most characteristically divine. But this is only half of God's "word" to humanity. For if abasement was an essential component of Jesus's ultimate glorification, so must it be also for his followers. Ironically, Paul's congregants have pursued the right methodology in the wrong direction. In seeking to identify with the God of Jesus, they have embraced the self-glorification typical of their culture. While this is a thoroughly "human" thing to do, it is nonetheless mistaken, for it represents an attempt to evade or overcome the limitations of creaturely existence by force of human strength, instead of acceding to them so as to allow God to accomplish the same goal. To follow Jesus in a cruciform manner implies being as fully "human" and creaturely (that is, dependent on God) as Jesus himself chose to be. This is neither theological masochism nor pathological self-denial; it is simply a return to our rightful place in the order of creation. Paul depicts himself, the Corinthians, and all humanity in such terms as a simple acknowledgment of human limitations in regard to the things of God, "to show that the transcendent power belongs to God, and not to us" (2 Cor. 4:7 RSV). Reflecting on his own long ministry of faithful proclamation, Stott puts it this way:

> This is not an invitation for us to suppress our personality. It is not an invitation to pretend that we feel weak when we don't. It is not an invitation to cultivate a fake frailty. Nor is it a renunciation of rational arguments since, as Luke tells us in Acts 18, Paul continued to argue the Gospel when he came to Corinth. No, it is rather an honest acknowledgment that we cannot save souls by ourselves, whether by our own personality, our own persuasion, or our own rhetoric. Only the power of God can give sight to the blind, hearing to the deaf, and life to the dead, and he does it through the gospel of Christ crucified, proclaimed in the power of the Holy Spirit.[2]

While it imposes unwelcome death on a humanity in search of life, the Christian gospel simultaneously interprets human weakness, suffering, and failure from the perspective of life-giving grace. Even as it proclaims a resounding "No" to competing claims of Lordship, and alternative descriptions of human identity, Paul's apostolic preaching offers a hermeneutic of grace, choosing to view the Corinthians and all of creation as having been reconciled "in Christ"—and thus either subject to or in process of actual reconciliation—to a gracious Creator. Those who proclaim the "word of the cross" therefore stand poised between the universality of Christ's work and the particularity of its individual embrace, offering on God's

2. Ibid., 137.

behalf the prospect of present and future glory that their hearers would otherwise have sought by more conventional and creaturely means.

This theological framework sets the agenda for Christian preaching, establishing direct lines of continuity between the content and method of proclamation, the personal experience of the proclaimer, and the life of the one proclaimed. At the risk of oversimplification, these lines of continuity may be expressed as a series of methodological principles, practical guidelines for preaching after the manner of Paul.

First, Paul's vision of preaching is inescapably christocentric and cruciform. Paul is unequivocal that the "Christ event" itself—not some more recent or congenial philosophical system with which it might be correlated—provides the conceptual framework for interpreting the situation of the believer, and of humanity as a whole. Not only the preacher's message or theology, but also the preacher's life and specific method of preaching are interpreted and shaped by the cross. "I have been crucified with Christ," he insists; "it is no longer I who live, but Christ who lives in me; and the life I now live in the flesh I live by faith in the Son of God" (Gal. 2:20 RSV). Thus Paul sees the dual principles of human frailty—even death—and divinely given life simultaneously at work in his own experience: in repeated rescue from hardship and persecution, in his surprising boldness and trust of God despite overwhelming odds, even in the effectiveness of his ministry among converts who actively oppose him.

Paul's challenge to preachers of the gospel is therefore (second) that we continually endeavor to discern the contours of encroaching death and divine renewal within our own lives. Preaching is an exercise in theological integration and an expression of lived theology, as we seek to discover consistent patterns of grace (as well as our ongoing need of grace) both in scripture and in personal experience. This implies, surely, a challenge to appropriate self-disclosure on the part of those who proclaim the gospel, a willingness to be as honest as is Paul about the true joys and difficulties not only of Christian discipleship, but of Christian leadership as well. Like Paul, preachers are constrained to embody the gospel as much as declare it, to bespeak Christ with their lives as much as speak of Christ in their sermons.

Therefore (third) to preach Christ is, like the life of faith in general, essentially an exercise in yielding oneself in all circumstances to God, trusting God to bestow an unearned and unrepayable gift of life. As we have argued from the outset, the human act of preaching is, before all else, an expression of spirituality, of the speaker's fundamental orientation to God by means of trust and hope in Christ. It both proceeds from the experience of grace and expresses dependence on grace in the very act of speaking. In this sense, preaching is of a piece with classic spiritual disciplines such as prayer, meditation, simplicity, fasting, confession, and service, to name only a few. For, like preaching itself, the common purpose of all such exercises is the practitioner's intention to yield and remain consciously open to the gracious embrace of God.

By the same token, cruciform preaching proceeds on the assumption that God is vitally active in the lives of its hearers (so Phil. 2:13). No less than they rely on grace to inspire their own speech, preachers rely on grace to sustain and transform their hearers. We may think of this as not only a hermeneutic of grace, but also a hermeneutic of hope: whether our audience appears cooperative or recalcitrant, Paul encourages us to view them (and ourselves) in light of the resurrection, as recipients of grace, and as creatures whom God continues to transform "from one degree of glory to another" (2 Cor. 3:18).

Even so (fourth), preaching does not impose a theological regimen on its hearers so much as testify to the sustaining mercy of God, inviting others to find for themselves in Christ what God through Christ has made available to all. It avoids coercion and invites trust—not so much in the speaker, however, as in God. Apostolic preaching, like crucifixion, is thus an exercise in weakness. It is an intentionally foolish activity that acknowledges its inability to achieve the ends of which it speaks. Yet while it is essentially foolish, it is not futile, insofar as it relies on the fidelity of God. Nor, for this reason, can we claim that preachers are altogether "without authority" (as proposed by the title of Fred Craddock's influential study); on the contrary, they may appeal to divine authority.[3] The essential distinction, however, is that any such authority is not their own, or theirs alone. Any claim to the authority of the preacher or the preached word must be set under the rubric of Paul's all-important "not ourselves."

This implies (fifth) that Christian proclamation does not exalt preachers above their hearers, but rather establishes them on the same level, as joint recipients of divine mercy—joint heirs with Christ and one another of

3. Fred B. Craddock, *As One Without Authority: Fourth Edition Revised and with New Sermons* (St. Louis: Chalice, 2001). See further P. T. Forsyth, "The Authority of the Preacher," in Richard Lischer, ed., *The Company of Preachers: Wisdom on Preaching, Augustine to the Present* (Grand Rapids: Eerdmans, 2002), 99–103, esp. 101 (from Forsyth's *Positive Preaching and the Modern Mind*, 1907).

God's kingdom (cf. Rom. 8:17). For this reason (much like the incarnation itself) a sermon typically expresses the preacher's identification with the circumstances of his or her audience, and is marked by sympathy and compassion as the consequences of such identification. This is precisely what we see Paul doing in the opening verses of 2 Corinthians, and in this sense preaching is indeed an exercise in pastoral care.

Sixth, apostolic preaching on the Pauline model unexpectedly refuses to pronounce final judgment (whether morally or as to the meaning of particular experience), since final judgment is the sole prerogative of Christ. This premise in particular seems contradictory, given that Paul is hardly shy of making forceful moral and theological assertions when the situation calls for it. Yet even while doing so he nonetheless acknowledges that, ultimately, only Christ is competent to offer a definitive assessment of human conduct and experience (1 Cor. 4:3–5).[4] Thus while preachers are free to assert moral values and assign theological meaning to human events in light of the gospel, they do so humbly and provisionally, admitting that Christ himself, not their interpretations of Christ, provides the key to Christian understanding.

Lest any of the foregoing be taken to imply a primarily individualized spirituality, it is important to recall (seventh) the implications of Paul's appeal to "new creation." That is, the preacher's field of vision is as wide-ranging as the scope of Christ's redemptive accomplishment, alike addressing issues of personal discipleship, the cruciform church as a "colony" (*politeuma*, Phil. 3:20) of God's reign on earth, and the renewal of the cosmos as a whole. No topic, however bland or controversial, falls outside the scope either of Christ's dominion or the preacher's interest.

By yielding absolutely to the pattern and rule of Jesus, apostolic preaching is, no less paradoxically, characterized (eighth) both by silence and by bold courage in speaking. It refuses to speak a merely human word, recognizing the futility of bare words, yet stubbornly insists on fully articulating the "word of the cross" (1 Cor. 1:18 RSV), however inexpedient or contrary that word may seem. The preacher's silence is not occasioned by theological timidity, or by concern for preserving personal benefit or avoiding rejection, but by the recognition that even Jesus falls silent on the cross. Yet, because it is governed by the cross, that silence is neither final

---

4. Although in fairness it must be said that Paul is not entirely consistent in this regard (e.g., 2 Cor. 11:13–15).

nor absolute; it is only temporary and provisional, ultimately reversed by its contingence upon the full dimensions of God's self-articulation in the person of Jesus, both crucified *and* risen. In very practical terms, preachers must therefore weigh their words carefully—not just for cadence or comprehensibility, but for the clarity of their testimony to an awkward, counterintuitive, glorious Christ. They must weigh them especially so as to ensure (as far as possible) that by means of such words they are working "together with" God (2 Cor. 6:1), and not against him.

Ninth and last in our series of broad methodological principles, Paul's description of the consequences of apostolic preaching reveals a further paradox. Even as the preacher must first be caught up by and become subject to Christ in order to speak of Christ to others, so faithful preaching is marked by the transformation of its hearers. Again, this is not a result of the speaker's personal charm or skill in speaking, but of the fact that God remains faithful in continuing to act according to the pattern of Jesus's cross and resurrection. The final test of faithful preaching, in other words, is the fact that preacher and hearers alike are changed by the saving action of God to which it testifies. They are conformed both individually and corporately to the pattern of Jesus's own death and vindication, and express in their lives together the contours of God's new creation and new humanity. Preaching is thus attended by "glory"—by revelation of the character of God, and by the transformation that results from knowing and yielding to a characteristically gracious Savior. On the other hand, such transformation is painfully gradual and imperfect, as Paul (and we with him!) knows only too well both from his own life and from the lives of his fractious congregants.

This brings us back to the starting point of our study. Even in translation, Paul's language is dense and his theology sufficiently complex that it is best digested in small portions. The secondary literature on Paul—or even a single letter such as 2 Corinthians—is vast and even more difficult to take in, much less do justice to. Homiletic theory is likewise a broad and ever-changing field. Even literature on the relationship between the two (that is, Paul's contribution to the method and content of Christian preaching) is too large to account for here. Thus a book that set outs with an ostensibly simple aim—explaining what Paul has to say about preaching in 2 Corinthians—turns out to be complicated, sometimes confusing, possibly even contradictory in places. Yet for all this, Paul's aim is clear and the purpose of our investigation relatively straightforward: to explore the implications of Jesus's death and resurrection for the manner in which we are called to proclaim it.

For some, no doubt, this discussion of Pauline homiletic will prove methodologically inadequate. There are no instructions detailing the correct manner of exegesis, no directions on how to compose a preachable manuscript, and few guidelines on the selection of suitable illustrative material. But this is as it must be, for the essence of Pauline homiletics, and Pauline spirituality, concerns an orientation and an outlook more than the method or mechanics of faithful proclamation. Most infuriating in this regard is the fact that Paul's ample skill as a theologian, pastor, apostle, and preacher of the gospel seems frequently directed to acknowledging the limitations of merely human endeavor, where we might have preferred him to offer guidance on the best means of redressing such shortcomings. Yet in this consists the true value of his approach.

In a culture—particularly a religious culture—that values status, success, and personal well-being, Paul offers a firm word of reassurance and hope. The many reversals that typically characterize the life of faith (both the preacher's own and that of the congregants) indicate neither lack of faith on their part nor lack of blessing on the part of God. On the contrary, Paul proposes that these are the normal conditions of discipleship from which faithful testimony and proclamation arise. Reversals are not ends in themselves so much as occasions for grace, opportunities for acknowledging the proper limitations of human endeavor, and for yielding to the steadfast faithfulness of Christ. According to Jesus's example, which the apostle imitates in turn, only by embracing the cross do we become open to the embrace of resurrection; only by following the way of the crucified Messiah do preachers begin to understand, to exemplify, and thus to lead their hearers in turn toward the life and new creation of Christ. This is the blessing that Paul offers to Corinth and to us, and that we offer those to whom we in turn are called and sent:

> Blessed be the God and Father of our Lord Jesus Christ, the Father of mercies and God of all comfort, who comforts us in all our affliction, so that we may be able to comfort those who are in any affliction, with the comfort with which we ourselves are comforted by God. For as we share abundantly in Christ's sufferings, so through Christ we share abundantly in comfort too.
>
> 2 Corinthians 1:3–5 RSV

Postscript

In the course of our study, we have had occasion to quote preachers (as well as scholars) both ancient and modern whose sermons and outlook exemplify the approach Paul advocates. These were most frequent in the first chapter, among them Martin Luther, Teresa of Ávila, St. Paul of the Cross, Lilias Trotter, Hudson Taylor, Mona Khauli, Nicholas Wolterstorff, and James van Tholen. But we have also heard from a United Methodist congregation in Prague, from Karl Barth, Helen Roseveare, Henri Nouwen, Kathy Black, Martin Luther King, Jr., Lauren Winner, and John Stott, among others. The contributions of each are recognizable because they have been published and made public. But as we noted at the outset, the vast majority of preachers throughout the entire history of the Christian church have conducted their ministries in either relative or absolute obscurity. And they, by virtue of such obscurity, best exemplify cruciform preaching as Paul intends it. Wherever preachers stand before their congregations conscious of the folly of the Christian message, the weakness of their efforts, and the apparent impossibility of the entire exercise—yet at the same time trusting deeply in God's life-giving grace to transform their limited resources—there, Paul's apostolic homiletic of cross and resurrection is at work. The one resource that genuinely faithful preachers of the gospel have in abundance is a parade of daily reminders as to their own inadequacy, unworthiness, and—dare we admit it?—lack of faithfulness. Yet these are the preconditions for grace, the foundations for preaching that relies on God "who raises the dead." Accordingly, the best and most frequent illustrations of the approach Paul takes are to be found not in published sermons (or books like this one!), but in churches of every shape, size, and theological stripe, wherever preachers confess that their sufficiency rests in Christ alone. In fact, readers are likely to recognize this dynamic repeated in their own experience of Christian discipleship, above all in their experience of Christian ministry. To the extent that this is so, we will each serve as living illustrations, "little Christs," to our respective congregations, who will thereby see right through us—and Paul—to the one we seek to proclaim.

Scripture and Ancient Writings Index

Name Index

Brazos Press is grounded in the ancient, ecumenical Christian tradition, understood as living and dynamic. As legend has it, Brazos is the Spanish name explorers gave to a prominent Texas river upon seeing how its winding waters sustained fertile soil in an arid land. They christened this life-giving channel Los Brazos de Dios, "the arms of God."

Our logo connotes a river with multiple currents all flowing in the same direction, just as the major streams of the Christian tradition are various but all surging from and to the same God. The logo's three "streams" also reflect the Trinitarian God who lives and gives life at the heart of all true Christian faith.

Our books are marketed and distributed intensively and broadly through the American Booksellers Association and the Christian Booksellers networks and bookstores; national chains and independent bookstores; Catholic and mainline bookstores; and library and international markets. We are a division of Baker Publishing Group.

Brazos Book Club and Border Crossings

Brazos books help people grapple with the important issues of the day and make Christian sense of pervasive issues in the church, academy, and contemporary world. Our authors engage such topics as spirituality, the arts, the economy, popular culture, theology, biblical studies, the social sciences, and more. At both the popular and academic levels, we publish books by evangelical, Roman Catholic, Protestant mainline, and Eastern Orthodox authors.

If you'd like to join the Brazos Book Club and receive our books upon publication at book club prices, please sign up online at **www.brazospress.com/brazosbookclub**.

To sign up for our monthly email newsletter, Border Crossings, visit **www.brazospress.com**. This email newsletter provides information on upcoming and recently released books, conferences we are attending, and more.

BrazosPress
The Tradition Alive